Fossil Forensics

Fossil Forensics
Separating Fact from Fantasy in Paleontology
by Jerry Bergman

Copyright © 2017 Jerry Bergman

Published in the United States by BP Books,
an imprint of Bartlett Publishing

Library of Congress Control Number: 2017944121
ISBN: 978-1-944918-10-1

For author inquiries, please send email to info@bartlettpublishing.com.

Bookstore bulk order discounts available. Please contact
orders@bartlettpublishing.com for more information.

http://www.bartlettpublishing.com/

1st Printing

Fossil Forensics

Separating Fact from Fantasy in Paleontology

Jerry Bergman, Ph.D.

With contributions by
Philip Snow, Frank J. Sherwin,
Fred Johnson, and MaryAnn Stuart

Endorsements

Fossil Forensics by Professor Jerry Bergman is an absolutely extraordinary book. I have had the great privilege and honor of proofreading books for him for many years now. This book, in particular, I believe will be important evidence in helping to deal the death blow to evolution's use of the fossil record to advance their theory of the evolution of simple molecules-to-man fairy tale. I predict it will be a best-seller, and profoundly impact this and future generations.

—**Bryce Gaudian, Development Manager for Agilis Corporation.**

As a biology researcher who has published in the peer reviewed scientific literature, and also a lifetime college biology professor for 40 years, I am pleased to state that, as I read the draft of the manuscript of this book, I was so intrigued that, when finishing each chapter, I eagerly looked forward to the next fascinating chapter!

—**Professor Wayne Frair, Ph.D.**

Acknowledgements

First, I acknowledge the many contributions of my students and the rewards gleaned from our fossil expeditions and the joy of discovery that we all savored in spite of the heat and dust that often goes along with fossil digs. Second, I am very grateful to Fred Johnson, PhD, Wayne Frair, Ph.D, Bryce Gaudian, and MaryAnn Stewart, M.A. for reviewing the manuscript and providing much insight into improving the manuscript. I also wish to thank Bert Thompson Ph.D., Clifford Lillo, M.A., Jody Allen, R.N., John Woodmorappe, M.A., Ted Siek, Ph.D., Eric Blievernicht, B.S., Gary Byerly, Mary Ann Stuart, Dennis Englin, Ph.D., and several anonymous reviewers for their comments on the earlier drafts of this book. And too, I also thank Emmett L. Williams, Ph.D., for helping me locate earlier papers on the creation view of arthropod origins and the anonymous referees for several helpful suggestions. I also wish to thank Andrew Fabich, Ph.D., Jody Allen, R.N., Joel Klenck, Ph.D., Don DeYoung and John Upchurch for their feedback on an earlier draft of the dinosaur chapter and Dr. Don Moeller, D.DS., M.D., George Howe, Ph.D., Bert Thompson, Ph.D., and Clifford Lillo, M.A., for reviewing an earlier draft of the chapter on teeth. Last, I thank Norbert Smith and 2 anonymous herpetologists for their comments on an earlier drafts of chapters and George F. Howe for editorial assistance.

About the Author — Jerry Bergman, Ph.D.

Dr. Bergman has taught biology, anthropology, geology, anatomy and other courses at the college level for over 40 years. He is currently an adjunct Associate Professor at the University of Toledo Medical College. He has 9 earned degrees, including a doctorate from Wayne State University in Detroit, Michigan. A member of MENSA, listed in *Who's Who in the Midwest* and *Who's Who in Theology and Science*, he has over 950 publications in both scholarly and popular science journals and has written 32 books and monographs. Dr. Bergman's work has been translated into 12 languages, including French, German, Italian, Spanish, Danish, Polish, and Swedish.

Among his many books is a monograph on the creation-evolution controversy published by Phi Delta Kappa, the honor society in education, and a college textbook on evaluation (Houghton, Mifflin Co.), and he has contributed chapters to numerous others. Other books include *Slaughter of the Dissidents*, *The Dark Side of Darwinism*, *Hitler and the Darwinian Worldview*, and the forthcoming *Darwinism's Blunders, Frauds, and Forgeries,* all available on Amazon.

Dr. Bergman has presented over one hundred scientific papers at professional meetings. His research has made the front page in newspapers throughout the country four times, has been featured by Paul Harvey several times on national radio, and has been discussed by David Brinkley on national television. He has been a featured speaker on many college campuses throughout the United States, Canada, Africa, and Europe and is also a frequent guest on various radio and television programs to discuss his research.

Dr. Bergman was on both the undergraduate and graduate faculty at Bowling Green State University and the University of Toledo, for a total of fourteen years. He has resided with his wife, Dianne, and his four children in Montpelier, Ohio since 1985. He now has 10 grandchildren. His hobbies include woodworking, fossil collecting, collecting books, photography, and reading.

Additional Contributors

1. Philip Snow is an author and/or illustrator of over 60 books, articles, and other publications on birds and wildlife. Some include *The Design and Origin of Bird's* (Day One Publishers UK/USA); *Collins Field Notebook of British Birds; Light & Flight - Hebridean Wildlife & landscape Sketchbook; Birdwatching on Mull and Iona and Birds and Forestry*. He has worked in many public and private collections, including HRH Prince Charles, USAF Museum, American Falconry Archives, Welsh Assembly, Welsh National Collection, and Gulf Royalty etc.

2. Frank J. Sherwin (M.A.) received his B.A. in Biology from Western State College in Colorado and a M.A. in Zoology with a specialty in parasitology and was active in research in his field at the University of Northern Colorado. Sherwin has published widely on the fossil record and is a frequent speaker on creation/evolution issues around the country. He is an experienced biology instructor at college level and now is an Assistant Professor at the Institute for Creation Research Graduate School where he teaches and writes creation based curriculum.

3. Fred Johnson (Ph.D.) received a Ph.D. in pathology at Vanderbilt University and served on the faculty of pathology and comparative medicine at the Bowman Gray School of Medicine (now Wake Forest School of Medicine) for 10 years. He moved into the pharmaceutical industry in pharmacology at Burroughs Wellcome Co. for 5 years and then into clinical research with Inspire Pharmaceuticals for 13 years. He currently is working as a medical writer at Grifols Therapeutics.

4. MaryAnn Stuart (M.S.) has a master's degree in Biology/Paleontology, has worked in various rolls with creation museums for over twenty years, and has for over a decade has served as an editor of numerous books and journal articles.

Table of Contents

Chapter 1

Introduction

This is volume one of a projected multi-volume set that will explore in some detail the fossil record of most all life forms. As a biology professor for over 40 years, I have always been fascinated by the wonder of animal design, and wanted to document its amazing marvels and diversity both in the present and in the fossil record, as well as separate out what we *know* from evidence from the *speculations* that are often accompanied with the evidence, and often given the same weight.

In this series, each volume will consist of an overview of the findings related to the fossil record as presented in the scholarly literature by recognized authorities. This volume focuses on general categories such as invertebrates, arthropods, fish, amphibians, whales, etc. The next volume will cover specific animals such as giraffes, woodpeckers, camels, and pandas. I have now looked at the evidence in detail for the fossil record of over 100 life forms and have discovered that a lot of the discussion of their origins dealt in fantasy instead of fact.

In college, one text used for a graduate class at Wayne State University in Detroit was C. Loring Brace and Ashley Montague's 1965 book titled *Human Evolution*, which included many illustrations of the life forms that linked humans to what many biologists believe is our common ancestor, an ape of some type. After reading the text and studying the illustrations, I was quite convinced that the author's information and conclusions were reliable. However, science requires validation, not mere assertion, so I continued to read the literature, and soon realized that taking their word for what the evidence shows was naïve, to say the least.

One of the main areas of speculation in the fossil record is in the origin of various types of creatures and the connections between them. Darwin's theory of evolution has been one of the major themes of biology since its inception in the 1800s. Darwin's theory, while it has many nuances, can be boiled down to four major points — that all organisms are descended from a single, universal common ancestor, that the present species are the result of gradual changes to previous species over long periods of time, that these changes are entirely accidental (i.e., there was no purpose inside or outside the organism that caused the change to happen), and that the way that these accidental changes can lead to complex functions and adaptations is through natural selection (the idea that organisms that are better fit for their environment will be more likely to reproduce). These ideas together form the modern theory of evolution, which is often termed as "Darwinism." There are other theories of evolution, but most of them tend to refer back to Darwinism to cover their own gaps and problems.

Unfortunately, this domination of the field by a single theory has caused many biologists to make or accept claims lacking substantial evidence. By most biologists, the fossil record is thought to be a major source of evidence for evolution. However, as I researched life as related to its putative evolution, I realized that the fossil record is actually one of evolution's major problems. As this work documents, the fossils tell a very clear account of the history of life quite in contradiction to the story of Darwinism. The reason is because,

> the most striking fact about nature is that it *is* discontinuous. When you look at animals and plants, each individual almost always falls into one of many discrete groups. When we look at a single wild cat, for example, we are immediately able to identify it as either a lion, a cougar, a snow leopard, and so on. All cats do not blur insensibly into one another through a series of feline intermediates. And although there is variation among individuals within a cluster (as all lion researchers know, each lion looks different from every other), the clusters nevertheless remain discrete in "organism space." We see clusters in all organisms that reproduce sexually. (Coyne, 2009, p. 184)

This has always been a major problem for Darwinism, and still is, as this book documents.

Controversy in Physical Paleontology

One thing I have learned in my lifelong study of Darwinism is that a great deal of controversy exists in the field of physical paleontology. My primary role in this work was to study carefully the peer reviewed scientific literature on evolution and to attempt to synthesize it in a way that was readable and understandable to educated adults. For several reasons, this was no easy task. Even the leaders in the field have come under fire from other leaders, as documented in my book *Evolution's Blunders, Frauds, and Forgeries* (Bergman, 2017).

The fact is, according to Professor Henry Gee, a senior editor of paleontology for *Nature,*

> Scientific research gets trapped in more box canyons than the Lone Ranger; does more U-turns than the average government; falls to certain death more often than Wile E Coyote; has more women in it than you might at first imagine (though probably not nearly enough); and generally gets the wrong answer. (Gee, 2013)

This is especially true of paleontology. Furthermore, a major part of the problem is that the lay public

> are told, very often, and by people who ought to know better, that science is a one-way street of ever-advancing progress, a zero-sum game in which facts are accumulated and ignorance dispelled. In reality, the more we discover, the more we realize we don't know. Science is not so much about knowledge as doubt. Never in the field of human inquiry have so many known so little about so much. (Gee, 2013)

I do not claim to be more knowledgeable or better informed than the experts that I relied on to write this book. And for this reason I relied heavily on them for my conclusions. In many cases I also relied on their conclusions, which are often quoted.

One esteemed researcher I respect is the late Ned Colbert, who was one of the most important figures in the field of vertebrate evolution for decades and the author of a leading text in the field, *Evolution of the Vertebrates.* Yet some of the reviews of his work from fellow paleoanthropologists were blistering, such as those by Professor Donald R. Prothero, Department of Geology at Occidental College in Los Angeles, California.

Accepted conclusions in the paleontology discipline constantly change, at times drastically, as a result of new discoveries and new insight, or even as the result of changing attitudes and assumptions. Within the field, there are always numerous contrasting and contradicting opinions by various scholars. With so many contradictory claims, even only a review of the scientific literature (as done here) is bound to offend certain persons in the field.

Most all of the scientists quoted were evolutionists. Many evolutionists acknowledge that the fossil record in their specialty lacks evidence for evolution, but maintain their faith in the theory because they believe that other specialties have shown evolution to be true. Therefore, by considering a number of different areas of the fossil record, I hope to better show the pattern of the fossil record, and its difficulty for reconciling with evolution. Even Darwin recognized the fossil record as one of several difficulties with his theory that he discussed, namely

> not finding in the successive formations infinitely numerous transitional links between the many species which now exist or have existed; the sudden manner in which whole groups of species appear in our European formations; the almost entire absence, as at present known, of fossiliferous formations beneath the Silurian strata, are all undoubtedly of the gravest nature. We see this in the plainest manner by the fact that all the most eminent palaeontologists, namely Cuvier, Owen, Agassiz, Barrande, Falconer, E. Forbes, &c., and all our greatest geologists, as Lyell, Murchison, Sedgwick, &c. have unanimously, often vehemently, maintained the immutability of species. (Darwin, 1859)

Georges Cuvier and Comparative Anatomy in the Fossil Record

The conclusions in this book are not new. As Darwin noted, they were expressed in the 1800s by Georges Cuvier, a man widely considered "France's grand old man of biological science" (Gregory, 2008, p. 50). As a youth it "soon became clear that young Georges was intellectually gifted" and was destined for greatness (Gregory, 2008, p. 53). Cuvier's family and friends were not disappointed. Due to his fact gathering and hard-nosed reasoning based on the results of his research, he would earn a sterling reputation as a careful scholar. This scientific "attitude would pervade all his work as a natural philosopher, be it on fossils, or on anatomy, or on anything [that] he took up. Know what you're dealing with before you start trying to explain things [was his philosophy]" (Gregory, 2008, p. 55).

History of science professor Frederick Gregory added that Cuvier wrote a large number of papers on fossils during his lifetime; and, as his "knowledge increased, his authority grew, and he proceeded to develop a whole new science" today called the

> science of comparative anatomy, which Cuvier used to extract from fossil remains an amazing amount of information. What he realized was that if you know enough about the anatomical structure ... the parts of that structure tell you a lot about what he termed the conditions of existence in which the animal lived. The relations among the anatomical parts of living things were in no way the product of chance. No, they were interconnected with the conditions of existence in a necessary way. Cuvier's job became to master his knowledge of the manner in which the anatomical parts went together so that he could tell what conditions

would have supported such a structure. For example, from the teeth he could tell what kind of vegetation must have been present [when the animal was alive]. (Gregory, 2008, p. 56)

In 1812, Cuvier was finally ready to publish his extensive scientific research work on fossils. Based on his extensive knowledge of fossils, he was

adamantly opposed ... [to] what the French called "transformism" ... another word for evolution. Cuvier did not approve of evolution. To him, it was like those speculative systems of the previous century, Buffon's and Hutton's. It was not based on empirical investigations but on flights of fancy, and that was not his idea of science. He referred to "some who think of the earth as alive, with mountains being the globe's respiratory organs and volcanoes the vehicle for removing excrement." His words, though polite ...The reader knew he felt it was all nonsense. (Gregory, 2008, p. 58)

Cuvier, the leading expert on fossils in his day, concluded from his extensive fieldwork that evolution was not supported by the evidence. The major reason why he opposed evolutionism was because the

fossil record did not support the notion that life had gradually evolved over time. "If species had changed by degrees," he wrote, "then we ought to be able to find some traces of these gradual modifications; we ought to be able to find intermediate forms between the time of the prehistoric world and the present day. But that," he says, "has not happened at all, up to now." (Gregory, 2008, p. 58)

Building on Cuvier's Legacy

Nor, as this review documents, has that happened since then. The result of 200 years of research has uncovered over 250 million catalogued fossils, and these have shown the fact that "individual kinds of fossils remain recognizably the same throughout the length of their occurrence in the fossil record, [a fact that] had been known to paleontologists long before Darwin published his *Origin*" (Eldredge and Tattersal, 1982, pp. 45-46).

Darwin himself was so "troubled by the stubbornness of the fossil record in refusing to yield abundant examples of gradual change" that he devoted two whole chapters to the fossil record problems in his *Origin* book. In order to salvage his arguments for evolution, Darwin

> was forced to assert that the fossil record was too incomplete, too full of gaps, to produce the expected patterns of change. He prophesied that future generations of paleontologists would fill in these gaps by diligent search and then his major thesis—that evolutionary change is gradual and progressive—would be vindicated. (Eldredge and Tattersal, 1982, pp. 45-46)

The fact is, 120 "years of paleontological research later, it has become abundantly clear that the fossil record will not confirm this part of Darwin's predictions. Nor is the problem a miserably poor record. The fossil record simply shows that this prediction was wrong" (Eldredge and Tattersal, 1982, pp. 45-46). They add that by assessing differences and resemblances between the fossils and both living animals and plants, paleontologists attempt

> to define taxonomic and evolutionary relationships, the underlying idea being that the closer animals correspond in their anatomical structure, the closer they are related from the point of view of evolutionary

descent. We now know that this view is far too simple, since relationships which are inferred on the basis of comparative anatomy may not necessarily correspond to true genetic relationships. Nevertheless, lack of other information makes it inevitable that the bulk of our views about evolutionary relationships has to be based on the evidence of structure. (Zuckerman, 1971, p. 64)

One major problem is

the names of ancestral human fossils can't be taken too seriously. Like theology, paleoanthropology is a field in which the students far outnumber the objects of study. There are lively—and sometimes acrimonious—debates about whether a given fossil is really something new, or merely a variant of an already named species. These arguments about scientific names often mean very little. Whether a humanlike fossil is named as one species or another can turn on matters as small as half a millimeter in the diameter of a tooth, or slight differences in the shape of the thighbone. The problem is that there are simply too few specimens, spread out over too large a geographic area, to make these decisions with any confidence. New finds and revisions of old conclusions occur constantly. (Coyne, 2009, p. 197)

As a result, comparative anatomists

need to exercise great forbearance, as well as great humility both in the area of fact and in that interpretation, simply because the inferences they draw about evolution are in the final analysis speculations— speculations that can only be checked by recourse to the facts from which they are derived. (Zuckerman, 1971, p. 64)

Another problem is "in the final analysis, the answer to the question of" evolutionary

> descent always depends upon preconceptions about the way this evolution occurred. For example, no scientist could logically dispute the proposition that man, without having been involved in any act of divine creation, evolved from some ape-like creature in a very short space of time — speaking in geological terms — without leaving any fossil traces of the steps of the transformation. (Zuckerman, 1971, p. 64)

Consequently, a problem is, "in general, students of fossil primates have not been distinguished for caution when working with the logical constraints of their subject." (Zuckerman, 1971, p. 64). This problem extends far beyond just primates, as will be documented in this present volume.

Reading This Book

Each chapter of this text was written to stand alone so as to allow the reader to first read those sections that are of most interest to him or her. For this reason, some minor repetition exists in the chapters in this book.

Although this manuscript was reviewed by numerous scholars, any errors that remain are mine, not those of my reviewers. Any and all comments by readers are welcome and will be considered in future editions of this work, which is the result of almost a half-century of reading and research.

References

Coyne, Jerry. 2009. *Why Evolution is True*. New York: Oxford University.

Eldredge, Niles and Ian Tattersall. 1982. *The Myths of Human Evolution*. New York: Columbia University Press.

Gee, Henry. 2013. Science: the Religion that Must Not be Questioned. *The Guardian*, London. September 19, 2013.

Gregory, Frederick. 2008. *The Darwinian Revolution*. Chantilly, VA: The Great Courses.

Zuckerman, Sir Solly. 1971. *Beyond the Ivory Tower: The Frontiers of Public and Private Science*. New York: Taplinger Publishing Company.

PART I:

General Fossil Considerations

Chapter 2

Teeth—Witness to the Fossil Record

Introduction

Evidence for evolution of vertebrates "is derived largely from the fossil record, and much of it is provided by teeth" (Butler, 2000, p. 201). As Jernvall, Keränen, and Thesleff noted "the study of mammalian evolution often relies on detailed analysis of dental morphology" (2000, p. 14444). The same is true for most other vertebrates. Many evolutionary conclusions, such as elephant evolution, are based largely on comparative dental morphology (Maglio and Ricca, 1977).

The importance of teeth in human evolution is so great that "were it not for teeth, anthropology would be a different subject" (Jernvall and Jung, 2000, p. 172). Fossil teeth are ideal objects to study evolution because they preserve extremely well in the fossil record, much better than even bone (Teaford, *et al.*, 2000; Smith and Tchernov, 1992; Zhu, 1935; Wilson, 1943). As a result of their abundance, teeth play a major role in helping to distinguish between different extinct species (Johanson and Shreeve, 1989). In Gould's words, "Since *enamel is far more durable than ordinary bone, teeth may prevail* when all else has succumbed to the whips and scorns of geological time. *The majority of fossil mammals are known only by their teeth* [emphasis mine] (1989, p. 60).

Deterioration of fossils is caused by water, weather, and temperature. Bone mineral crystals tend to be long and narrow and, as a result, the needle-shaped splinters that form from water trapped in the pore spaces that exist in all bone causes these pores to widen. As they widen, even more water is allowed to enter, forming yet larger crystals (Calcagno, 1989). Within a few weeks to a year in moist environments, the bone is rapidly damaged. The major causes of deterioration of animal body parts including bone include:

1. Drying and wetting (very important in all semi-arid, arid, and temperate areas, or in humid areas with monsoonal climates)

2. Formation of salt crystals during drying (and the analogous formation of ice crystals during freezing)

3. Freezing and thawing (an important process, especially at high altitudes and latitudes or for short periods of time)

In contrast to bone, tooth enamel is far better preserved because enamel is extremely dense, with virtually no space between the crystals, and very few pores (Patterson, 1956; Smith and Teaford, 2000). Therefore, it requires about 10 to 100 times longer for the same deterioration effects to occur in tooth enamel as it does in bone. Even dentine takes longer to break down—usually 2 to 10 times longer on average—than bone. Conversely, cementum tends to be easily destroyed and, consequently, is rarely found preserved on teeth in the fossil record. Because the anchoring bone for teeth decays more rapidly than the teeth themselves, separate teeth are very common in the fossil record. Often, when a fossil is discovered, the teeth are among the best-preserved parts of the animal. Consequently, much of our understanding of animal history is a result of the study of teeth, and many animals are known *only* by their teeth (McCollum and Sharpe, 2001).

The more than 50 basic teeth types that have been classified come in so much variety that they often can be used to identify a mammal's taxonomic order (Miles, 1972, p. 10; Forstén, 1973; Denison, 1974; Cocke, 2002; Matthew and Harmsted, 1924; Patterson, 1956; Raschkow and Hillam, 1973; Scott, 1892). Teeth are a major means by which to differentiate humans from other primates. Often an attempt is made to identify an animal solely on the basis of its teeth. This is sometimes very difficult, as the classic case of the *Hesperopithecus* illustrates — peccary teeth are very similar to human teeth and, as a result, have been mistaken for human teeth (Bergman, 1993).

Mammals are heterodonts, which means that their teeth vary even within one animal. In fish and reptiles, however, the teeth are all nearly identical, except for size (homodonts). Even closely related mammals can have very different tooth morphology, depending on their diet and food-chewing needs. The Darwinian origin of teeth assumes that the evolutionary status of an animal's teeth is an excellent index of its body evolution. The stage of evolution of an animal's teeth, though, is not always directly related to the stage of the supposed evolution of its entire body (Frayer, 1977; Oxnard, 1987).

Teeth Structure

Although they appear to be simple organs, teeth actually are complex, well-designed, living structures that require proper care to keep healthy, especially in humans. As Stokstad noted, "in whatever form they take, teeth are a marvelous invention, enabling us to rip into drumsticks or chew a caramel with abandon" (2003, p. 1164). Paleontologist Peter Unger wrote that teeth are " among the most important innovations in the evolution of life... [that]

reached a new level of complexity and variations with the radiation of mammals" (2010, p. 73). Although many animals can effectively chew a wide variety of materials, their teeth often are *designed* to fit the normal diet of the animal (Lucas, 1982).

The general design of teeth is given in Figure 2.1. The exposed part of the tooth is called the *crown*; the tooth part in the jaw is the *root*. The outer part of the tooth, the enamel, is the hardest structure in the body. Enamel is composed of numerous microscopic crystalline structures that resemble soda straws set parallel to each other (Moeller, 2003, p. 119).

Below the enamel is the *dentine*, a substance that resembles bone, except that it is much harder (Shier, *et al.*, 2004, p. 652). Dentine is living cellular tissue that requires adequate blood circulation, which is provided by the veins and arteries located in the root canal. The root is enclosed by a thin layer of material similar to bone called *cementum*, which helps to bond the tooth firmly in the bone socket. The tooth is firmly attached to the bone by thick bundles of collagenous fibers called *periodontal ligaments*. The ligaments contain nerves that prevent the animal from applying excess forces to the teeth.

Although mammalian teeth are both more complicated and more efficient than those of other vertebrates, "all teeth are basically similar, formed in essentially the same way from enamel" (Butler, 2000, p. 208). Almost all vertebrates have teeth, but a few totally lack them. In all toothed vertebrates except mammals (fish, reptiles, a few extinct birds such as *Archaeopteryx*, and amphibians), the teeth develop to fill the jaw space that was designed to hold them.

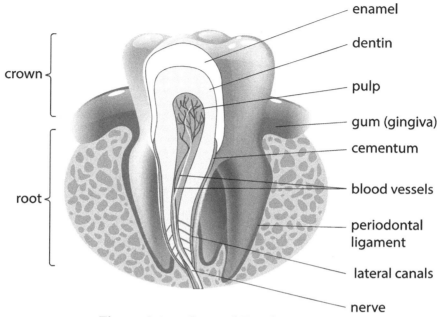

enamel

dentin

pulp

gum (gingiva)

cementum

blood vessels

periodontal ligament

lateral canals

nerve

crown

root

Figure 2.1 — General Tooth Anatomy[1]

In sharks, some amphibians, and even some other animals, no matter how many teeth are lost, new ones normally develop in the same way a cut heals in a healthy animal. In these vertebrates the animal either has an endless supply of teeth or does not develop any teeth.

The complex development of teeth is not well understood (Zhao, *et al.*, 2000). Teeth are merely the final product of a cascade of metabolic procedures that produce a complex structure designed to develop at a specific location in the body. Tooth evolution cannot be understood apart from the development of the entire dento-maxillary system. The periodontal ligament co-development, the root growth development, the condylar growth, the jaw basal bone,

---

[1] Image Credit: Elen Bushe / Shutterstock.com

the enamel microcrystal structure, and the simultaneous development of the opposing arch all are part of this complex pattern of co-development that results in properly placed teeth. This method of evaluation is called the complex systems approach because all organs require a complete system to function (Moeller, 2003, p. 1). Moeller (2003) concluded that "You cannot prove or disprove either evolution or Creation ... outside of the system approach. This is evolution's gross failure" (p. 1).

Mammals that have teeth also are unique because two sets of teeth form during their development—the first set, called *primary teeth* or *milk teeth*, erupt at regular intervals between about six months to two or three years of age. These teeth are later replaced with larger secondary or *permanent teeth*. Some mammals develop primary teeth, but do not produce permanent dentition replacements. The monotreme *Ornithorhynchus*, duck-billed platypus, has "two pairs of upper teeth and three pairs of lower molariform teeth, but these are shed before maturation and are functionally replaced by a leathery beak (Carroll, 1988, p. 420).

In humans, the primary teeth are both fewer in number (20) and smaller than the secondary teeth (32). The 32 secondary teeth are arranged as follows: *molars* (for grinding) are in the back; *premolars* on the side; *cuspids* (or canines) for tearing or stabbing are located on the side towards the front; and *incisors* (for cutting and biting off chunks of food) are located in the direct front of the mouth.

The complexity of teeth indicates that the number of genes involved in their formation is "undoubtedly large" (Butler, 2000, p. 208). All this variation is "genetically controlled to a high degree" and is little influenced by the environment (Butler, 1982, p. 44). If primarily environmentally influenced, it would effectively adapt to local conditions, and genetic selection would be less important. Therefore, this trait is ideal for Darwinists to study and is another reason why the fossil record should show an abundant number of clear transitional forms.

The Evolution of Teeth

In the most widely held theory of tooth evolution, it is hypothesized that marginal oral skin produced small knobs (denticles) that eventually evolved into tooth-like conodonts (McCollum and Sharpe, 2001). The conodonts eventually evolved into primitive teeth and then, after many more eons, into modern teeth (Teaford, *et al.*, 2000; Miles, 1972).

Many new discoveries have challenged this view. Even the theory that teeth evolved by co-option of external skin denticals at the margins of the jaws has recently come under attack by Smith and Johanson (2003, p. 1235) who examined the need for functional teeth to survive.

Teeth as Evidence for Evolution

Because they preserve so well, teeth are an excellent means of evaluating Neo-Darwinism (Young, *et al.*, 1929; Smith and Tchernov, 1992; Kurtén, 1982; Osborn and Gregory, 1907; Butler and Joysey, 1978; Balkwill, 1893; Butler, 1982). The wide diversity of morphology (shape and size), enamel, and other microstructures of teeth among the extant and fossil animals indicates that a large number of clear transitional forms should exist to confirm their evolutionary path (Moeller, 2003).

A problem is that, although size changes can be observed, the fossil record reveals no evidence of tooth evolution, either from primitive teeth or from some theorized precursors. As Stokstad noted regarding teeth: "These complex structures are always organized—into sturdy rows of molars" (2003, p. 1164). Even accessory structures, such as dentine, are found in the fossil record. Dentine extends back to the late Cambrian (Smith and Sansom, 2000, p. 70).

As a result of the good fossil record in the "Cambro-Ordovician vertebrates, we know that there was great diversity" of dentine tissues even in the Cambrian (Smith and Sansom, 2000, p. 79). Furthermore, recent evidence challenges the classical view of teeth evolution (Smith and Coates, 1998). An example is the finding that living and fossil animals either have fully developed teeth, or none at all, and that "complex structures with dentin and enamel have been described in the earliest jawless vertebrates, conodonts" (McCollum and Sharpe, 2001, p. 153).

All living amphibians have ridges on their jaws that can function as teeth, but they lack even very primitive teeth. Such ridges are interpreted as "transitional features," but they are, in fact, fully developed structures (Miles, 1972, p. 6). Some jawed vertebrates caught their prey with "bumpy gums or bony cutting blades and cuff-like structures made of so-called semi dentine" (Stokstad, 2003, p. 1164).

These structures were not teeth, nor were they constructed out of dentine, enamel, or other modern tooth structures. They were merely bumpy gingival, often covered by horny plates, and nothing more. Nonetheless, these horny plates were well-developed systems, and not transitional forms. They functioned very effectively for grasping and slicing (Miles, 1972, p. 7). Modern examples include turtles and tortoises.

Another major problem facing the theory that teeth evolved from bone is that in teeth there are at least two different types of proteins that are not found in bone. Furthermore, most all of the internal structures of teeth are considerably different from those of bones (Shier, *et al.*, 2004, p. 650).

Did Teeth Evolve Once or Many Times?

The complexity of teeth and the small likelihood they could have evolved even once in history have caused many researchers to "assume that teeth evolved just once, in the common ancestor of jawed vertebrates" (Stokstad, 2003, p. 1164). A recent reevaluation of teeth, however, now has caused many researchers to question this monophylogenetal assumption. The extended jawed fish called placoderms, for example, have teeth that differ greatly from other fish teeth. The difficulty in fitting these teeth into a single, viable evolutionary scenario has posed such serious difficulties that the researchers involved argue that teeth must have evolved more than once (Smith and Johanson, 2003, p. 1235).

This poses no small challenge to Darwinism, however, and has caused some researchers to question the position of "a significant portion" of animals on the current vertebrate family tree. In Stokstad's (2003) words, "scientists may need to shake up a significant portion of the vertebrate family tree" (p. 1164) as a result of these and other findings, by which he meant that the order and phyletic relationships of many groups on the tree may have to be changed.

Some researchers agree with tooth evolution expert Jukka Jernvall that "multiple origin of all the things that have something to do with teeth seem to be an emerging theme in evolutionary biology" (as quoted in Stokstad, 2003, p. 1164). This polyphyletic view renders tooth evolution less plausible because, as noted, tooth evolution long was considered extremely unlikely, forcing the conclusion that teeth must have evolved only once, and all teeth types have evolved from this one type.

To conclude that they evolved *many* times indicates that something very unlikely must have happened often and forces one to question the whole scenario. Such an unlikely trend towards the multiple origins of teeth in separate taxonomic groups fits well with the concept of the creation of many distinct kinds (baramins).

This newfound parallelism of teeth does not "reveal how teeth came about" and, consequently, complicates and does not help to solve the evolutionary conundrum (Smith and Johanson as quoted in Stokstad, 2003, p. 1164). Generally, teeth of living and extinct animals are lined up according to criteria that appear to be based largely on size and complexity. The teeth then are assumed to have evolved largely along this pattern. A major problem with this approach, however, is the large amount of intraspecific variation in dental features found in some animals (Metz-Muller, 1995).

Another evolutionary theory for the origin of teeth is the belief that they did not arise as chewing structures, but for other purposes, such as a superior method to capture prey (Smith, 2003). This event is theorized to have occurred in a primitive animal that then gave rise to all of the other groups of jawed vertebrates, including sharks, osteichthyes (bony fishes), and certain extinct animals.

Figure 2.2 — A Fossilized Shark Tooth[2]

---

[2] Photo Credit: Ivan Smuk / Shutterstock.com

Placoderms are considered the most basal group of jawed vertebrates, and for this reason their study is critical in researching the evolutionary origins of teeth (Smith and Johanson, 2003). Fortunately, many well-preserved examples of early placoderms with teeth are available for study. Careful evaluation of placoderm teeth revealed that the animals with teeth all had true teeth, not primitive, less-evolved teeth as had been expected. Once again, an evolutionary prediction was falsified.

In a study of well-preserved placoderm specimens, Smith and Johanson concluded that the same tooth pattern in placoderms they studied also is found in modern lung fish. The placoderm teeth were not primitive bony projections but rather conical structures arranged in defined rows (Smith and Johanson, 2003, p. 1235). Thin slices made of the teeth showed that they were fully developed and made of "regular dentine, not semi dentine" (Stokstad, 2003, p. 1164). Some placoderms, though, totally lacked teeth. So far no evidence of transitional tooth forms between the no-tooth condition and completely developed teeth has been discovered. One of the leading experts on the evolution of teeth found "a remarkable flurry of research on the origin or origins of vertebrate teeth. While this work is progressing, the details of when, where, why, and how teeth first appeared still elude consensus. Indeed, there is not even agreement on the fundamentals, such as how we define a tooth" (Unger, 2010, p. 73).

A Computer Literature Search on the Evolution of Teeth

A literature review of all articles having both the keywords "teeth" and "evolution" (some overlapping exists in these databases, and Biological Abstracts contains many journals devoted totally to evolution) were located and reviewed (see Table

2.1). Most of the articles located fell into these categories: discussions of the growth and development of teeth in infants and children, theoretical/speculative discussions, studies of individual teeth, review articles, or discussions of new fossil finds.

None of the articles provided clear evidence for tooth evolution but, at most, involved discussions of minor changes in the size and shape of fully developed teeth from different animals. But even here, much controversy existed (for example, see Frayer, 1977). Many studies comparing the teeth of animals in hypothetical evolutionary lineages suggested, at best, saltation (evolutionary jumps) — evidence that would fit equally well with the creation of separate kinds worldview.

Database	Records	Hits	%
Biological and Agricultural Index	1,080,522	0	0.0
Biological Abstracts	6,469,420	20	0.00031
Medline (1966 to present)	12,402,978	3	0.00002
Anthropological Literature	507,779	59	0.0116

Table 2.1 — Results of Literature Search[3]

The Use of Living Animals to Study Evolution of Teeth

In contrast to many evolutionary hypotheses, one can create a mental picture of the development of teeth from bone into teeth. This picture, in turn, gives us an idea of what to look for in the fossil

---

[3] Date of search – Nov. 21, 2003

record. Because teeth are the hardest structure in the body, teeth evolution evidence should, therefore, be very apparent in the fossil record. As indicated earlier, very few reports of plausible fossil evidence of tooth evolution exist in the literature (see Table 2.1). Hypothetical scenarios are freely postulated, but all lack empirical evidence (Miles, 1972).

Many evolution studies are based on living animals such as primates and operate under the assumption that some living primates are "primitive," and others are more "modern." (The terms "primitive" and "advanced" in this context, however, have meaning *only* if Darwinism is true.) The teeth of living animals then are compared, and evolutionary trends are deduced from these comparisons (Butler, 2000, p. 201). This, though, is not proof of evolution, but can merely provide plausible "just-so stories."

Of the hundreds of thousands of fossil teeth that have been evaluated so far, all are fully developed compared to their modern forms, and evolutionists even have claimed that very few were transitional. Although teeth vary considerably, no fossils have been proposed as clearly transitional from non-teeth to fully developed teeth. One problem, as described by Smith and Sansom, is that, in the past, many descriptions of teeth have used

> terminology, either based solely on these interpretations, or on comparison with bone, based on the assumption that an evolutionary series exists as a fossil record of the transformation of bone into dentine. Terms such as mesodentine, semidentine and metadentine have been used unrealistically in phylogenies with this assumption (2000, p. 79).

As noted, complex structures with both dentine and enamel have been found in "the earliest jawless vertebrates" (McCollum and Sharpe, 2001, p. 153). The major difficulties in documenting teeth evolution, especially the fact that traits considered both "primitive" and "modern" are found in both ancient and modern teeth, are explained by some Darwinists as resulting from "convergent evolution." Jernvall and Jung conclude that the distolingual cusp in the upper molars (called the hypocone) has evolved "at least 20 times in mammals" and even "among primates, the hypocone has evolved multiple times" (2000, p. 181). But, as noted earlier, such polyphyletic schemes in which teeth arise independently many times are extremely unlikely.

Morphogenesis: The Evolutionary Origin of Different Shapes and Types of Teeth

Teeth exist in a bewildering variety of shapes, seemingly every possible shape (Garcia and Miller, 1998, pp. 95-128). In fish and reptiles, all of the teeth in any one animal are very similar in shape (homodonts). In contrast, mammals are heterodonts (use many different kinds of specialized teeth). Moeller claimed that thousands of morphological variations and what can be called eruption sequence variations, together within other developmental cascades, exist. Thus, even though two teeth appear to have similar morphology, they could have major developmental differences (2003, p. 121).

Some morphological differences include teeth that are specially designed to scissor, stab, grind, dig, chisel (as in beavers), sieve (as in some aquatic animals), and lift (such as elephant tusks). Some "fangs" have a complex mechanism to effectively deliver poison (Miles, 1972, p. 8). The largest teeth in a living animal are elephant tusks, which are greatly enlarged incisors composed of a type of dentine called Ivy (Garcia and Miller, 1998). One documented elephant tusk was 16.5 feet (5m) long and weighed 465 lbs. (211 kg). Walrus tusks, which are teeth, can grow up to 1 meter long, and can weigh up to 12 pounds (5.4 kg).

In addition, many other interesting teeth oddities exist, such as the Narwhale *Monodon monocerus* (order Odontoceti) that has two teeth in its upper jaw, but only one of these (normally the left one) grows out. This tooth grows long enough to serve as a tusk, while the other tooth remains small.

Other significant variables among the different animal kinds include the dento-maxillary complex and the eruption sequence. The enamel microstructure differs widely and includes radial enamel, prismatic enamel, and synapsid columnar enamel (Moeller, 2003a, p. 1). Even the periodontal attachment system varies enormously (Moeller, 2003, p. 119). Moeller (2003) argued that the fossil record should contain not only mutational improvements, but also even more mutational failures that include such obvious changes as dental crowding, hypereruption, and hypoeruption. He concluded as follows:

> Considering the enormous amounts of fossil dental and jaw material available, it is statistically unrealistic to assume that no fossil evidence exists of any intermediate dental types. Just because it is possible to arrange different appearing dentitions in a phylogeny, this does not indicate support for the position that they evolved. The engine of evolution, that being genetic mutations, has great difficulty in accounting for the gradual modification of a highly complex integrated and coupled system in small increments. Genetic theory has an even greater difficulty in accounting for such changes (Moeller, 2003, p. 125).

Each of the many various tooth types is believed to have evolved from the basic pre-reptile reptilian tooth type, but evidence for an evolutionary sequence of these many teeth variations finds no support in the fossil record. This "problem of tooth morphogenesis," concerning which Salazar, Ciudad, and Jernvall noted that the "Generation of morphological diversity remains a challenge for evolutionary biologists because it is unclear how an ultimately finite number of genes involved in initial pattern formation integrates with morphogenesis" (2002, p. 8116).

"Transitional Stages" Lacking

Evolutionists would expect to find many fossil transitional teeth between the basic kinds of teeth, such as between elephant tusks and common mammal teeth, for example. Models of morphogenesis exist, so we have some idea what to expect in the fossil record, but clear examples of linking steps never have been found in the millions of fossil teeth uncovered so far. This is a serious gap in the fossil record.

Another problem is confirming the identity of a transitional tooth. Would it be a tooth that is smaller than a tooth in a modern animal? Would it be one with half the enamel, half the periodontal ligament, half the dentin, or half erupted compared to a non-transitional tooth? Or would transitional teeth be like malformed teeth as we often see in humans with genetic abnormalities?

Several mammal groups lack teeth, including the ten species of whales in the order Mysticeti, eight species of Pangolins family Manidae, and three species of anteaters of the family Myrmecophagidae within the order Edentata. Modern toothless mammals and certain other animals such as birds are theorized to have lost their teeth during evolution, a conclusion that is also unsupported in the fossil record and hard to rationalize, considering how critical teeth are for defense, grooming, procuring food, and use as tools. The only exception I have been able to locate is one reptile that evidently lost its teeth in the distant past: the Triassic turtle *Proganochelys*. It had rows of small homodont palatial teeth, whereas modern turtles have none (Romer, 1974, p. 115). This animal could be an extinct turtle like the extinct Archaeopteryx.

Irreducible Complexity

One argument against Darwinism is "irreducible complexity," the observation that a complex organ first must exist in a fully formed condition to function, otherwise it will afford no selective advantage to its possessor. Some claim that this argument from irreducible complexity is less successful in the case of the evolution of teeth than for almost any other body parts because a less developed tooth may be better than no tooth at all, and small bone protuberances might be better than no bone protuberances for chewing food and self-defense. Evolutionists claim that *any* improvement would be selected for, and most all transitional forms would seem to provide a survival advantage. If this were true, we would expect transitional forms commonly to occur, but they are unknown in the fossil record.

As noted, teeth do not exist in a vacuum, but are part of a complex "functional system that necessarily has remained operational throughout evolutionary change" (Butler, 2000, p. 209). Irreducible complexity is therefore a valid concern because all of the basic parts of the dentomaxillary complex must exist for the system to be functional. University of California biologist Richard Goldschmidt (1982) even "challenged the adherents of the strictly Darwinian view ... to try to explain the evolution of ... teeth ... by accumulation and selection of small mutants" (pp. 6-7). Importantly, no evidence of malocclusion exists even in the first jawed fish, the placoderms: the first jaws articulated perfectly. To achieve perfect occlusion from day one is a huge task for Darwinism (Cuozzo, 2004).

In a paper published the same year as Goldschmidt's, Butler (1982) discussed the many problems of tooth evolution, concluding that their complexity severely limits the number of ways teeth can evolve. Moeller (2003) added that the dentomaxillary system is very resistant to the effects of random mutations (p. 124). Of the about 100 known human and animal mutations that affect the dentomaxillary system, almost all are loss mutations. No known genetic mechanism can selectively modify tooth morphology, but rather typically causes a variety of damaging changes to the gingiva, the jaw, and related structures.

This research has caused Moeller (2003) to conclude that the claimed "transitional" teeth involve various modifications that place them in hypothetical "phylogenies," that are then retrofitted into a scheme to "demonstrate" evolution. He added that no evidence of beneficial mutational changes in the developmental cascade exists. He concluded that the claimed "tooth only" fossil record demonstrates only trivial modifications of previously created tooth forms.

What the fossil record does demonstrate is "quantum leap dental-maxillary morphologic changes" which are apparent only by considering the dento-maxillary system as a single identity. An example Moeller gave is that elephants (proboscidians) have an entirely different method of tooth eruption than ungulates. He concluded that evolutionists need to demonstrate fossil evidence for changes in tooth eruption patterns. The dento-maxillary system ought to provide untold examples of fossil intermediate malerupted teeth. The fact that there is no evidence of any such transitional modification of the dento-maxillary subsystems lends strong support for the Creation model (2003, p. 1).

Summary

Because teeth are comparatively well preserved in the fossil record, evidence for their evolution should be found if it exists. Teeth enamel is "the most enduring animal substance in the entire living world, defying the vicissitudes of time and subterranean burial, taking "first rank among Nature's hieroglyphics of the past" (Osborn, 1925, pp. 40-41). Yet, in spite of a century of intensive searching, evidence for evolution of teeth has never been found. The claimed support for macroevolution usually amounts to nothing more than very ambiguous evidence, such as bone fragments which, in living animals, generally make-up much less than ten percent of the mass of the entire animal body.

As a result, it is on the basis of bones rather than fossil teeth that claims for evolutionary change usually are made. In the case of teeth, it is very unlikely that more fossil discoveries will fill in the enormous number of missing links required to prove an evolutionary origin. Millions of fossil teeth have been discovered, and not one has provided clear evidence that teeth originated by macroevolution. Conversely, the fossil record for teeth, as well as the complex structure of teeth, provide clear evidence for intelligent design according to separate animal kinds.

References

Balkwill, Francis Hancock. 1893. *The testimony of the teeth to man's place in nature; With other essays on the doctrine of evolution.* Kegan Paul, Trench, Trübner and Company, London.

Bergman, Jerry. 1993. "The History of *Hesperopithecus, Haroldcookii Hominidae." CRSQ*, 30(1): 27-34.

Butler, Percy Milton 1982. Directions of evolution in the mammalian dentition. *Systematics Association* 21:241.

_____. 2000. Chapter 14: The evolution of tooth shape and tooth function in primates, pp. 201-211 in *Development, Function and Evolution of Teeth,* edited by M. F. Teaford, M. M. Smith, and Mark W. J. Ferguson. 2000. Cambridge University Press, New York.

Butler, Percy Milton and Kenneth Alan Joysey. 1978. *Development, Function, and Evolution of Teeth.* Academic Press, New York.

Calcagno, James M. 1989. *Mechanisms of human dental reduction: A case study from post-Pleistocene Nubia.* Dept. of Anthropology, University of Kansas, Lawrence, KS.

Carroll, Robert L. 1988. *Vertebrate paleontology and evolution.* W.H. Freeman, New York.

Cocke, Joe. 2002. *Fossil shark teeth of the world: A collector's guide.* Lamna, Torrance, CA.

Cuozzo, DDS, Jack. 2004. Personal communication.

Denison, Robert Howland. 1974. *The structure and evolution of teeth in lungfishes.* Field Museum of Natural History, Chicago, IL.

Forstén, Ann-Marie. 1973. *Size and shape evolution in the cheek teeth of fossil horses.* Societas pro Fauna et Flora Fennica, Helsinki.

Frayer, D.W. 1977. Metric dental change in the European upper paleolithic and mesolithic. *American Journal of Physical Anthropology* 46(1):109-120.

Garcia, Frank A. and Donald S. Miller. 1998. *Discovering fossils: How to find and identify remains of the prehistoric past.* Stackpole Books, Mechanicsburg, PA. Illustrations by Jasper Burns.

Gould, Stephen. 1989. *Wonderful life.* W. W. Norton, New York.

Goldschmidt, Richard. 1982. *The material basis of evolution.* Yale University Press, New Haven, CT. Introduction by Jay Gould.

Jernvall, Jukka. 2000. "Linking development with generation of novelty in mammalian teeth." *Proceedings of the National Academy of Science,* 97(6):2641-2645, March 14.

_____ and Han-Sung Jung. 2000. "Genotype, phenotype, and developmental biology of molar tooth characters." *Yearbook of Physical Anthropology* 43:171-190.

_____, Soile V.E. Keränen, and Irma Thesleff. 2000. "Evolutionary modification of development in mammalian teeth: Quantifying gene expression patterns and topography." *PNAS,* 97(26):14444-14448, December 19.

Johanson, Donald and James Shreeve. 1989. *Lucy's child: The discovery of a human ancestor.* William Morrow, New York.

Kurtén, Björn. 1982. *Teeth: Form, function, and evolution.* Columbia University Press, New York.

Lucas, P.W. 1982. Chapter 12: "Basic Principles of Tooth Design" pp 154-162 in *Teeth: Form, function, and evolution,* edited by Björn Kurtén. Columbia University Press, New York.

Maglio, Vincent J. and Anthony B. Ricca. 1977. *Dental and skeletal morphology of the earliest elephants.* North-Holland, Amsterdam, Oxford, New York.

Matthew, William Diller and Samuel Harmsted. 1924. *Evolution of the horse. In Two Parts: Evolution of the horse in nature by W.D. Matthew, [and] the horse under domestication: Its origin and the structure and growth of the teeth by S.H. Chubb.* American Museum of Natural History, New York (Reprinted in 1928).

McCollum, Melani and Paul T. Sharpe. 2001. Evolution and development of teeth. *Journal of Anatomy* 199(1-2):153-159.

Metz-Muller, Florence. 1995. Evidence of intraspecific variation in dental features within anancus arvernesis (proboscidea, mammalia) from the locality of dorkovo (early pliocene of Bulgaria, biozone MN14). *Geobios (Lyon)* 28(6):737-743.

Miles, Albert Edward William. 1972. *Teeth and their Origins.* Oxford University Press, London.

Moeller, Don. 2003. Dental fossils and the fossil record. *TJ* 17(2):118-127.

_____. 2003a. Letter dated October 6, 2003.

Osborn, Henry Fairfield. 1925. *The earth speaks to Bryan.* Scribners, New York.

_____ and William K. Gregory. 1907. *Evolution of mammalian molar teeth to and from the triangular type including collected and revised researches trituberculy and new sections on the forms and homologies of the molar teeth in the different orders of mammals.* Macmillan, New York (Reprinted in 1966).

Oxnard, Charles E. 1987. *Fossils, teeth and sex: New perspectives on human evolution.* University of Washington Press, Seattle.

Patterson, Bryan. 1956. Early cretaceous mammals and the evolution of mammalian molar teeth. Natural History Museum, Chicago, IL.

Raschkow, Isaac and Christine Hillam. 1973. *Studies on the evolution of mammalian teeth (1835).* Birmingham.

Romer, Alfred S. 1974. *Vertebrate paleontology,* 3rd Ed. The University of Chicago Press, Chicago, IL.

Salazar-Ciudad, Isaac and Jukka Jernvall. 2002. A gene network model accounting for development and evolution of mammalian teeth. *Proceedings of the National Academy of Science* 99(12):8116-8120.

Scott, W.B. 1892. *The evolution of the premolar teeth in the mammals*. Academy of Natural Sciences, Philadelphia.

Shier, David; Jackie Butler, and Ricki Louis. 2004. *Hole's human anatomy and physiology*. Tenth edition. McGraw Hill, New York.

Simmons, Geoffrey. 2004. *What Darwin didn't know*. Harvest House, Eugene, OR.

Smith, Moya Meridith. 2003. Vertebrate dentitions at the origin of jaws: When and how pattern Evolved. *Evolution and Development* 5(4):394-413.

_____ and M. Coates. 1998. Evolutionary origins of the vertebrate dentition: Phylogenetic pattern and developmental evolution, *European Journal of Oral Science* 106(Suppl 1):482-500.

_____ and I.J. Sansom. 2000. Chapter 5: Evolutionary origins of dentine in the fossil record of early vertebrates: Diversity, development and function in *Development, Function and Evolution of Teeth*, Teaford et al. (editors), pp. 65-81.

_____ and Mark Franklyn Teaford. 2000. *Development, function and evolution of teeth*. Cambridge University Press, Cambridge.

_____ and Cerina Johanson. 2003. Separate evolutionary origins of teeth from evidence in fossil jawed vertebrates. *Science* 299:1235-1236.

Smith, Patricia and E. Tchernov. 1992. *Structure, function, and evolution of teeth*. Freund Publishing House, London.

Stokstad, Erik. 2003. Primitive jawed fishes had teeth of their own design. *Science* 299:1164.

Teaford, Mark Franklyn; Moya Meridith Smith, and Mark W.J. Ferguson (editors). 2000. *Development, function, and evolution of teeth*. Cambridge University Press, New York.

Tompkins, Robert L. 1996. Relative dental development of upper Pleistocene hominids compared to human population variation. *American Journal of Physical Anthropology* 99(1):103-118.

Unger, Peter. 2010. *Mammal Teeth; Origin, Evolution, and Diversity*. Baltimore, MD: Johns Hopkins University Press.

Wilson, Robert. 1943. *The evolution of mammalian molar teeth: An exhibit in geology hall, University of Colorado Museum*. University of Colorado Museum, Boulder, CO.

Young, William G.; R. Jupp, and B.J. Kruger. 1989. *Evolution of the skull, jaws, and teeth in vertebrates*. Dept. of Oral Biology and Oral Surgery, University of Queensland, St. Lucia, Qld, Australia.

Zhao, Z.; K.M. Weiss and D.W. Stock. 2000. Development and evolution of dentition patterns and their genetic basis" in *Development, function, and evolution of teeth*, Mark F. Teaford, Moya Meridith Smith, and Mark W.J. Ferguson (editors). Cambridge University Press, New York.

Zhu, Yuanding. 1935. *Comparative studies on the scales and on the pharyngeals and their teeth in Chinese cyprinids: With particular reference to taxonomy and evolution*. St. John's University Press, Shanghai, China.

Chapter 3

Feathers — A Case Study in Complex Structures

Introduction

All adult birds, and only birds and certain turkey-sized putative theropods, and no other animals, have feathers (Parkes, 1966, p. 77). Furthermore, even the "amino-acid composition, shape, and behavior of feather keratins are unique among vertebrates" (Brush, 1996, p. 131). For strength and efficiency, the most efficiently engineered airplane ever built cannot compete with birds. Birds are "custom designed for flight," and one critical component is their feathers (Bishop, 1997, p. 8). The fact that birds use feathers to fly "affects virtually every aspect" of their design and construction (Witmer, 1995, p. 9). Feathers are the "most complex epidermal appendages found in animals" (Prum and Williamson, 2001).

These precision-designed structures are highly effective, yet extremely light, insulators that are designed to enable birds to fly.

Bird wing feathers themselves are one of the most beautifully designed structures existing in the world (Compton, 1987, 3:244-245). Feathers have such "striking diversity in size, shape, color, and texture" that very few human art masterpieces can compare with them in harmony of colors, liveliness, and softness (Prum and Williamson, 2001). Often copied but never equaled, the pattern and color beauty of feathers has been appreciated by humans the world over, as is evident from the fact that since ancient times feathers have been used by humans to adorn themselves.

Producing a Rainbow of Colors

The black, brown, and gray feather pigments are from the bird's blood, and the red and yellow pigments from its fat. **Lipochrome** pigments produce red, orange, and yellow colors, and **melanin** produces black, brown, red-brown, and gray colors (Hickman, et al., 2001, p. 588). The rainbow of colors, including the blue shimmering on the birds' throat and tail feathers, is due to both pigments and differential scattering of light. Referred to as **structural colors**, this method uses particles within the feather to scatter short wavelengths (the scattering intensity is proportional to the inverse fourth power of the wavelength).

The microscopic ridges on the feathers function as light diffraction grating to break up the light that falls on them into all the colors of the light spectrum. These systems all combine to produce the vibrant rainbow of colors that birds commonly display. Their colors serve a variety of functions, including seemingly contradictory functions such as to attract mates and yet blend in with their surroundings as camouflage.

Many individual birds use thousands of feathers to cover their body; a *Plymouth Rock Hen* has an estimated 8,000, and a *Whistling Swan* 25,000. Even a small bird such as a wren has over 1,000 feathers (Taylor, 1993, p. 5). Furthermore: "Birds account for a disproportionate amount of our perception of nature not only because their flight, song and colors make them noticeable as well as appealing but because they are nearly ubiquitous" (Ogburn, 1957, pp. 66-67). The reason why they are so ubiquitous, Ogburn notes, is because, just as the airplane "has enabled men to extend their realm to the farthest reaches of the planet," so to the feather, the "masterpiece" of nature, also has enabled birds to do the same (pp. 66-67).

Types of Integuments

All animals have some type of integument covering to maintain the integrity and integration of their bodies and protect them from pathogens, the weather, and other adverse environmental conditions. The four basic types of integument structures that function to protect eukaryotes are:

1. **Skin**. Skin can be extremely *thin,* such as that covering many worms, of *medium* thickness, such as the skin covering humans, or *thick* and tough, such as the hide covering cows and elephants.

2. **Hair.** Many animals also possess some type of hair (fur) growth in or over their skin or hide. Most mammals are abundantly covered with thick hair for warmth and insulation.

3. **Scales**. Scales, such as those on reptiles, range from thin-but-strong scales covering snakes to thick iron-like scales protecting armadillos. Scales overlap like house roof shingles and function in much the same way to keep water out and trap body heat while still allowing the animal to move.

4. **Feathers**. Feathers are a unique structure found *only* in birds and, some Darwinists claim, possibly some feathered dinosaurs. All birds (class Aves), have feathers (Bock, 2000). Feathers are considerably different from scales and all types of skin, whether the skin is thin and hairy, or thick and hairless.

Feathers, scales, hair, fingernails, and claws are all outgrowths of the skin and are all as devoid of feeling as are animal hair or nails.

It is for this reason, no pain is produced when hair is cut or nails are trimmed. Feathers and hair both form in pits called *papillae* located underneath the skin and often cover almost the entire body just as hair and scales do. Each pit is abundantly supplied with blood to nourish the growing feather. The feather, a strong-but-light structure, is constructed from keratin, a strong-yet-flexible protein.

Most birds "shed" or lose their feathers at regular intervals, usually once a year, a process called *molting*. Molting "is a highly orderly process" that occurs gradually to insure no bare spots develop (Hickman, et al., 2001, p. 588). Its placement is so highly ordered that the "flight and tail feathers are lost in exact pairs, one from each side, so that balance is maintained" (Hickman, et al., p. 588).

The Structure of a Feather

The most common theory of feather origins suggests that feathers evolved from reptile scales. The anatomy of feathers is radically different from that of skin or scales and is most similar to hair, yet much more complex. Bishop notes, "Feathers may look simple, but they're really very complicated. Each one can have more than a million tiny parts" (1997, p. 9). The complex anatomy of a feather varies, depending on the feather's function. For example, the "complex morphology" of the *flight* or *contour feather* includes a long shaft that usually is hollow and always strong, and a web that flares out from the shaft in the form of roughly planar *vanes* on either side (Bock, 2000, p. 478). The shaft consists of a hollow, stiff structure, often called a quill or vein, termed the *rachis* that serves as a solid-but-flexible support for branches called *barbs*. The rachis and barbs are analogous to a tree trunk and tree branches (Terres, 1980).

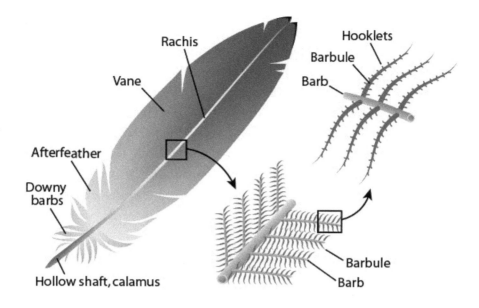

Figure 3.1 — Anatomy of a Feather[1]

Each parallel barb slants diagonally from the shaft, and has numerous smaller side branches or *barbules* (or *webs*) of different types that overlap those of the neighboring barbs in a herringbone pattern resembling a miniature replica of the whole feather (Peterson, 1963). The flight feather of a large bird can have as many as a million barbules (Denton, 1986, p. 202). The *barbules* (or *webs*) in flying birds are held firmly to the next web by "hooklets" called **hamuli** that function much like Velcro®. These branches and hamuli form a web sufficiently flexible, yet also stiff, and dense enough so that when the bird flies, very little air or water is able to seep through the spaces (Bock, 2000, p. 478).

---

[1] Image Credit: Copyright 2017 Arizona Board of Regents / ASU Ask a Biologist. Available under the Creative Commons Attribution-ShareAlike 3.0 Unported License. Image can be further recopied under this same license.

The branches and hooklets contain *barbicles*. The feather barbules also must be strong, yet flexible enough so that they will not break in the wind. Their design enables birds to ride air currents more gracefully than the best glider human engineers have ever designed. If the hooklets are lacking, such as in the plumes of the ostrich, the bird cannot fly. Hooklets are designed so that *they can separate* under certain conditions, preventing wind damage to the wing and feathers, but can be easily reattached when the bird preens its feathers. Ruffled feathers normally prompt preening behavior. Humans can repair a ruffled feather simply by drawing it between their fingers. Preening behavior is part of the irreducible complexity of the total feather design.

Feathers are designed to give the bird "lift" by causing the air on the top wing surface to flow *faster* than the air on the bottom wing surface. This results in lowered air pressure above the wing called the Bernoulli effect. To achieve this, flight feathers must be asymmetric, with the smaller vane on the leading edge in direct contact with the air during flight. The "sophisticated aerodynamic principles in the design of the bird's wing" include a mechanism that reduces the adverse effect of turbulence—a major cause of airplane crashes (Denton, 1986, p. 202).

Specially designed slots in the bird's airfoil cause part of the air stream to smooth out the airflow, an innovation imitated by aeroengineers in modern airplanes by designing small subsidiary airfoils in the wing. The bird also can vary its wing shape and flow traits to facilitate take-off, flight control, and landing. One way of achieving this is by an intricate system of tendons that allows the bird to twist its feathers so as to alter their resistance to air (Denton, p. 202).

Birds must have feathers to fly, but feathers also give the bird much-needed protection against adverse weather, especially cold air and water. Overlapped like shingles and coated with a layer of oil, feathers protect the bird from water and heat loss much like roof shingles help to protect a house. As Peterson notes, the feather is a marvel of natural engineering. It is at once extremely light and structurally strong, much more versatile than the stretched skin on which a bat supports itself in flight or the rigid structure of an aircraft's wing—and far more readily repaired or replaced when damaged....Though nearly weightless it has strength. The stiff shaft of the quill provides rigidity where support is needed, yet it is supple towards its tip, when flexibility is required for split second aerial maneuvering. Feel the sleekness of the web, soft yet firm. Separate the barbs; zipper them together again by running them through the fingertips as a bird would preen with its bill. The intricacy of the design that allows this can be appreciated by putting the feather under a microscope (1963, p. 33).

Feathers are connected together, along with other structures, to form the plumage. The plumage, dermal and subdermal cutaneous muscles, ligaments, the brain and sense organs all form an "interconnected" structure that must work as an irreducibly complex unit in order for the feather system to work at all. During construction it is critical that even such details as the angle, thickness, shape, and construction of all the feather parts are held to within narrow tolerances (Tarsitano, et al., 2000). Most minor deviations can render the entire flight system nonfunctional. A theory of feather evolution must even account for "the structure and complexity of the follicle" that produces and sustains the feather (Prum, 1999, p. 292).

Lacking Evidence of Feather Evolution

The main problem is little to no evidence exists for Feather evolution. In the words of one Columbia University biologist, "we lack completely fossils of all intermediate stages between reptilian scales and the most primitive feather" (Bock, 2000, p. 480). So far, not one of the required, hypothetical transitional types has been discovered in the fairly abundant bird fossil record. Millions of fossilized birds exist, and all of them have perfectly formed feathers. It is for this reason that the origins of feathers is considered an enigma by Darwinists (Turner, 1973).

Another major problem with all Darwinist theories of both feather and bird evolution is the fact that functional integrity is required for life, just as it is for any complex machine involving not only the feather, but also its many support structures (including the follicle, muscle, and nervous systems). In other words "organisms at every stage in the evolutionary sequence must be functional wholes interacting successfully with selective demands arising from the particular environment of the organisms at each stage in the evolutionary sequence" (Bock, 2000, p. 482).

Flight requires not only the evolution of feathers, but also a total redesign of almost the entire animal. In chicken embryos, feather development begins at day six and is intimately connected to the bird's entire development (Chuong, et al., 2000). As a result, birds are "the most clearly distinct of all vertebrate classes," and there is an "enormous gap in anatomy and way of life" between birds and their putative closest relatives, the reptiles (Carroll, 1997, p. 306). For example, the "metabolic rate and sustained body temperature are higher than in all other" vertebrates. Carroll concludes that the "geometry and mechanics of their respiratory system are unparalleled" (p. 306).

Reptiles have bellow-like lungs, birds have a complicated system of air sacs that keep air flowing in one direction through special tubes (*parabronchi*) in the lung, and blood moves through the lung's blood vessels in the opposite direction for efficient oxygen uptake (Schmidt-Nielsen, 1971).

As an Oregon State University respiratory physiologist argues, this is an excellent engineering design.

> Recently, conventional wisdom has held that birds are direct descendants of theropod dinosaurs. However, the apparently steadfast maintenance of hepaticpiston diaphragmatic lung ventilation in theropods throughout the Mesozoic poses a fundamental problem for such a relationship. The earliest stages in the derivation of the avian abdominal airsac system from a diaphragmatic-ventilating ancestor would have necessitated selection for a diaphragmatic hernia [i.e. hole] in taxa transitional between theropods and birds. Such a debilitating condition would have immediately compromised the entire pulmonary ventilatory apparatus and seems unlikely to have been of any selective advantage (Ruben, 1997, p. 1267).

Ruben's statement was in reference to the theropod origin of birds, but is an equally effective criticism of all reptile-to-bird origin theories. A related problem is that "the sequence of evolutionary steps must be continuous and gradual with no large saltational changes" (Bock, 2000, p. 482). These two problems have proved lethal to all past and present theories of both feather and flight evolution.

Special muscles on their skin enable birds to exercise detailed, controlled movement of their feathers. This system aids in flying and sometimes in protection. Some birds fluff their feathers for various reasons, such as to give the appearance of more mass to frighten enemies, to keep them warmer, or to attract other birds during their mating season. The famous feather spread of the male peacock is an excellent example of the high level of control that birds have over their feathers (Burgess, 2001). A further problem is that feathers are useless for flying (or most other functions) unless (and until) they are properly arranged on the bird. A specific pattern for the wing, tail, and other parts of the bird is required.

For all of these reasons "it is not realistic to discuss the evolution of the avian feather independently of the evolution of the avian integument with all of its interconnected features" (Bock, 2000, p. 479). Evolution of feathers, and all of the many other structures required to fly as separate structures is unlikely and clearly counterproductive because, as separate structures, they would impede survival. Lone feather shafts clearly would interfere with the animal's survivability. Only a complete set of the required parts and a complete set of feathers will produce flight.

The Basic Feather Types

Over a dozen different kinds of feathers exist to achieve the many functions feathers serve, including not only flight, but also signaling, courtship, waterproofing, streamlining the body, protective coloration, insulation, and even chemical defense (Bock, 2000, p. 479). And *none* of these many kinds of feather variations have properties which provide evidence that they evolved from scales, as would be expected by Darwinists. Nor is there any evidence of transitional forms between *any* of the feather types. One of these variations is what is known as **down feathers**, where little or no shaft is present, and the barbs interlock far less often than in non-down feathers.

Powder-down feathers are down feathers that release a talc-like powder to help waterproof the feathers and provide them with metallic-like luster (Hickman, et al., 2001). **Filoplume feathers** contain hair-like projections on the end of each shaft that are used for decoration, courtship, sensory input, and other purposes. In other types of feathers, such as the **bristle feathers** found on a flycatcher, the vein may be nearly or totally absent. Yet in other types, such as on the penguin the vein may be solidified.

Another feather type is the flight or wing feathers (*reimages*), often called contour feathers, and tail feathers (*rectrices*) that function to help the bird guide its flight (Bock, 2000). Two basic types of flight feathers exist — *fast* and *slow*. The fast type are strong, trim feathers used in birds that travel at high speeds, such as pigeons and hawks. The slow type consists of a soft and loose-edged structure and is used on birds, such as owls, that fly and soar at relatively slow speeds. The advantage of slow feathers is that they produce flight that is far *quieter* than that allowed by fast feathers. Quietness is far more important to an owl's hunting success than speed.

The belief in feather evolution requires evidence for the evolution of *each kind* of feather, or evidence for the evolution of each feather from the first feather, which requires speculation about "feasible selective demands acting on evolution of feathers," a task no one has yet achieved (Bock, 2000, p. 479). The evolution of feathers is considered so improbable — even by evolutionists — that they conclude "feathers evolved only once in the history of the vertebrata" (Bock, 2000, p. 480). Much speculation also exists about this putative first feather — was it a simple contour feather, a downy feather, or a flight feather (Bock, 2000, p. 483)?

A major problem with feather evolution is that "it is difficult to account for the initial evolution of feathers as elements in the flight apparatus since it is hard to see how they could function until they reached the large size seen in *Archaeopteryx*" (Carroll, 1997, p. 314). In other words "the chief difficulty in thinking about the evolution of the first feathers is the difficulty in accounting for the genesis of the structure through a continuous sequence of selective forces and with a continuous series of hypothetical morphological steps that are functionally plausible" (Regal, 1975, pp. 35-36). The common solution is to argue that feathers may have first evolved to provide insulation by a gradual increase in the size and the protofeather traits of scales (Carroll, 1997, p. 314). Known as the *insulation theory*, this idea has received a great deal of attention in recent years.

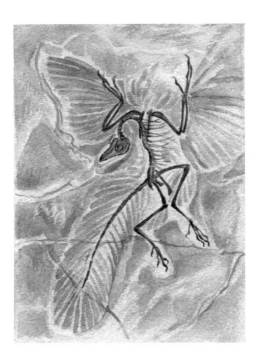

Figure 3.2 — Drawing of *Archaeopteryx* Fossil Imprint[2]

The Insulation Function of Feathers

Since birds are endotherms (warm-blooded), to survive in cooler climates they must effectively prevent much of their heat-loss — especially the loss from underneath their breast feathers. The air spaces between the feathers are highly effective insulators of the bird's body. This function is so critical that many Darwinists have theorized that feathers actually originated primarily as an insulating device and only later facilitated flight (Tucker, 1938; Ostrom, 1974; Bock, 2000). The first step in bird evolution,

---

[2] Image Credit: Panaiotidi / Shutterstock.com

therefore, is believed to be *not* the development of their ability to exploit the air, but for a light and effective "thermostat mechanism" to maintain constant temperature — with part of this system later evolving into feathers (Tucker, 1938).

Much disagreement exists about the role thermoregulation had, if any, in feather evolution partly because relatively little is known about early birds (Brush, 1996, p. 132). In contrast to this hypothesis, Parkes reasoned if "the primary 'need' of the avian ancestor" was for "an epidermal outgrowth ... useful as a thermoregulatory mechanism ... why 'bother inventing' anything as complex as a feather? Hair would have been much simpler!" (1966, p. 81). Actually a hairlike structure is much *better* for insulation, which explains why flightless birds have feathers superficially similar to hair (Feduccia, 1999, p. 130). In some cases this may be explained by loss of information for the complexity of flight feathers due to loss of selection pressure to maintain aerodynamic structure (Feduccia, 1999, p. 130), a conclusion compatible with the creation model.

Another problem is that "primitive" down feathers are a very poor means of temperature control. Flight feathers that use trapped air achieve much better insulation. Dewar (1957) concluded that the insulating theory is erroneous because the assumption of a cold-blooded creature becoming warm-blooded is problematic for many reasons, including the fact that the transformation from cold- to warm-blooded was theorized to have taken place in the tropics where temperatures are both fairly consistent and close to that of the blood in warm-blooded animals (37°C).

For this reason, some argue that feathers evolved, not to help birds keep warm, but to cool the bird by functioning as "sun shades" that block the sun to reduce the level of heat absorption (Bock, 2000, p. 481). Bock concludes that the thermal theory of feather evolution is, at best, "a poorly tested theory" (2000, p. 484).

Another problem that requires some explanation is the origin of the extremely complicated mechanism that birds use to avoid becoming overheated while in pursuit of their quarry. It is widely recognized that the heat-regulating mechanism of birds is poorly understood and that no viable theory exists as to its origin. Problems include the fact that flight feathers *reduce* dissipation of the heat generated by the bird's high metabolism.

To overcome this problem birds have unique air sacs to assist in dissipating heat generated during periods of high activity. But these structures alone usually cannot maintain a constant temperature. Some speculate that, to help maintain a cool temperature, a complex nervous mechanism exists to regulate both the oxidation level and the amount of blood supplied to each organ. Evolutionary theories relating to the origin of feathers and flight (and even heat conservation) are all inadequate, and evidence for such an evolutionary origin is nonexistent (Regal, 1975, p. 35).

Because of this problem, theories of feather origin recently have multiplied. Some researchers now argue that feathers evolved for water repellency, to function as a sink for excess sulfur waste, as a heat shield, or to streamline the body for greater speed. But none of these theories come even close to explaining their aerodynamic structure. Prum, in an extensive review of these theories, concluded that they all are "insufficient to explain the origin and diversification of feathers" and added that they are actually a "hindrance to evaluating" new fossil finds (1999, p. 292).

The Fossil Record

The common assumption that birds and feathers do not preserve well because of their hollow bones is incorrect. Their bone and feather fossil impressions can actually be preserved in certain environments, especially lacustrine (lake) environments, inland water habitats, and marine locations. As a result, a relatively abundant fossil record of both birds and feathers exists, thus enabling us to draw some fairly firm conclusions about bird and feather history (Davis and Dyke, 1999, p. 162; Davis and Briggs, 1995).

Literally millions of impressions of a large variety of small animals—even insects and feathers—have been found in stone, clay, peat, tar, and amber. The scales of dinosaurs and reptiles, the feathers of birds, the leaves of plants, and even the wings of insects all are often clearly outlined in detail in the fossil record, enabling us to study these life forms in detail.

Feathers also are preserved by carbonized traces (present in about 70% of deposits), bacterial autolithification (conversion to rock involving bacteria), imprintation (such as *Archaeopteryx*), in coprolites (animal dung), and in amber (Davis and Briggs, 1995). In general, the *better* the fossil record in terms of preserving morphology for a class of life, the *weaker* the case for Darwinism for that class. In the case of animals for which only bone fragments are preserved, such as those fossils used to support human and whale evolution, the ambiguity of the bones from extinct forms has been used in an effort to argue for transitional forms.

The Fossil Evidence and Feather Evolution

What is consistently found in the fossil record are fully developed scales, feathers that are fully feathers, and skin that is unequivocally skin. No transitional structures consisting of feathers that are part feather and part scale, or even feathers that are less than modern types, have ever been uncovered (Stahl, 1985, p. 350). Nor are "recognized intermediates" found in the fossil record (Brush, 1996, p. 132). All of the earliest birds discovered, including *Protoavis*, have fully modern feathers: "the oldest known feathers ... are already modern in form and microscopic detail" (Martin and

Czerkas, 2000, p. 687).

Archaeopteryx, of which 11 specimens or fragments have been confirmed so far, had perfectly developed "completely modern" feathers that are "nearly identical with those of modern birds" in spite of the fact that *Archaeopteryx* was a very different kind of bird compared to modern birds (Prum, 1999, p. 291; Carroll, 1997, p. 315). For this reason, *Archaeopteryx* "does not provide much information about the origin of feathers because its feathers are almost identical to those of living birds" (Zhang and Zhou, 2000, p. 1957).

Furthermore, fully functional "feathers clearly existed prior to the existence of *Archaeopteryx*" (Brush, 2000, p. 632). *Archaeopteryx* is important because it was until recently "the only direct evidence ... of the earliest stages of avian evolution" (Ostrom, 1974, p. 27). Other fossil feathers evolutionists date as far back as the Cretaceous and the "earliest feathers in the fossil record are modern in every respect, and no contemporary feather structure is unequivocally identifiable as primitive" (Carroll, 1997; Brush, 1996, p. 132).

Extensive study of one *Archaeopteryx* feather, a 69 millimeter-long, perfectly preserved example dated by evolutionists to be 150 million years old, is identical in all major details to modern feathers (Parkes, 1966, p. 77). As early as 1910, Pycraft concluded that the *Archaeopteryx* feather differed "in no way from the most perfectly developed feathers known to us" (1910, p. 39), and the wealth of discoveries since then has not altered this early view. Furthermore, a large number of skin impressions from dinosaurs have been uncovered, and evaluations of the extant samples conclude that they are "unlikely to represent a predecessor to a feather bearing integument" (Martin and Czerkas, 2000, p. 687).

Attempts by Darwinists to hypothesize *how* feathers could have evolved have produced "a morass of contradictory theories and muddy thinking" (Parkes, 1966, p. 77). Early evolution textbooks, such as Osborn (1918, p. 228), discussed a set of transformations or "intermediate feather types" that scientists were certain they would soon find in the fossil record. So far, none have been found. Nonetheless, most evolutionists still theorize that feathers evolved from reptile scales (Maderson, 1972).

One text confidently claims that "a feather is nothing but a further development of the scale (Heilmann, 1927, p. 128). One early scientific account concluded that scales gradually became longer, fimbriated, and "more and more efficient in the work of carrying the body through space" until birds could fly with ease (Pycraft, 1910, p. 39). The present scenario involves the elongation of reptilian scales, which then subdivide into a set of lateral plates that subdivide again to form the feather framework (Maderson and Alibardi, 2000, p. 514). These feather-evolution schemes, although they may appear plausible, all tend to obscure crucial difficulties, and often are too vague to provide grounds to criticize their specific claims (Denton, 1986, p. 216).

Since major morphological, tissue, and biochemical differences exist between feathers and scales, a large number of functional transitional forms would have had to exist (Brush, 1996, p. 132). Furthermore, "little to nothing can be said from the fossil record on functions and roles of feathers, especially the intermediate stages between the reptilian scale and the primitive avian feather" (Bock, 2000, p. 480). One major problem Klotz notes is the fact that feathers "cannot correspond to a whole scale but only to the outer half of the scale. The inner half or vascular core is believed [by evolutionists] to have atrophied" (1970, p. 460). Even speculating on the "most primitive stages of the evolution of feathers" is very problematic (Bock, 2000, p. 479).

Feathers are not only "strikingly different from scales in their structure," but also their developmental path also is radically different (Klotz, 1970, p. 460). The many problems with scale-to-feather evolution have motivated the development of new theories of feather origins, such as their evolution from a "cylindrical epidermal invagination around the base of a dermal papilla" (Prum, 1999, p. 291).

Brush even concludes that feathers must have evolved from a conical shaped, tubercle-like follicle rather than a plate-like structure (2000, p. 631). One reason he argues for this view is due to the fact that the most primitive feather must have a hair-like follicular mechanism to produce feather proteins, which then must be properly assembled to produce the many molecular structures needed to form the feather's complex gross anatomy. Therefore, the complex follicular mechanism must have evolved first.

Feathers have many more similarities, both morphologically and biochemically, to hair than to scales (Sawyer, et al., 2000). Although no evidence exists for this primitive follicular structure in the abundant bird fossil record, Brush's theory demonstrates a major failure of current scale-to-feather evolution theories. Hair-to-feather evolution is actually more logical for many reasons, including the fact that a hair follicle already exists. The major argument against this theory is that birds are speculated to have evolved from reptiles, not from mammals. Therefore, almost all researchers have totally ignored the hair-to-feather theory.

Feathers found in Amber

One of the oldest feathers, found in amber, dates back to the Cretaceous and is "an almost complete beautifully preserved" feather (Grimaldi and Case, 1995, p. 1). This example is a fully developed semiplume (one that occurs at the margin of feather tracts and apteria (naked spaces between the feathered areas of birds) and usually the contour feathers overlay it (1995, p. 2). The rachis and barbs were perfectly formed, and it is sometimes possible to identify the bird from which the amber-entombed feather has come.

Unfortunately, many specimens have not yet been carefully studied. Further studies no doubt will aid in the identification of many others. Although many fossil feathers and amber-preserved feathers (some dating back to the Cretaceous) have been located, no clues of feather evolution have ever been found in the fossil record; and consequently no physical evidence exists of the many changes that feathers would to have undergone if they evolved.

New Discoveries

It is still much too early to evaluate the numerous recent claims of feathers on dinosaurs or other animals, some of which have been shown to be forgeries. Others may also prove to be forgeries, and yet others offer very debatable evidence for feather evolution (Dalton, 2000). In China, the source of all of the new feather finds, one researcher claimed "assembly line factories" exist to assemble fossil forgeries that sell for large sums of money (Dalton, 2000a, p. 932).

The most infamous of these is *Archaeoraptor liaoningensis*, which was proven by computerized tomography scans to be a composite of several fossils (see Sloan, 1999, pp. 98-107 for the announcement of the find; Dalton, 2000a, pp. 689-690). Once "proclaimed as a key intermediate between carnivorous dinosaurs and birds but now known to be a forgery" (Zhou, Clarke, and Zhang, 2002, p. 285).

Many of the alleged "intermediates" are actually either fully formed, modern feathers, or structures that are not feathers but other structures (see Dalton, 2000b; Yu, et al., 2002). For example, *Sinosauropteryx* (also called *Sinornithosaurus*) "feathers" are actually "filaments" (Brush, 2000, p. 632). Other ancient fossil feather discoveries—such as on the oviraptorosaur *Caudipteryx* and *Protarchaeopteryx*—are "true feathers" (Padian, 2000, p. 30). These animals in some ways are more similar to non-flying birds, such as the ostrich, than flying birds. Other new discoveries — such as the hair-like filamentous integumental appendages on *Sinornithosaurus millenii*, a non-avian dinosaur — have only complicated the Darwinian theory (such as discussed by Zhang and Zhou, 2000). For instance, Feduccia concluded that one recent find, known as *Apsaravis*, contributes little

> to our understanding of avian evolution, and its lack of a clear relationship with any kind of modern bird makes its significance ambiguous. If *Apsaravis* is not related to any modern ornithurine, how can it tell us anything important about the evolutionary questions raised by [its discoverers] Norell and Clarke? (2001, p. 508).

The latest discovery of feathers on the bird-like, turkey-sized "theropods" *Caudipteryx* and *Protarchaeopteryx* indicate that they are flightless birds (Ross, 1998, p. 2). Touted by some as a dinosaur, *Caudipteryx* has been dated back to the early Cretaceous and is estimated to be 30 million years younger than *Archaeopteryx* yet is "more like modern birds than the undoubtedly Volant [flying] Archaeopteryx" (Woodmorappe, 2003, p. 90).

Evolutionary paleo-ornithologists Alan Feduccia and Larry Martin are staunch critics of the dinosaur-to-bird theory. They "believe that *Protarchaeopteryx* and *Caudipteryx* are more likely to be flightless birds similar to ostriches. They have teeth like some extinct birds and lack the long tail seen in theropods. *Caudipteryx* even used gizzard stones like modern plant-eating birds, but unlike theropods" (Sarfati, 1999, p. 61). Far from being ancestors of Archaeopteryx, cladistic evidence points [under evolutionary presuppositions] to their being more bird-like, and secondarily flightless *descendants* of Archaeopteryx (Swisher, et al., 1999, pp. 58-61).

Much debate exists about this and related finds (Yu, et al., 2002). Some consider these animals to be bird-like dinosaurs, or other dinosaur-like, flightless birds that have lost their full flight plumage (or never developed it). Conclusions on these finds will require much more study and yet already have produced much debate and controversy.

Much disagreement still exists about *Archaeopteryx*, a discovery now close to a 150 years old. Likewise, the placement by evolutionists, if any, of the recent finds may never be settled. Many of these finds are from a province of China, and already one find from this area has proven to be a hoax. Consequently, much more study is necessary to determine the value of these finds. So far, none of these finds challenge the conclusions presented in this chapter, and early study of these finds has strongly supported the findings reviewed here.

Flight Evolution

Connected to the topic of feather evolution is the evolution of flight. Many theories exist to explain flight evolution, including the gradual elongation of scales to produce a large surface for parachuting, then gliding, and finally flight (the *tree-down* or *arboreal hypothesis*). Tarsitano, et al., (2000) show that from a functional, morphological standpoint the tree-down theory is superior and that serious problems exist with the major opposing model.

Other authorities argue for the opposite hypothesis, called the *ground-up* or *cursorial theory*. Yale University Professor John Ostrom, after explaining why the tree-down theory is fatally flawed, argued eloquently for the ground-up theory, a position that he admitted was a distinctly minority view (1979). But yesterday's heresy is often today's orthodoxy, and the cogent arguments by the arboreal advocates against the cursorial theory now are largely ignored.

Since no evidence exists for any of these theories, they remain speculative at best and in most cases are largely guesswork (for a review of the history of bird evolution theories, see Witmer, 1995).

As Carroll concludes, "neither structural nor physiological arguments have yet settled this controversy conclusively" (1997, p. 314), and many of these evolutionary hypotheses are difficult or impossible to test. Regal (1975, p. 35) concludes that all existing "theories relating the origin of feathers to flight ...[are] inadequate." Marden adds that "theorists have spent half a century fiercely debating whether avian flight evolved from 'the trees down,' via gliding intermediates, or from 'the ground up,' via running, leaping intermediates, with no resolution in sight" (1975, p. 27).

Conclusions

Even though fossil impressions of feathers are abundant in the fossil record and much has been written speculating on how scale-to-feather evolution could have occurred, not a shred of fossil or other evidence has ever been found to support the scale-to-feather evolution theory (Parkes, 1966; Regal, 1975). In the words of Prum, understanding "the evolutionary origin of feathers has been constrained by the lack of any known ancestral feather morphologies or structural antecedents" (1999, p. 291).

The evidence supports Klotz's early conclusion that the "origin of feathers is still a real problem" for Darwinism, and all contemporary theories of feather origin are hypothetical ideas that "can only be characterized as judicious speculation" (1970, p. 460). In short, nothing has changed since Regal stated that "although most textbooks include some sort of speculation on the evolutionary origin of feathers ... [a] morass of contradictory theories and muddy thinking ... occurs in ... much of the literature on this subject" (1975, p. 35).

Although much speculation and major disagreements exist on how feathers "could have" evolved, all existing theories are "just-so stories," unsupported by fossil or historical evidence. The profound evolutionary enigma of feathers noted by Darwin and also by Heilman (1927) remains, even today. The lack of evidence for feather evolution is not only a major problem for Darwinism, but the design and function of feathers provides evidence for both intelligent design and irreducible complexity. Flight and feathers are indeed a "miracle" (Cromer, 1968).

Feather evolution is related to the question of bird evolution. Periodically, new bird fossils are found, but most of them have been of little or no use as evidence of bird evolution, and the few claimed examples typically generate much debate.

In conclusion, we agree with Brush: "Uncountable numbers of words have been written in attempts to ... reconstruct the primitive feather and explain why feathers evolved" (2000, p. 631). So far, all of these attempts have not only failed, but also have led to the conclusion that how feathers "arose initially, presumably from reptilian scales, defies analysis" (Stahl, 1985, p. 349). A more poetic summary was penned by Cavagnardo:

> The fossil record is a narrow window. Through it we view the past as if it were a movie snipped from the reel of life, frame by random frame, and spliced together again by some capricious hand. The feather—like the flower, which replaced the cone almost without trace of transition—springs full-blown upon the screen of time, unanticipated among the scaly creatures that for eons had impressed the young and forming rocks with their skin casts, footprints, and often giant bones. There is no hint of feathers upon the flaps that carried gliding reptiles for the first time into the perilous but promising sky (1982, p. 42).

References

Aymar, Gordon. 1935. *Bird Flight*. New York, Dodd, Mead.

Bishop, Nic. 1997. *The Secrets of Animal Flight*. Boston: Houghton Mifflin.

Bock, Walter J. 2000. "Explanatory History of the Origin of Feathers." *American Zoology*, 40:478-485.

Brush, Alan H. 1996. "On the Origin of Feathers." *Journal of Evolutionary Biology.*, 9:131-142.

_____. 2000. "Evolving a Protofeather and Feather Diversity." *American Zoology*, 40:631-639.

Burgess, S. 2001. "The Beauty of the Peacock Tail and the Problems with the Theory of Natural Selection." *Tech Journal*, 15(2):94-102.

Carroll, Robert. 1997. *Patterns and Processes of Vertebrate Evolution*. New York: Cambridge University Press.

Cavagnardo, David. 1982. *Feathers*. Portland, OR: Graphic Arts Center.

Chuong, C.-M, N. Patel, J. Lin, H.-S. Jung and R. B. Widelitz. 2000. "Sonic Hedgehog Signaling Pathway in Vertebrate Epithelial Appendage Morphogenesis: Perspectives in Development and Evolution." *Cellular and Molecular Life Sciences*, 57:1672-1681.

Compton. 1957. *Comptons Encyclopedia*. Chicago: The University of Chicago., Vol.4.

Cousins, Frank W. 1971. "The Alleged Evolution of Birds." Chapter 4 in *A Symposium on Creation*, Vol. III. Grand Rapids MI: Baker. Ed. by Donald Patten.

Cromer, Richard. 1968. *The Miracle of Flight*. Garden City, New York: Doubleday & Company.

Dalton, Rex. 2000a. "Chasing the Dragons." *Nature*, 406:930-932.

_____. 2000b. "Feathers Fly over Chinese Fossil Birds Legality and Authenticity." *Nature*, 403:689-690.

Darwin, Charles. 1859. *The Origin of Species*. London: John Murray.

Davis, Paul and D. Briggs. 1995. "The Fossilization of Feathers." *Geology*, 23(9):783-786.

Davis, Paul and Gareth Dyke. 1999. "Birds" in *The Encyclopedia of Paleontology*. Chicago, IL: Fitzroy Dearborn.

Denton, Michael. 1986. *Evolution: A Theory in Crisis*. Bethesda, MD: Adler and Adler.

Dewar, Douglas. 1957. *The Transformist Illusion*. Murfeesboro, TN: DeHoff.

Editorial. 2000. "Disappearing Discovery of the Year: Archaeoraptor." *Science*, 290:221.

Feduccia, Alan. 1999. *The Origin and Evolution of Birds*. 2nd Edition. New Haven: Yale University Press.

_____. 2001. "Fossils and Avian Evolution." *Nature,* 414:507-508 (with Mark A. Norell and Julia A. Clark replying on p. 508).

Grimaldi, David and Gerard R. Case. 1995. "A Feather in Amber from the Upper Cretaceous of New Jersey." *American Museum Novitiates*, 3126:1-6, April 5, 1995. New York: American Museum of Natural History.

Heilman, Gerhard. 1927. *The Evolution of Birds*. New York: D. Appleton.

Hickman, Cleveland, Larry Roberts, and Allan Larson. 2001. *Integrated Principles of Zoology*. New York: McGraw-Hill.

Klotz, John. 1970. *Genes, Genesis and Evolution*. St Louis: Concordia.

Maderson, Paul F. 1972. "On How an Archosaurian Scale Might Have Given Rise to an Ovian Feather." *American Naturalists*, 146:424-428.

_____ and Lorenzo Alibardi. 2000. "The Development of the Sauropsid Integument: A Contribution to the Problem of the Origin and Evolution of Feathers." *American Zoology*, 40:513-529.

Marden, James. 1975. "How Insects Learned to Fly." *The Sciences*, 35(6):26-30.

Martin, Larry and Stephan A. Czerkas. 2000. "The Fossil Record of Feather Evolution in the Mesozoic." *American Zoology*, 40:687-694.

Ogburn, Charlton. 1957. *The Adventure of Birds*. New York: William Morrow.

Osborn, Henry Fairfield. 1918. *The Origin and Evolution of Life*. New York: Charles Scribners.

Ostrom, J.H. 1974. "*Archaeopteryx* and the Origin of Flight." *Quarterly Review of Biology*, 49(1):27-47.

_____. 1979. "Bird Flight: How did it Begin?" *American Scientist*, 67:45-56.

Padian, Kevin. 2000. "Dinosaurs and Birds — An Update." *National Center for Science Education Reports*, 20(5):28-30.

Parkes, Kenneth. 1966. "Speculations on the Origin of Feathers." *Living Bird*, 5:77-86.

Peterson, Roger Tory. 1963. *The Birds*. New York: Time.

Prum, Richard O. 1999. "Development and Evolutionary Origin of Feathers." *Journal of Experimental Zoology (Molecular, Developmental, Evolution)*, 285:291-306.

_____ and Scott Williamson. 2001. "Theory of the Growth and Evolution of Feather Shape." *Journal of Experimental Zoology (Molecular, Developmental, Evolution)*, 291:30-57.

Pycraft, W.P. 1910. *Animal Life: An Evolutionary Natural History, Vol II — A History of Birds*. Methuen London.

Regal, Philip. 1975. "The Evolutionary Origin of Feathers." *The Quarterly Review of Biology*, 50(1):35-66.

Ross, Hugh. 1998. "Darwinism's Fine Feathered Friends — A Matter of Interpretation." *Reasons to Believe*, 12(3):1-3.

Ruben, J.A., et al. 1997. "Lung Structure and Ventilation in Theropod Dinosaurs and Early Birds." *Science*, 278(5341):1267-1270.

Sarfati, Jonathan. 1999. *Refuting Evolution*. Green Forrest, AR: Master Books.

Sawyer, Roger H., Travis Glenn, Jeffrey O. French, Brooks Mays, Rose B. Shames, George L. Barnes, Jr., Walter Rhodes, and Yoshinori Ishikawa. 2000. "The Expression of Beta (ß) Keratins in the Epidermal Appendages of Reptiles and Birds." *American Zoology*, 40:530-539.

Schmidt-Nielsen, Knut. 1971. "How Birds Breathe." *Scientific American*, 225(6):72-79.

Scholander, P.F. 1957. "Engineers Make Much Use of This Principle of Counter-Current Exchange which is Common in Living Orgainisms as Well." The Wonderful Net. *Scientific American*, April, pp. 96-107.

Sloan, Christopher. 1999. "Feathers for T. Rex?" *National Geographic*, 196(5):98-107, Nov.

Stahl, Barbara J. 1985. *Vertebrate History: Problems in Evolution*. New York: Dover.

Swisher, Carl C., III; Yuan-qing Wang, Xiao-lin Wang, Xing Xu, and Yuan Wang. 1999. "Cretaceous Age for the Feathered Dinosaurs of Liaoning, China." *Nature*, 400:58-61. Tarsitano, Samuel F., Anthony P. Russell, Francis Horne, Christopher Plummer and Karen Millerchip. 2000. "On the Evolution of Feathers from an Aerodynamic and Constructional View Point." *American Zoology*, 40:676-686.

Taylor, Barbara. 1993. *The Bird Atlas*. New York: Dorling Kindersley.

Terres, Hohn. 1980. *The Audubon Society Encyclopedia of North American Birds*. New York: Alfred A Knopf.

Tucker, B.W. 1938. "Functional Evolutionary Morphology: The Evolution of Birds." In *Evolution*, pp. 330-332, edited by G.R. DeBear. Oxford: Clarendon Press.

Turner, C.E.A. 1973. *"Archaeopteryx*, A Bird: No Link." *Evolution Protest Movement*, Sept.

Wallace, George and Harold D. Mahan. 1975. *An Introduction to Ornithology.* New York: Macmillan.

Witmer, Lawrence. 1995. *The Search for the Origin of Birds.* New York: Franklin Watts.

Woodmorappe, John 2003. "Bird Evolution: Discontinuities and Reversals." *TJ,* 17(1):88-94.

Xing Xu, Hong-he Zhou, and Richard O. Prum. 2001. "Branched integumental structures in Sinornithosaurus and the Origin of Feathers." *Nature,* 410:200-204.

Yu, Mingke; Ping Wu, Randall B. Widelitz, and Cheng-Ming Chuong. 2002. "The Morphogenesis of Feathers." *Nature,* 420:308-312.

Zhang, Fucheng and Zhonghe Zhou. 2000. "A Primitive Enantiornithine Bird and the Origin of Feathers." *Science,* 290:1955-1959.

Zhou, Zhonghe; Julia A. Clark, and Fucheng Zhang. 2002. "Archaeoraptor's Better Half." *Nature,* 420:285.

Chapter 4

Intermediate Forms and Functions

Introduction

This putative great grandfather of all life was a simple life form that evolved from some simple pre-life form that spontaneously generated itself millions of years ago in some hypothetical "primordial soup." Newer ideas place the location of *abiogenesis*, the origin of life from non-life by natural and not supernatural, means, at various other places, including in clay, deep-ocean hot vents, and even in land surface hot springs.

Since Darwin's time, billions of fossils have been found. The Smithsonian Institute alone contains about 15 million fossils. These fossils give us a very good idea of what life was like eons ago. In all of these millions of fossils, no clear transitional forms have ever been located. Virtually all of fossils found are those of clearly established types. Thousands of plant and animal types that are now extinct have been unearthed, but all are either extinct types or, at best, only minor variations of existing types. Of the new fossils that are claimed by some to be transitional forms, almost all are very similar to existing types. The fossil evidence clearly shows that all life did not evolve from simple primitive organisms as Darwinism requires.

Problems with the Fossil Record

A good example of the types of transitional forms that scientists expect to find in the fossil record, that is if evolution were true, are bones showing the supposed evolution of the giraffe. All other mammals have extremely short necks, and in most all cases the head is not more than a few inches away from the trunk of their body. It is hypothesized that giraffes also once had very short necks in the distant past and at least in this respect were similar to other mammals. Due to the competition for food, scientists hypothesized that there would be found more leaves, the diet of giraffes, at the *higher* levels of the trees. This is because it is assumed that the short-necked animals who consume leaves tend to defoliate the lower parts of trees. Darwinism argued that this situation confers an advantage to the animals with longer necks, and the giraffe's neck would, in time, evolve to the length that it is today. Darwin concluded, as man breeds dogs, horses, and cows for certain traits by selecting for breeding those animals with the desired traits, so nature does the same thing.

The many problems with this theory include the fact that large amounts of low level foliage typically exists in much of Africa. And, as far as is known, there has never been a population of mammals tall enough to defoliate most of the lower levels of the tall trees in a large area. Most mammals are grazers or meat eaters; very few consume tree leaves. Even the giraffe relies on a diet of grass (the giraffe and the koala bear, a marsupial, are the most common examples), there is no evidence that there ever was a lack of foliage close to the ground in most non-desert areas.

The second major problem is that the fossil record does not support the theory of giraffe neck evolution. If the giraffe's neck evolved, we would expect to find fossils of giraffes with short necks at the lower levels of the theoretical geological column. And as we progressed up the geological strata, we would expect to find fossil evidence of the same animal with longer and longer necks, eventually bringing us to the modern long-necked giraffe. However, as of yet, *not a single fossil* has been unearthed that has even been claimed to be strong evidence of giraffe evolution. Given the fact that literally billions of fossils have been unearthed (admittedly, mostly of smaller marine animals), it seems extremely unlikely that any will ever be found. This is good evidence that no intermediate fossils have ever existed and that giraffe evolution never occurred. The question of why other animals did not evolve long necks to reach the abundant supply higher up in the tree is another problem.

Darwinists have frequently claimed that transitional forms have not been found because many animals, such as worms and insects, do not have substantial hard body parts, and the parts most likely to be preserved in the fossil record are hard parts, such as teeth, bones, and shells. This claim would not explain the lack of evidence for giraffe evolution — giraffe neck bones are an excellent measure of the neck length. If evidence for Darwinism for an animal were dug up, it clearly would be the hard parts such as bone. The same lack of clear transitional forms of the type required exist for every type of chordate, including fish, amphibians, reptiles, birds, and mammals.

Evolutionists at one time believed that, if we just kept looking for fossils, eventually the many "missing links" would be located. But our museums are full of fossils and, of the millions that have been found, no true missing links have ever been identified. It is true that lack of evidence for evolution does not mean evidence for the only competing theory, creationism. Nonetheless, the fossil record is exactly what we expect to find if the creationist position (i.e., different animal kinds were created separately) were true. Creation predicts that we would *not* find transitional forms between phyla, class, and possibly even genera, and this is exactly what is found.

Scientific research, pursued with the goal of proving evolution, has, in fact, proved quite the opposite. Although much but not all of the evidence is in, and not all of the questions have been answered, an impressive case can be made for the creationist position. This review agrees with the conclusion made over 50 years ago by Professor Corner of the University of Cambridge:

> Much evidence can be adduced in favor of the theory of evolution — from biology, biogeography and paleontology, but I still think that, to the unprejudiced, the fossil record of plants [and animals as well] is in favor of special creation ... The evolutionist must be prepared with an answer, but I think that most [attempts to answer] would break down before an inquisition. (Corner, 1961, p. 97)

Twenty years later, Harvard paleontologist Stephen J. Gould concluded that

> The extreme rarity of transitional forms in the fossil record persists as the trade secret of paleontology .... Paleontologists have paid an exorbitant price for Darwin's argument. We fancy ourselves as the only true students of life's history, yet to preserve our favored account of evolution by natural selection we view our data as so bad that we never see the very process we profess to study. (Gould, 1980, pp. 181-182)

Gould's answer is punctuated equilibrium, a solution that does not solve the problem of "the extreme rarity of transitional forms."

Do Existing Putative Transitional Forms Prove Evolution?

Many living and extinct animals have been used as evidence of evolution. A few animals with fully developed features typical of other classes, which is what all fossil finds are, is not what is required to prove evolution. What is required are thousands of *intermediate* forms that clearly show *gradual* evolution from, for example, a monkey type to a man. And these transitional forms have not and, it is becoming increasingly obvious today, will not be found. There exist no "half-fish, half-bird" fossils, only animals with some unique structures, like flippers on mammals, i.e. whales, that evolutionists try to "force" into a transitional form category. The fact that some evolutionists do not accept many of the claimed transitional forms as truly transitional shows the critical importance of interpretation.

Many life forms are clearly part of a group of unique animals, but do not fit the requirement for a transition. One living example is the duck-billed platypus, an emphatically interesting creature—it lays eggs and has a duck bill like a bird and a tail like a beaver, is furry like a cat, and stores its young like a kangaroo. The duck-billed platypus would be a perfect transitional form if it was known only as a fossil. No one claims that this living Australian anomaly is evolving from, for example, a bird to a mammal, or from an amphibian to a bird. It is well established that ducks did not descend from a platypus, neither did mammals. There are no transitional forms whatsoever that lead to it or from it, and it is still very much alive and well. The platypus is simply an animal that has many interesting characteristics, several of which are more typical of other types of animals, such as birds. It is, indeed, an enigma, and there exist many other living enigmas.

Likewise, the same is true of the Archaeopteryx. Many bones belonging to the Archaeopteryx bird have been discovered (at least nine fairly complete sets and one perfectly formed feather) and even here no evidence of evolution exists, only a very unique bird. It's unusual features are its small size, the fact that it had teeth (no modern bird has teeth, although a few extinct forms do) and a longer tail than most birds, which some evolutionists claim indicates its reptilian ancestry. Some ancient and modern birds have long tails, and some had teeth, but many reptiles have no teeth.

If scientists discovered only penguin fossils, would they conclude that they were evidence of mammals evolving into birds because they appear to be developing wings which, on superficial examination, does seem to be the case. Actually, Darwinists claim that penguins are de-evolving from birds, an assumption for which, again, there is no evidence. Penguins are not evolving or de-evolving into anything. They are perfectly adapted to their environment, and their supposed "de-evolving wings" are not wings, but highly functional flippers to facilitate swimming.

Evolution from Gills to Lungs

An example of a transitional form would be the evolution from gills to lungs. We would expect the early stages of the gill-to-lung transition to have some system that could function as lungs, enabling the animal to stay out of water for more than a few minutes. In time, the lung tissue would expand and develop so that the so-called lung-gill creature will enable later generations to stay out of the water for longer and longer periods of time. No animal has ever been found to have anything like this structure. Animals either have fully developed gills or fully developed lungs, and no intermediate examples are known, anywhere, in living or fossil animals. Some animals exist that in *one stage* of their life have gills, and in another stage have lungs, but *each* stage is separate, and gills, which are totally different structures from lungs, are completely developed, as are also the lungs in the next stage. The so-called lung fish, such as the mudskipper, although they can swim, they live out of water in the atmosphere about 90% of the time. They breathe by forcing air to pass through their skin, which traps air to supply oxygen to their cells (Rake, 2015, p. 28). Although they have gills, they use them not to breathe, but rather to excrete waste products. They also have gill chambers that they use to store water, allowing them to remain out of the water for significant periods of time.

It seems that evolution would favor animals with *both* functional gills *and* functional lungs. This animal could more effectively escape from their predators then animals with only gills or lungs—those in the water could jump out on land and quite effectively escape predators, and those that normally lived on the land could run into the water to escape predators. Lions don't normally run into water while chasing their prey. It would seem that this structure would also develop *if* Darwinism were true, but none exists.

Some marine animals live out of the water in a state of "suspended animation" until the water rises to engulf them. There is no animal, though, that is equally comfortable on land or in the water as Darwinism would expect to develop by survival of the fittest theory. They have either perfectly formed lungs or perfectly formed gills, just as there are airplanes or automobiles; and no "auto-planes" yet developed have been able to *effectively* transverse on both land and in the air.

Evolutionism is supposed to proceed in ways that is often presented somewhat magically. Humans are often said to have developed a larger brain because we needed one, yet extra arms would also give us a clear selective advantage, and wings would be even better. Humans *could* develop wings, according to evolution, simply through some mutations that gave him a "wing like protuberance" somewhere on his shoulder, back, front, etc., like they theorize birds once had. If this protuberance enabled humans to jump slightly higher, or land slightly slower, the theory says it would, confer on them a survival advantage, if ever so slight. In time other mutations would occur that lengthen the size of the wings, and eventually humans would be able to fly.

The only problem is the theory does not work. There is no evidence of any animal anywhere "developing" wings or any other new organ, although evidence exists of losses. All the animals found in the fossil record either have wings or do not. A few birds have very useful fully developed wing-like structures that are not used for flying, but for other purposes, such as the ostrich. Ostriches can run about 50 miles-per-hour, and their wings serve as excellent balancing organs, although they are also very useful for other functions. An example is frightening predators by lifting their feathers up causing the animal to look much larger. Evolutionists, though, contend that, given enough time and an enormous number of mutations, almost anything can, and will, evolve. That claim is simply not true. Like a multiple choice question, if a student doesn't know the answer, staring at the page beyond a few minutes will not help him. No matter how long he stares, the correct answer will simply never come if he did not learn the material.

The Evidence for Human Evolution

The most crucial evidence required to prove Darwinism is linking humans to so-called lower life forms. The few claimed transitional forms that have been found are *all* hotly debated — and they are incredibly sparse. It has been said that all of the fossils "proving" human evolution could fit comfortably on a kitchen table. Professor Watson stated, "The fossils that decorate our family tree are so scarce that there are still more scientists than specimens. The remarkable fact is that all the physical evidence we have for human evolution can still be placed, with room to spare, inside a single coffin!" (Watson, 1982, p. 44)

Since 1982, many new discoveries have been made, and many of the human evolution fossils have been reclassified as ape or another human variety, such as Neanderthals. These fossils are typically extremely old and consist of distorted bits and pieces of bone and teeth. Only a few partial skeletons have been found. The most complete skeleton is Lucy, which is claimed to be about 40 percent complete, but because many bones are only broken fragments, if one compares its total weight with the total weight of a complete skeleton, it is actually less than ten percent complete. Another problem is the fossil record claims are riddled with fraud—Piltdown man and Java man are among the most famous examples[1]. The result of this state of affairs is, as Watson notes, not surprising because

> despite the diligent research done in East Africa by paleontologists Richard Leakey and Donald Johanson, there are gaping holes in the evolutionary record, some of them extending for 4 to 6 million years. Modern apes, for instance, seem to have sprung out of nowhere. They have no yesterday, no fossil record. And the true origin of modern humans—of upright, naked, tool making, big-brained beings—is, if we are to be honest with ourselves, an equally mysterious matter. There is, therefore, plenty of room for an alternative explanation. (Watson, 1982, p. 44)

Why Darwin's Theory Does Not Work

Proof of Darwin's theory was beguilingly simple— one would eventually find in the fossil record the predecessors of today's more perfectly adapted life forms. These predecessors were less adapted, less able to survive, and weaker in comparison with those around them that did survive. The weaker, less fit, animals were wiped out by natural selection.

---

[1] See Millar, 1972; Janus, 1975; and Shapiro, 1974.

The only problem with the theory of survival of the fittest is that it is simply not true. Hitching concludes that "Darwinism is a theory that seeks to explain evolution. It has not, contrary to general belief, and despite very great efforts, been proved" (Hitching, 1982, pp. 14-15). We now have a fairly accurate picture of most major life forms, including extinct animals, and there seems to be little difference between those that went extinct and those that survived. Many extinct animals actually seem like they would be better fit to survive than animals that are still with us today — the dinosaurs and the other ferocious monsters of old are good examples. Scientists are still searching for the cause of the dinosaurs' extinction, although the asteroid hypothesis hypothesis is now the most popular.

Animals that become extinct are most often the victim of circumstances — chance and unforeseen occurrences. Actually, we have no idea why most animals went extinct. Their senses were not less developed, nor was there anything else about them that we have been able to determine to that was inferior. All their sense organs, body structures, etc. were very similar to those animals alive today. Some were different, but often not much from most animals today. It often takes an expert to find the differences, and even then their differences are often very small and debated by scholars.

A few animals with fully developed features typical of other classes is not what is required to prove evolution. What is required are thousands of *intermediate* forms that clearly show *gradual* evolution from a dog-like animal to, for example, a monkey-like primate, to, eventually, humans. And these transitional forms have not and, it is becoming increasingly obvious today, will not be found. Most fossils that are claimed to be intermediary are actually simply variations of types that are commonly found today or animals that have features commonly found on other types. There are no "half-fish, half-bird" fossils, only some unique structures like flippers that Darwinists try to "force" into a transitional form category, and even most evolutionists do not accept many of the claimed transitional forms as truly transitional.

If enough fossils are found, obviously some variations from the extinct types will be located. Given a thousand North American adults, their height may range may range between 5' 1" and 6' 2". Given a hundred thousand people, the variation may be between 4' and 6' 11." Given several billion people, the range may be between around 28 inches and 7' 8" tall, which is close to the variation actually found today. Thus, the *more* fossils that are discovered, the greater variation one will find, and the greater the likelihood that a fossil form that seems to be a "transitional" will be uncovered. Generally, the larger the number objects of a specific category that are located, the greater range in their traits, which slowly increases to a point that further increases are increasingly small.

Scientists have also tried to "evolve" bacteria, a small life form with a short lifespan. A speck of bacteria transferred on a toothpick tip placed in blood serum will produce two billion per cubic centimeter for every cubic centimeter of blood in the body every four days. By comparison, the vaccine used against influenza contains 12.4 billion germs in each 15.5 drops. Furthermore, bacteria are in an excellent position to evolve, i.e., the numbers of mutations are high, and billions are rapidly reproduced; thus the level of favorable mutations would also normally be high.

Scientists have bred bacteria for many billions of generations and *the bacteria are still bacteria* although the ratio of types changes, but they always only produce "after its kind." Why bacteria have not evolved is not explainable — but, of course, if they evolved into a higher life form, life on earth could not exist anywhere because life is dependent on bacteria to recycle most everything. There is no evidence that any species has changed, or can change, into another kind of animal.

Some people note the harm that various bacteria have done, asking, "Why would a loving God create disease-causing bacteria?" We now know in order for higher forms of life to exist, lower forms of life must also exist. There is an incredible balance in the natural world, and the vast majority of bacteria are not pathogenic. Actually, most do a myriad of important tasks, most notably return the carcass of animals to the soil by breaking them down by a process called decay, which is actually a process of chemically incorporating the animal body into the bacteria (ingestion) and then chemically changing it into elements that plants can use.

Without decay, life would soon cease to exist on the earth. There exist thousands of kinds of bacteria, most which are very useful and many live within humans. The problem of sickness is not caused by the presence of bacteria (they are everywhere) but by a few mutant bacteria plus a poor diet, and other factors; thus some people succumb to illness, but in most cases most people do not, even during plagues. Bacteria would obviously not have any higher forms of life to break down if they evolved first and lived only among other bacteria for a significant amount of time.

Conclusions

The evidence has shown that no transitional forms are known between any of the major phyla of animals and plants." Harvard's the late George Gaylord Simpson added that, in spite of some claimed examples, "it remains true, as every paleontologist knows, that *most* new species, genera, and families, and that nearly all new categories above the level of families, appear in the record suddenly and are not by known, gradual, completely continuous transitional sequences" (Simpson, 1953, p. 360; emphasis in original). And as Smithsonian scientist Austin A. Clark concluded, "The complete absence of any intermediate forms between the major groups of animals, which is one of the most striking and most significant phenomena brought out by zoology, has hitherto been overlooked, or at least ignored" (quoted in Funk, 1929, p. 7).

It is evident that, as a criminologist needs sufficient physical evidence to link an accused with the crime (fingerprints, photos, eye witness identification, etc.), likewise, Darwinists need sufficient physical evidence to support their hypothesis. As the physical evidence is clearly lacking, it behooves the jury to dismiss the theory as unsubstantiated. Creation predicts that we would *not* find transitional forms between phyla and class and this is exactly what is found.

Scientific research, often pursued with the goal of proving Darwinism, has proved quite the opposite. Although much, but not all, of the evidence is in, and not all possible questions have been answered, an impressive case can be made for the creationist position. The evidence has vindicated the beliefs of theists since Adam and Eve. And, as an examination of the evidence has been quite intensive for the past century and a half, it is now evident that the required evidence for Darwinism will likely never be found because it never existed.

References

Corner, E.J.H. 1961. "Evolution" in MacLeod and Cobley's *Contemporary Botanical Thought*, pp. 95-114.

Gould, Stephen Jay. 1980. *The Panda's Thumb: More Reflections in Natural History*. New York: W.W. Norton & Company.

Funk, Willard. 1929. "New theory of man in the making?" *Literary Digest*, Feb. 18, 100:27-28.

Hitching, Francis. 1982. *The Neck of the Giraffe: Where Darwin Went Wrong*. New York: Ticknor and Fields.

Janus, Christopher. 1975. *The Search for Peking Man*. New York: MacMillan.

Millar, Ronald. 1972. *The Piltdown Men*. New York: St. Martin's Press.

Rake, Jody S. 2015. *Mudskippers and Other Extreme Fish Adaptations*. North Mankato: Capstone Press.

Raup, David. 1985. *Extinction: Bad Genes or Bad Luck?* New York: Norton.

Shapiro, Harry. 1974. *Peking Man*. New York: Simon and Schuster.

Simpson, George Gaylord, 1953. *The Major Features of Evolution*. New York: Columbia University Press.

Watson, Lyall. 1982. "The Water People" *Science Digest*, 90(5):44.

PART II:

The Invertebrates

Chapter 5

Invertebrates — An Overview

Introduction

Most of the fossil record evidence used as support for Neo-Darwinism consists of bone fragments of vertebrates that require much interpretation and, as a result, produce much controversy among vertebrate paleontologists and other evolutionists. Yet, of the estimated 1.7 million known species of animals, fully 95 percent are invertebrates (Barnes, 1987, p. 1). These invertebrates usually are divided into 22 different phyla (Milne and Milne, 1976).

Fortunately, an abundant number of invertebrate fossils exist — easily in the millions — many of which show excellent external morphology (Eldredge, 2000, p. 83; Hallam, 1977). Furthermore, a good invertebrate fossil record has been known to exist for many decades (see Easton, 1960; and Twenhofel and Shrock, 1935, p. 17). The rich record of fossil invertebrates that are preserved in amber, tar, or frozen in ice (all of which are excellent preservatives) often show exquisite detail of even minute body parts such as eyes and hair (Gayrand-Valy, 1994; Alonso, et al., 2000). Even soft-bodied worms such as Phoronids have left excellent mud casts (Anderson, 1998, p. 345). Soft-bodied animals are most often preserved as impressions, often in coarse-grained sediments (Jensen, Gehling and Droser, 1998).

This excellent fossil record allows accurate comparisons of ancient and modern forms that can be used to evaluate Darwinism. This chapter evaluates evidence for evolution in each of the major invertebrate phyla, excluding insects and arthropods, which are reviewed later. A major problem in determining evolutionary relationships is the lack of consensus on exactly what defines a specific phylum or other taxonomic rank (Meglitsch and Schram, 1991, p. 300).

Another problem is that much disagreement exists even about basic information such as the adequacy of the fossil record. For example, the "fossil record of the Crustacea is often stated in textbooks to be poor, but the truth is that the record is good. All four classes of crustaceans have fossils.... The record is so extensive, in fact, that limitations of space do not allow much discussion" (Meglitsch and Schram, 1991, p. 490).

As we will document, an enormous fossil record does exist, and invertebrate fossils are found in greater profusion in the Paleozoic, Mesozoic, and Cenozoic than any other organism. A major problem for Darwinism is the fact that "some of the oldest forms of animal life that are found in the fossil record [are] also some of the most complex" (Eldredge, 2000, p. 42). As will be discussed, little disagreement exists about the facts, but much disagreement exists about the implications of these facts.

The Burgess Shale and Invertebrate Evolution

One of the most important fossil-finds is a formation known as the Burgess Shale that was popularized by Gould's 1989 book *Wonderful Life*. Discovered in 1909, the fruitful geological site located in southwestern Canada revealed dozens of creatures very different from all present known life forms. Many soft-body animal structures were preserved in fine detail, allowing scientists to produce accurate pictures of the strange life forms that they discovered that are mostly invertebrates (Cook, 1995).

Examples include the five-eyed *Opabinia*, a flattened oval creature called *Waxia hallueigenia*, which had seven pairs of spines on one side and seven tentacles on the other, and *Anomalocaris*, whose mouth was shaped like a circular nutcracker (Meyer, 2013). The mostly sea-bottom-dwelling animals were dated to the mid-Cambrian (Latham, 2005, p. 32). Fifteen of these creatures were so different, both from each other and from modern life forms, that they were placed in new phyla (Cook, 1995).

The discoverer, Professor Charles Walcott, knowing that his fossil discovery would upset orthodox evolutionary conclusions, tried to compromise this fact by forcing these strange new life forms into existing phyla. His tortured efforts to accommodate these many strange new life forms to evolution by attempting to shoehorn the fossils into the then conventional categories of worms and arthropods were re-evaluated over a half century later by Professor Harry B. Whittington and his two graduate students, Simon Conway Morris and Derek Briggs (Gould, 1989, p. 24).

Over 73,300 specimens were found; 87.9 percent were animals, and most of the rest were algae — a total of 119 genera and 140 species have now been identified (Gould, 1989, p. 222). The result was a revolution in the invertebrate fossil record that approximately doubled the number of phyla — all of which appeared fully developed at the beginning of the Cambrian and lacked a fossil record before this (Meyer, 2013). The Burgess Shale fossils are a major embarrassment to Darwinists because, as Gould wrote, Darwin admitted that he knows of "no greater challenge to the iconography of the cone [the theory of evolution of life from a few simple animals to many kinds of complex life forms] and, hence, no more important case for a fundamentally revised view of life — than the radical reconstructions of Burgess anatomy ... they have turned the traditional interpretation on its head" (Gould, 1989, pp. 46-47).

The reason why is because the many unique body plans discovered in the Burgess shale showed "designs so far beyond the modern range" that they inverted the cone of life and invertebrate variety. As Gould explains the

> anatomical variety reached a maximum right after the initial diversification of multicellular animals. The later history of life proceeded by elimination, not expansion. The current earth may hold more species than ever before, but most are iterations upon a few basic anatomical designs. (Taxonomists have described more than a half million species of beetles, but nearly all are minimally altered Xeroxes of a single ground plan.) In fact, the probable increase in number of species through time merely underscores the puzzle and paradox. Compared with the Burgess seas, today's oceans contain many more species based upon many fewer anatomical plans (Gould, 1989, pp. 46-47).

Gould concludes that the Burgess Shale shows that the history of life, rather than starting with one or two roots and constantly diversifying into other life forms as evolution predicts, started as an incredibly prolific bush that rapidly decreased its width with time. Ever since then life forms have become extinct by a process that is more like a lottery than a weeding out due to a lack of evolutionary fitness.

In other words, instead of a morphological tree that was small at the bottom when life began and branched out as evolution produced new life forms, the evidence produced an inverted tree, like a Christmas tree. Many basic animal forms existed at the start of life, and fewer as time progressed. This is the exact opposite of that predicted by evolution (Latham, 2005).

Cambridge Paleontologist Conway Morris goes even further, arguing that the Burgess Shale discoveries actually "cast considerable doubt on various mechanisms of microevolution" (1998, p. viii). The Burgess Shale fossils are one reason why "organic evolution excites continuing debate and disagreement" (Morris, 1998, p. 3). Another problem is that many of the early life forms found in the Burgess shale not only had unique body plans, but also were evolutionarily advanced. University of California, Berkeley paleontologist James Valentine noted that it was "troubling to Darwin and early evolutionists that such seemingly complex forms as trilobites were to be found in the most ancient rocks that had yielded fossils at that time" (Valentine, 2000, p. 513).

Metazoa

Metazoan life forms include all multicellular animals. The metazoa is divided into *Parazoa* (animals with poorly differentiated tissues and no organs, namely the porifera or sponges) and *Eumetazoa* (metazoa animals with tissues and organs, excluding the porifera and worm-like metazoans). The Eumetazoa possess multicellular reproductive structures that develop via a set of distinct embryonic stages, such as in brachiopods. According to orthodox Neo-Darwinism, both vertebrates and invertebrates evolved from ancestral metazoans.

Evidence from the fossil record, developmental biology, and metazoan phylogeny

concluded that the major metazoan body plans originated rapidly during the late Neoproterozoic and earliest Cambrian (Valentine, et al., 1996). After noting that the metazoan ancestry remains enigmatic, Willmer concluded the many competing theories that exist to explain metazoan origins can be divided into two large families, *colonial* and *syncytial*, theories (Willmer, 1990, pp. 187-193).

After noting that "zoologists disagree about the origin of metazoans," Meglitsch and Schram conclude that, due to a lack of fossil evidence, metazoan evolution

> must be based on other kinds of information. Elaborate theories have been based on analyses of developmental patterns and the erection of hypothetical animals to explain animal history. Although many of these theories are interesting — some approach a type of biopoetry — very few are based on consideration of the meaning of form and function.... It is far more effective for the student of invertebrate zoology to consider the animals themselves: which characters they share and which are unique, and what animals do and how they do it, to discern possible paths of animal history. One should not try to analyze animals within the confines of the many old theories of invertebrate evolution where fancy [hypotheses] often had to make up for lack of facts (1991, p. 48).

The reason for these difficulties when speculating about evolutionary relationships among metazoan phyla is that the phyla are morphologically very distinct from each other, making the production of plausible evolutionary trees very difficult (Anderson, 1998, p. 422). Anderson also concluded that the "methods used to infer evolutionary relationships" have improved greatly, and, as a result, new information has forced us to reevaluate much of what was assumed for decades. He also notes that evolutionists

> have no reliable way of testing for the correctness of phylogenies. The lack of consensus is all too evident. For example, a group of researchers has recently collected the major metazoan phylogenies (based on morphological features) produced since the 1950s. The result was 13 different phylogenies for the animal phyla.... We cannot tell by inspection which of these conflicting hypotheses (if any) is correct ... molecular data offer a possible source of new data, and renewed hope of resolving phylum-level relationships (Anderson, 1998, p. 422).

The result of the lack of fossil record evidence results in the conclusion that "morphologically complex metazoans appear abruptly during the Cambrian explosion" (Valentine, 2000, p. 513). An important means of constructing phylogenetic trees for parasitic invertebrates is not only morphology, but also their parasitic traits and mode of life. Because this information is difficult to determine from the fossil record, the fossil record is less useful for deducing parasitic evolutionary relationships for most invertebrates.

Nonetheless, what has been found provides "no information as to how the group evolved" parasitic or other traits because even early fossil forms are very similar to living forms (Meglitsch and Schram, 1991, p. 194). This conclusion can be stated with confidence because many excellent invertebrate examples are preserved in amber, often as a result of the parasites trying to escape their host (Poinar and Poinar, 1999, p. 30).

Phylum Porifera

The porifera (sponges) are considered the most primitive multicellular life forms. More than 900 fossil genera have been described, and approximately 5,000 living sponge species are known. They lack a mouth, but have a unique feeding system that uses tiny pores for bringing water into their bodies by the use of beating flagella. The animal thereby filters nutrients out of the water. Although they have an excellent fossil record dating from the late Precambrian (Gehling and Rigby, 1996), about all that evolutionists can conclude with confidence from this record is that they must have "evolved along a line different from other Metazoa," and are speculated to have arisen from some prostistan or choanoflagellate — and beyond this, little can be known with much confidence (Meglitsch and Schram, 1991, p. 66).

Fossil representatives of all classes of porifera apparently date back to the Cambrian. The earliest probable sponge is similar to modern sponges. Since few, if any, transitional forms are even claimed, the evolutionary relationships "within the phylum are uncertain" (Meglitsch and Schram, 1991, p. 66). Nonetheless, much speculation about their origins exists.

Coelenterata

Coelenterata includes the phyla Cnidaria and Ctenophora. The Cnidaria are a large group of aquatic, mostly marine, animals that includes corals, jellyfish (medusa), sea anemones, hydrozoan (Hydra), Obelia, Metridium, and Astrangia. Many have stinging cells (cnidoblasts), from which the phylum gets its name. Found throughout the aquatic world, both in the distant past and today, this large phylum is very common in the fossil record. These putative very primitive multicellular life forms are also considered to be numerically one of the most successful of all phyla. Approximately "3,000 living species of corals, and probably twice that number of fossil forms" exist (Meglitsch and Schram, 1991, p. 93).

Cnidaria have left "an extensive fossil record, especially among the Anthozoa," dating all the way back to the Cambrian (Meglitsch and Schram, 1991, p. 93). Their fossil remains are found "all over the world" in very diverse types of sediments (Prokop, 1995, p. 22). Corals are extremely durable fossils that are "commonly preserved in the fossil record" (Doyle, 1996, pp. 246-247). Although "the fossil record of cnidarians is good ... it contributes at present little to our understanding of the evolution of Cnidaria," and debates have continued for decades over even such basic questions such as "whether the medusa or the polyp represents a more primitive condition" (Meglitsch and Schram,1991, pp. 93-94).

The reason for these debates is the absence of evidence for evolutionary change as required by Darwinism--the fossil evidence, instead, shows stasis. This problem has been noted back to the time of Darwin. Valentine concluded that it was "troubling to Darwin and early evolutionists that such seemingly complex forms such as trilobites were to be found in the most ancient rocks that had yielded fossils at that time" (Valentine, 2000, p. 513).

Figure 5.1 — Fossil Trilobite Imprint[1]

---

[1] Photo Credit: Merlin74 / Shutterstock.com

The Ctenophora (Greek for lamb-bearers) have eight comb-like rows of fused cilia arranged along their sides that beat synchronously, propelling the animals through their water world. Common examples include comb jellies, sea gooseberries, Venus's girdles and sea walnuts. The phylogenetic position is very disputed because researchers must rely on morphology for the reason that no evidence of their evolution exists in the fossil record. Furthermore, morphological and molecular data are contradictory, thus the controversy continues in spite of new genetic data that researchers hoped would solve the problem (Collins, et al., 2005). Fossil evidence supports an early origin of both the Ctenophora and a very early Cnideria (Collins, et al., 2005).

Phylum Bryozoa

The Bryozoa phylum includes lamp shells, lingula, and bugula, most of which are microscopic, but easily found because most lived in colonies. These lifeforms are called Lophophorates, a group of animals possessing a fan-shaped set of cilia surrounding their mouth. No fossils of the most primitive living Bryozoan, the phylactolaemates, are known. For this reason, ideas about their evolutionary history are largely speculation. Barnes concluded that the first putative marine bryozoan fossil dated to the late Cambrian, and that

> beginning with the Ordovician there is a rich fossil record, and thousands of fossil species have been described. Stenolaemates, of which there are three distinct orders, dominate the Paleozoic fauna, although there were Paleozoic ctenostome gymnolaemates. Cheilostomes, the dominant marine forms today, made their appearance in the late Jurassic (Barnes, 1987, p. 748).

This rich fossil record shows no evidence of evolution — the earliest known examples are undisputed examples of bryozoans.

Phylum Platyhelminthes (flatworms)

Phylum Platyhelminthes consists of worms with flat-body morphology. Their nervous system consists of cells concentrated at the head end. Many species in this phylum are parasites, including leaches, flukes, and some planarians. The fossil record is excellent, but shows so little evidence of change that many flatworms are considered to be "living fossils" that have not changed since they first appeared in the fossil record but, instead, still exist in their "primitive bilaterian body plan" (Anderson, 1998, p. 429).

Phylum Nematoda (round worms)

Most nematodes are small worms that resemble fine sewing thread (the Greek word for thread is *nema*. The majority were free living, but the few parasitic

types cause considerable health problems for humans on a global scale (the *Caenorhabditis elegans* is a worm that is a highly favored experimental animal). They normally live in both salt and fresh water and also in the soil. The fossil record of parasitic nematodes in amber dates back to the Eocene (Poinar and Poinar, 2002). The "absence of an informative fossil record" and "lack of clearly homologous characters" have made it very difficult to produce a plausible evolutionary tree (Blaxter, et al., 1998, p. 71). Thus, existing phylogenetic speculation is often based on genetic comparisons. One recent genetic study was in several cases at variance with previous phylogenies (Blaxter, et al., 1998). They conclude that "Although nematode parasites are generally assumed to have evolved from free-living ancestors, the precise origin and free-living sister taxa of each parasitic group are unknown" (1998, p. 74).

Phylum Nemertinea (proboscis worms)

Nemertinea are known as Nemertea or Rhynchocoela, and commonly are called "ribbon worms." Many Nemertinea are parasites. Their most distinctive character is a long muscular tube (a proboscis) that can be thrown out to grasp prey. The fossil record tells us "little about nemertine evolution except to suggest that the phylum has been around for a long time" (Meglitsch and Schram, 1991, p. 281). Modern nemertines are histologically fairly distinctive from each other, and "therefore, it is difficult ... to envision at this time how they are related to each other" (Meglitsch and Schram, 1991, p. 281). They add that, in spite of this major problem, Darwinists still have tried to at least hypothesize their evolutionary relationships.

Phylum Annelida (segmented worms)

Phylum Annelida is comprised of segmented worms that currently belong to four classes, *Polychaeta*, *Oligochaeta*, *Hirudinea*, and *Branchiobdellida*. They include Nereis, Lumbricus, and Hirudo. The most well known examples are the earthworms, which have soft, cylindrical bodies with metameric segmentation that is visible externally as a series of rings. The Annelids have an extensive fossil record and appear very early in the fossil record. In spite of this advantage for evolutionists, there exists "little evidence in the fossil record to aid in sorting out evolutionary relationships" (Anderson, 1998, p. 201). Of those that have been found, in "all cases, these fossils seem to be similar to known living polychaete groups." Because the fossil record shows little or no evidence of change, "consensus does not exist" about their evolutionary relationships "nor is there agreement over facts and events in annelid history" (Meglitsch and Schram, 1991, p. 344).

Phylum Echinoderm

Echinodermata phylum are marine invertebrates that includes a diverse variety of animals, including sea urchins, starfish (asterias), sand dollars (melitta), sea cucumbers (cucumaria), and brittle stars. They have "a long fossil record, extending to the early Cambrian," and their external morphology is "often beautifully preserved" in the fossil record (Anderson, 1998, p. 375). Many ancient forms have become extinct. Other ancient forms, such as starfish, still are common today and are considered living fossils because, evolutionists conclude, that they have "remained substantially the same over a period of 480 million years" (Prokop, 1995, p. 164).

One reason their fossil record is excellent is because all echinoderms possess large calcareous skeletal plates that are well preserved in the fossil record. Furthermore, "the relatively large size of many echinoderms, and the high population densities that echinoderms have achieved in the past have combined to make them among the most abundant invertebrate fossils" (Meglitsch and Schram, 1991, p. 559).

In spite of this abundant fossil record, speculations about their evolution abounds:

> There is probably no greater snake pit in the field of invertebrate phylogenetic speculation, with the possible exception of arthropods, than that of echinoderms. Mental gyrations on the subject have been rampant since the last century (Meglitsch and Schram, 1991, p. 560).

The speculation about their origins cannot be based on the fossil record, because it lacks evidence of the evolutionary origins of any invertebrate.

Phylum Mollusks

Phylum Mollusca is a large group of diverse, soft-bodied animals that often secrete hard, protective shells. They include snails, slugs, chitons, mytilus, and bivalves but also include Class Cephalopoda. The Cephalopod Class includes octopus, squid, cuttlefish, and nautilus. No evidence has yet been found for the evolutionary origins of cephalopods in its rich fossil record.

So far over 10,000 fossil species of mollusks have been identified, mostly from calcareous shells of Ammonoidea, Nautiloidea, and some Coleoidea (Clarke and Fitch, 1975). As Anderson (1998, p. 142) notes, despite the fact that "cephalopods have left an impressive fossil record from the late Cambrian to the Recent, the origin of the group and its relationships to other molluscan classes are still uncertain."

It is often speculated that cephalopods evolved from Monoplacophorans that first appeared in the early Cambrian. Other paleontologists argue for a very different cephalopod evolutionary lineage. Although an enormous fossil record exists for most mollusks, partly because their hard shells preserve very well, the lack of transitional forms has produced much controversy about their evolution (Anderson, 1998, p. 429). Although some are extinct, many other modern mollusks are only "slightly modified" from ancient fossil forms (Prokop, 1995, p. 62).

Other fossils are believed by some evolutionists to be evolutionary ancestors of modern mollusks, but other researchers argue that these fossils actually were evolutionary dead ends. Mollusks are believed by many to have evolved from some type of flatworm that evolved into a "primitive molluscan," the Monoplacophorans, but others argue that the evidence better supports the conclusion that their ancestor is a Rostroconchia (Anderson, 1998).

Figure 5.2 — Common European Cuttlefish[2]

Other paleontologists argue that mollusks belong on a common line with the Annelids, and yet others concluded that it is more likely that they are a separate evolutionary offshoot from a small ciliated acoelomate ancestor (Willmer, 1990, p. 258). Each group has what they feel are good arguments for their evolutionary position, and can enumerate what they feel are good reasons why the theories of other researchers are wrong.

Class Brachiopoda

The Gastropod class of Brachiopods include snails and slugs, animals protected by a single, calcaneous shell that usually is twisted to form a spiral (Prokop, 1995, p. 58). The bivalves class (Bivalvia) of Brachiopods have a laterally compressed body protected by two shell halves ("valves") that are hinged dorsally

---

[2] Photo Credit: David Litman / Shutterstock.com

and can completely enclose their body. Their shells preserve very well and, consequently, an enormously rich fossil record has been uncovered, including many interesting extinct gastropods (Montoya, et al., 1999). Brachiopod "fossils are known from the earliest Cambrian deposits onward" (Meglitsch and Schram, 1991, p. 521), and are "represented by distinctive and complex skeletal remains more or less continuously throughout the Phanerozoic record" (Williams and Hurst, 1977, p. 79).

In spite of their good fossil record dating all the way "back to the Cambrian...all the major bivalve groups appeared" in the Ordovician directly after the Cambrian (Doyle, 1996, p. 149). No evidence has been uncovered for their origin (or their evolution), although considerable variation within the divisions exists. Consequently, there exists much speculation and, as a result, much controversy about their evolutionary history because no plausible transitional forms have ever been identified.

Discussion

This literature review supports the conclusion about invertebrate evolution, namely that a discussion of the invertebrates would not

> be complete without some attempt at an overview of their evolution. No subject, however, has ever been marked by so much speculation as has that of invertebrate phylogeny. Hardly any workers agree. ...These widely disparate concepts are frequently juxtaposed against each other without comment in lecture presentations and reading assignments, and as a result students all too often become confused. The plethora of rival interpretations of anatomical facts and the confusing array of names applied to all manner of hypothetical ancestors, or paper animals, is intimidating (Meglitsch and Schram 1991, p. 588).

As a result, Meglitsch and Schram conclude that determining phylogenetic trees that show an invertebrate's evolutionary history "is an exercise in futility, with little hope of ever reaching a consensus" (1991, p. 591). They further conclude that "we have a story for animal evolution" but "whether or not this scenario is a true and accurate description of what really happened in the course of" invertebrate evolution cannot be demonstrated by fossils (1991, p. 599).

Another problem is that the lack of fossil evidence for invertebrate macroevolution allows Darwinists imagination free reign (Donovan, 1998; Clarkson, 1986). This is not unlike Darwin himself, who "had no fossil evidence to guide him ... simply his fertile and innovative imagination" that he freely used to develop his secular creation story (Swisher, Curtis, and Lewin, 2000, p. 141).

And as a result "it is therefore not surprising" that Darwin "got some things wrong" (p. 141). As Meglitsch and Schram argue, "Evolutionary Theory is the grand paradigm that holds all of biology together," and therefore a correct tree must exist (1991, p. 591). In other words, evolutionists believe that all life evolved from simple one-celled life, and then they try to use morphology to develop a plausible evolutionary tree. But, they admit that

> all too many family trees of the animal kingdom have been produced since the days of Haeckel.... All these theories, regardless of their details, have certain things in common. First, they attempt to deal with all phyla, but focus on only a few characters in their attempt to arrange the phyla. Second, they often start with *a priori* assumptions about hypothetical ancestors and what genealogical arrangements should be, and then seek facts to back up their position. Third, none of these theories really attempt to make testable statements about animal relationships, but rather prefer to focus

on producing definitive stories about animal history (1991, p. 589).

The whole invertebrate fossil record shows, as Eldredge found was true of trilobites, that stability was the norm throughout history, although small changes (microevolution) occasionally do appear (Eldredge, 2000, p. 84). Furthermore, a century of the study of fossils by paleontologists has consistently found "the persistence of stable species for millions of years" (Eldredge, 2000, p. 85). Eldredge, after noting that "paleontology has to date contributed almost nothing to evolutionary theory," proposed several reasons why this is true (Eldredge, 1977, p. 306).

The main reason for the lack of evidence for evolution in the fossil record, Eldredge concludes, is because speciation "typically happens so quickly that rarely do we catch it in midstream when we scour the fossil record for insights on how evolution occurs" (Eldredge, 2000, p. 85). Of course, this is not a conclusion based on direct evidence, but only speculation, based on, at best, very sparse or no evidence. This is why Gould concluded "the basic questions paleontologists have asked about the history of life" have "found no resolution within the Darwinian paradigm" (1977, p. 1).

Because of this problem, many researchers have tried to ignore the fossil record and have instead produced evolutionary trees by other means, such as DNA data of present-day organisms. Because these data are often very contradictory, others, such as Meglitsch and Schram, relied purely on the morphology of living animals and ignored both biochemical and DNA data in developing their evolutionary trees. Overcoming the fossil record problems by using other criteria produces a cladogram based heavily on comparisons of morphological traits. Largely ignoring both biochemical data and the fossil record does not solve the problem because neither provides consistent evidence for Neo-Darwinism.

Another major problem is that research has found "little correlation between gene number and morphological complexity in the invertebrates: relatively complex forms can have fewer genes than relatively simple forms" of life (Valentine, 2000, p. 513). The lack of fossil evidence required to produce a reasonable phylogeny has motivated using a totally new approach based on comparisons of genomes from modern organisms in harmony with the genetic clock theory (Meglitsch and Schram, 1991, pp. 591-599). As Willmer (1990, p. 75) concludes, "despite our best efforts" we have "not achieved very much understanding" of invertebrate evolution from our study of the fossil record. New conclusions overturning existing firmly established ideas are common in the field (Cowen, 2003, p. 292).

Conclusions

If evolution occurred, undisputed evidence would be abundant in the enormous invertebrate fossil record. But it is not. This literature review has confirmed invertebrate zoologist Robert Barnes's (date, and page) observation about invertebrates, namely that "the fossil record tells us almost nothing about the evolutionary origin of phyla and classes. Intermediate forms are non-existent."

Barnes's noted that the only exception to this generalization was an animal "which may be on the line leading to the cephalopods." He adds, optimistically, that he believes the needed intermediate forms exist, but are "undiscovered or not recognized," and that more work will reveal them (1980, p. 365). Over three decades later his conclusion still is valid, and the needed fossil forms he had hoped paleontologist would find have not been found. What the fossil record shows is the "rapid origination of major metazoan body plans" (Valentine, et al., 1996). Also what Raup cautiously states about marine invertebrates is true of all invertebrates, namely that the "number of marine invertebrate species has been reasonably constant throughout most of the last 600 million years" (1977, p. 50).

Although the fossil record "should be the final arbiter in deciding between opposing theories on major issues of phylogeny" (Willmer, 1990, p. 52), in fact, the fossil record is usually ignored, and whatever method seems to work is used to support the theory of common descent. As a result, Thomas admitted that the previous conclusions based on the fossil record have now been shattered by DNA research (see Nardi, et al., 2003). The major contradictions between the fossil and DNA approaches to determining evolutionary relationships has only created doubt in an evolutionary history tree based on the Darwinistic worldview.

References

Aguinaldo, Anna Marie A.; Turbeville, James M.; Linford, Lawrence S.; Rivera, Maria C.; Garey, James R.; Raff, Rudolf A.; Lake, James A. 1997. *Nature*, 387 (6632) pp. 489-493.

Alonso, Jesus; Arillo, Antonio; Barron, Eduardo; Corral, J. Carmelo; Grimalt, Joan; Lopez, Jordi F.; Lopez, Rafael; Martinez-Delclos, Xavier; Ortuno, Vicente; Penalver, Enrique; Trincao, Paulo R. 2000. A new fossil resin with biological inclusions in Lower Cretaceous deposits from Alava (northern Spain, Basque-Cantabrian Basin). *Journal of Paleontology*, 74(1): 158-178.

Anderson, D.T. (editor). 1998. *Invertebrate Zoology*. South Melbourne, Australia: Oxford University Press.

Barnes, Robert D. 1980. "Invertebrate Beginnings." *Paleobiology*, 6:365-370.

_____. 1987. *Invertebrate Zoology*. Fifth Edition. Philadelphia: Saunders.

Bergman, Jerry. 2004. "Insect Evolution: A Major Problem for Darwinism." TJ. 18(2):91-97.

_____. 2006. "The Fossil Record for Arthropod Evolution: A Major Problem for Neo-Darwinism." CRSQ.

Blaxter, Mark L., Paul De Ley, James R. Garey, Leo X. Liu, Patsy Scheldeman, Andy Vierstraete, Jacques R. Vanfleteren, Laura Y. Mackey, Mark Dorris, Linda M. Frisse, J.T. Vida, and W. Kelley Thomas. 1998. "A Molecular Evolutionary Framework for the Phylum Nematoda." Nature, 392:71-75.

Clarke, M.R. and John E. Fitch. 1975. "First Fossil Records of Cephalopod Statoliths." *Nature*, 257:380-381, October 2.

Clarkson, Evan Neilson Kerr. 1986. *Invertebrate Palaeontology and Evolution*. Second Edition. London: Unwin Hyman.

Collins, Allen G., Paulyn Cartwright, Catherine McFadden, and Bernd Schierwater. 2005.

"Phylogenetic Context and Basal Metazoan Model Systems." *Integrative and Comparative Biology*, 45:585-594.

Cook, Harry. 1995. "Wonderful Life: Burgess Shale and the History of Biology." *Perspectives on Science and Christian Faith*, 47:159, September.

Cowen, R. 2003. "Fossils Push Back Origin of Land Animals." *Science News*, 138:292.

Donovan, Stephen K.; Veltkamp, Comelis J. 1994. Unusual preservation of late quaternary millipedes from Jamaica. Lethaia, 27(4):355-362.

_____. 1998. *Invertebrate Palaeontology and Evolution*. Third Edition. London: Unwin Hyman.

Doyle, Peter. 1996. Understanding Fossils. An Introduction to Invertebrate Paleontology. New York: Wiley.

Easton, W.H. 1960. *Invertebrate Paleontology*. New York: Harper.

Eldredge, Niles. 1977. "Trilobites and Evolutionary Patterns." Chapter 9 in *Patterns of*

Evolution. Edited by A. Hallam, pp. 305-332. Amsterdam: Elsevier.

_____. 2000. The Triumph of Evolution and the Failure of Creationism. New York: W. H. Freeman.

Gayrard-Valy, Yvette. 1994. *Fossils: Evidence of Vanished Worlds*. New York: Abrams.

Gehling, J.G. and J.K. Rigby. 1996. "Long Expected Sponges from the Neoproterozoic

Ediacara Fauna of South Australia." *Journal of Paleontology*, 2:1 85-195.

Gould, Stephen Jay. 1977. "Eternal Metaphors of Palaeontology." Chapter 1 in *Patterns of*

Evolution, pp. 1-26. Edited by A. Hallam. Amsterdam: Elsevier.

_____. 1989. Wonderful Life: The Burgess Shale and the

Nature of History. New York, NY: W.W. Norton.

Hallam, Anthony. 1977. Patterns of Evolution; As Illustrated by the Fossil Record. Oxford, NY: Elsevier Scientific.

Jensen, Sóren, James G. Gehling, and Mary L. Droser. 1998. "Ediacara-Type Fossils in

Cambrian Sediments." *Nature*, 393:567-569, June 11.

Latham, Antony. 2005. *The Naked Emperor: Darwinism Exposed.* London: Janus Publishing Company.

Meglitsch, Paul A. 1967. *Invertebrate Zoology.* New York: Oxford University Press.

_____and Frederick R. Schram. 1991. *Zoology.* Third Edition. New York: Oxford University Press.

Meyer, Steven C. 2013. Darwin's Doubt: The Explosive Origin of Animal Life and the Case for Intelligent Design. New York: HarperOne.

Milne, Lorus and Margery Milne. 1976. *Invertebrates of North America.* New York: Doubleday.

Monastersky, R. 2003. "Fossils Push Back Origin of Land Animals" *Science News*, 138: 292.

Montoya, P.; Alberdi, M.T.; Blazques, A.M.; Barbadillo, L.j.; Fumanal, Ma. P.; Van der Made, j.; Marin, j.M.; Molina, A.; Morales, j.; Murelaga, X.; Penalver, E.; Robles, E; Ruiz Bustos, A.; Sanchez, A.; Sanchiz, B.; Soria, D.; Szyndlar, Z. 1999. The Lower Pleistocene Fauna at Sierra de Quibas (albanilla, Murciaprovince, Spain) *Estudios Geologicos* 55(3-4):127-161.

Morris, Simon Conway. 1998. *The Crucible of Creation: The Burgess Shale and the Rise of Animals.* Oxford, New York: Oxford University Press.

Nardi, Francesco; Giacomo Spinsanti, Jeffrey L. Boore, Antonio Carapelli, Romano Dallai, and Francesco Frati. 2003. "Hexapod Origins: Monophyletic or Paraphyletic?" *Science*, 299:1887-1889.

Penney, David. 2002. "First Fossil Record of Nematode Parasitism of Ants; A 40 Million Year Tale." *Parasitology*, 125(5): 457-459.

Poinar, George and Roberta Poinar. 1999. *The Amber Forest*. Princeton, NJ. :Princeton University Press.

Prokop, Rudolf. 1995. *Fossils*. Leicester, England: Magna.

Raup, David M. 1976. Species Diversity in the Phanerozoic: An Interpretation. *Paleobiology* 2(4):289-297.

_____. 1977. "Probabilistic Models in Evolutionary Paleobiology." *American Scientist*, 65:50-57.

Ruppert, Edward, Richard Fox, Robert Barnes. 2004. *Invertebrate Zoology: A Functional Evolutionary Approach*. Belmont, CA: Thomson/Brooks Cole.

Swisher Ill, Carl C.; Gamiss H. Curtis and Roger Lewin. 2000. *Java Man: How Two*

Geologists' Discoveries Changed Our Understanding of the Evolutionary Path to Modern

Humans. New York: Scribner.

Twenhofel, William H. and Robert Rakes Shrock. 1935. *Invertebrate Paleontology*. New York:McGraw Hill.

Valentine, James W. 2000. "Two Genomic Paths to the Evolution of Complexity in Bodyplans." *Paleobiology*, 26(3):5 13-519.

_____, Douglas H. Erwin, and David Jablonski. 1996. "Developmental Evolution of Metazoan Bodyplans: The Fossil Evidence." *Developmental Biology*, 173:373-381.

Williams, Alwyn and John M. Hurst. 1977. "Brachiopod Evolution." Chapter 4 in Patterns of Evolution, pp. 79-1 19. Edited by A. Hallam. Amsterdam: Elsevier.

Willmer, Pat. 1990. *Invertebrate Relationships*. Cambridge: Cambridge University Press.

Chapter 6

Arthropods — Progress or Persistence?

Introduction

Arthropoda is the largest and most diverse phylum in the entire animal kingdom, comprising over one million different species (Giribet and Ribera, 2000). Arthropods clearly are the most successful animals on earth, and the lifestyles and "ecological niches they inhabit are almost incomprehensibly diverse" (Marden, 1995, p. 26; Levine, 2002). They are found in freshwater, marine, and terrestrial habitats worldwide (Wills, et al., 1997). Arthropoda is not only the largest phylum in the animal kingdom, but also is the only invertebrate phylum that contains aquatic, terrestrial, and aerial members. It includes the trilobites, crustaceans, arachnids, myriapods, horseshoe crabs (not covered in this chapter — see Helder, 1997), and insects (also not covered in this chapter — see chapter 7, and Manning, 2003).

Arthropoda are so diverse that some entomologists have questioned whether or not they could have descended from a common ancestor as usually taught (Manton, 1973). Therefore, all assumptions about evolutionary descent must be produced from the study of either fossils (most of which are identical to modern forms) or living arthropods. Gamlin and Vines note under the subheading "Evolution of the arthropods" that the arthropod fossil history dates back to

> more than 600 million years, but, unfortunately, there are no fossils of their earliest ancestors. Because they share an exoskeleton and jointed limbs, biologists once assumed that all arthropods arose from the same stock. Yet *recent studies of living arthropods* suggest that there are three main lines which evolved independently: the Crustacea, the Uniramia and the Chelicerata (1987, p. 81, emphasis mine).

Lammerts concluded from his study of entomology that it is

> a source of constant wonder to me how such a remarkable array of creatures as are found in the order Coleoptera [beetles]could ever be considered as having arisen from a common ancestor. One of my [University of California, Berkeley] professors, Dr. E.C. Van Dyke, a world authority on this group, often was equally puzzled (1974, p. 125).

Arthropods are defined as "bilaterally symmetrical segmented animals with a characteristic tough chitinous protective exoskeleton that is flexible only at the joints; growth is by ecdysis" (Tootill, 1988). Ecdysis growth (often called molting) involves periodic shedding of the cuticle exoskeleton and growth of a new and larger exoskeleton. Each segment typically contains a pair of jointed appendages, modified so as to serve different functions. The arthropod coelom is a long fluid-filled cavity located between the gut and the body wall. The coelom in non-insect arthropods functions as a hydrostatic skeleton, and is reduced in size compared to the insect coelom. The main arthropod body cavity is blood-filled and termed the haemocoel.

Arthropods also have a ventral nerve cord, a pair of cerebral ganglia, and paired segmental ganglia (Tootill, 1988) and are the "only invertebrates that show a definite, individualized form of adipose [fat] tissue" (Kaufmann, 1977, p. 214).

The Arthropod Fossil Record in General

Darwin recognized that the fossil record was a major problem for his theory and expected that time would fill-in the many now-famous "missing links." Most of the fossil evidence used in an attempt to support neo-Darwinism consists of vertebrate bone fragments that require much interpretation. This has led to a great deal of controversy among vertebrate paleontologists. Of the estimated 1.7 million known animal species, fully 95% are invertebrates, and most of these are arthropods (Barnes, 1987, p. 1). An enormous fossil record—easily in the millions—exists for the invertebrates, including arthropods.

Many of these arthropod fossils show excellent external morphology (Eldredge, 2000, p. 83). Furthermore, "some of the earliest, most conspicuous and informative metazoan fossils are ... arthropods" (Wills, 2001, p. 187). They are found in greater profusion in rocks labeled Paleozoic, Mesozoic, and Cenozoic than any other group of organisms. Even plant-arthropod interactions have been documented as far back as the postulated Paleozoic Era (Chaloner, Scott, and Stephenson, 1991).

While there exist major problems with the vast time periods ascribed to these supposed geologic ages, they will be used throughout this chapter as a frame of reference. Arthropod larvae less than one millimeter long have been found in late Cambrian rocks (Anderson, 1998, p. 434). The rich arthropod fossil record includes examples in excellent preservatives such as amber, tar, or ice that often show exquisite detail of even minute body structures such as eyes and hair (Gayrard-Valy, 1994; Alonso et al., 2000). Another reason for the rich fossil record is that the skeletons of certain arthropods, including trilobites, malacostrancans, and ostracods, are reinforced with calcium carbonate, thus fossilize well under the right conditions (Wills, 2001).

Trackways left by trace-forming animals and arthropod borings are also common and important fossil evidence, especially for non-marine arthropods (Donovan, 1994, p. 200). Furthermore, ancient or fossil spider webs as well as wasp, bee, and ant nests all have been discovered.

The fossil record of terrestrial arthropods, according to the evolutionary time scheme, goes back to before the Early Devonian (Edgecombe, 1998, p. 174). This excellent fossil record allows accurate comparisons of ancient and modern arthropod forms that can be used to evaluate the validity of Darwinism. Professor Budd (1997) concluded that "what these fossils mean, however, both in terms of arthropod classification and the early evolution of the phylum is far from clear: no single opinion has won universal assent" because the fossil record shows no clear evidence of macroevolution (Budd, 1997, p. 125).

A major problem in determining evolutionary relationships of phylum Arthropoda is the lack of consensus on what exactly defines a phylum or other taxonomic rank (Meglitsch and Schram, 1991, p. 300). An even greater problem is determining if creatures now classified as arthropods actually belong to the single phylum Arthropoda (Anderson, 1998, p. 432). Disagreements exist even about such basic information as the adequacy of the fossil record to accurately determine phylogeny. The record is judged inadequate to evolutionists only because it shows no evidence of evolution. To an objective observer, the record is complete enough to evaluate evolution. Thus, evolutionists often claim that the "fossil record of the Crustacea is often stated in textbooks to be poor, but the truth is that the record is good. All four classes of crustaceans have fossils.... The record is so extensive, in fact, that limitations of space do not allow much discussion."[1]

Although an "abundance" of fascinating fossil arthropods is known (Meglitsch and Schram, 1991, p. 368), the record provides little evidence for either their origin or macro-evolutionary development. As a result, a "mind-boggling array of hypotheses and scenarios" exists for "arthropod evolution. Every authority seems to have his own version. There is not even agreement as to whether there is one phylum, Arthropoda" (Meglitsch and Schram, 1991, p. 369).

A significant problem for Darwinism is the fact that some of the oldest animal life forms uncovered in the fossil record are some of the most complex (Eldredge, 2000, p. 42). Little disagreement exists about the facts concerning fossil arthropods, but there is considerable disagreement about the *implications* of those facts (Morris, 2000: Hallam, 1977). Aguinaldo, et al., concluded that the

> arthropods constitute the most diverse animal group, but, despite their rich fossil record and a century of study, their phylogenetic relationships remain unclear. Taxa previously proposed to be sister groups to the arthropods include Annelida, Onychophora, Tardigrada, and others, but hypotheses of phylogenetic relationships have been conflicting (1997, p. 489).

So many fossils have been found that some paleontologists believe the "early terrestrial ecosystems were dominated by small arthropods" (Shear, et al., 1996, p. 555). In spite of the "excellent

---

[1] Meglitsch and Schram, 1991, p. 490.

preservation, there are many conspicuous gaps in the arthropod record," and, as a result, "enormous controversy has surrounded the relationships of the major groups" (Wills, 2001, pp. 188, 190). In fact the "phylogeny of the major extant arthropod subphyla have been an area of major interest and dispute, and the validity of many of the arthropod groups suggested in earlier works is being questioned" (Springer, and Holley, 2013, p. 546). For this and other reasons both "arthropod evolution and classification are controversial" (Solomon, et al.,, 2011, p. 662). Consequently evolutionary authors are forced, as two evolutionary authors admit, to present, a "highly speculative interpretation of arthropod phylogeny" in their textbook (Miller and Harley (2013, p. 280). For several suggested phylogenetic relationships of arthropods, see Valentine (1989) and Edgecombe (1998).

The Trilobita

The trilobites are extremely abundant in strata assigned to both the Cambrian and Silurian. So far, about 65 different genera and over 100 species have been named (Margulis and Sagan, 2002, p. 180). Trilobites have a flat, oval body divided longitudinally into three lobes — hence their name. In common with other arthropods, they have a head, a thorax, and an abdomen. Like dogs, they display a great deal of variety, yet the trilobites all possess three lobes and a chitinous exoskeleton (Sherwin and Armitage, 2003). Trilobites are easy to identify because many of their traits, such as their overall plan of limb organization, are unique to Trilobita when compared to other arthropod groups (Eldredge, 1977, p. 327).

Trilobites have been preserved extremely well, partly because their hard calcium carbonate carapace (body covering) is highly resistant to deterioration (Margulis and Sagan, 2002, p. 180). Their fossil record is for this reason one of the best of any ancient plant or animal. They are found in "trilobite beds" located many places, such as Kodiak Island, Alaska (Meister, 1968). For this reason they are by far one of the most carefully studied of all the invertebrate groups (Clarkson, 1986). Trilobites are "commonly preserved as chitinous plates" or as molds, and, in some cases, their "actual integument is so well preserved that the markings on the surface can still be seen" (Twenhofel and Shrock, 1935, p. 433).

Figure 6.2 — Several Trilobite Fossils[2]

Their numerous paired appendages have been studied extensively. Fortunately, their appendages have been preserved in enormous detail in the fossil record (See Levi-Setti 1993, pp. 45-54 for SEM photographs that show this detail). Trilobites' eyes consisted of *enormously* complex, compound-faceted structures that sometimes formed a continuous band that extended across their whole frontal margin (Prokop, 1995, p. 111). The trilobite eyes resemble those of modern insects and were probably at least as

[2] Photo Credit: Icrms / Shutterstock.com

complex, if not more so. Design features such as these strongly support the view that they were the handiwork of an intelligent Creator (Sherwin and Armitage, 2003; DeYoung, 2002).

Trilobites are important both to the neo-Darwinian and creation position (Cook, 1968). Eldredge claims that the Trilobita "are as compelling examples of evolution as any of which I am aware,"[3] yet they show only variations within the Genesis kind. Although millions have been found in wide size range (some reaching almost 39" or 1 m long), and many in excellent condition that allow an accurate reconstruction of their history, they show no support for macroevolution. Instead, the fossil record shows a "relatively sudden, abrupt appearance of trilobites and other complex forms of animal life at the base of the Cambrian" (Eldredge, 1977, p. 44). As Clarkson concluded, in spite of their excellent fossil record, "almost nothing is known about the ancestors of the trilobites. In common with other arthropods, it may be presumed that trilobites were possibly derived from the same ancestors as the annelids, but this is only speculation" (1986, p. 330). Many researchers argue that trilobites are most closely related to crustaceans.

Most trilobite types existed contemporaneously with each other, which precludes hypothesizing any clear evolutionary trends amongst existing trilobite fossils. Furthermore, "no evidence, such as a transition series of fossils," has been found to bridge the gulfs separating the various trilobite species from each other (Whittington, 1992, p. 85, and chart, p. 86). Lack of intermediate forms is consistent with a creation origins model.

Extensive study of their fossils has demonstrated that trilobite "species and subspecies tend to remain relatively unchanged ... throughout their stratigraphic ranges" and that there are "fewer long-term 'evolutionary trends' within lineages 'documented' for

---

[3] Eldredge, 2000, p. 122

trilobites than for many other groups" (Eldredge, 1977, pp. 309, 316). Some devolution, though, such as loss of eyes, is seen in the fossil record (Whittington, 1992, p. 89).

Because wholesale speculation by paleontologists is the norm, Whittington stated that there "is no lack of either interpretation or speculation" about trilobite evolution (1992, p. 85). Eldredge tried to account for the lack of fossil evidence for trilobite evolution by resorting to the punctuated equilibrium model — the theory that evolution proceeded for relatively short periods of time followed by long periods of stasis (2000, p. 44). Eldredge and Gould actually developed their punctuated equilibrium theory specifically to explain the lack of a fossil record for trilobite evolution (Eldredge, 1977, p. 331; 2000, p. 84; Gould, 1977).

The fossil record does not provide evidence of relatively rapid evolution followed by stasis, and then more rapid evolution, as punctuated equilibrium predicts. Instead, it shows "the *abrupt appearance* of different kinds of trilobites in the Lower Cambrian and the replacement of these early groups by new ones during the transition from Cambrian to Ordovician" (Whittington, 1992, p. 84, emphasis mine).

Large numbers of trilobites died off at the end of the Cambrian for unknown reasons. Professor Hand described mass kills of trilobites as distant as Oklahoma, Morocco, and Poland as, "smothering to death by tons of hurricane-generated storm sediment was so rapid that the trilobites are preserved in life position" (Hand, 2011). The fossil record indicates that a burst of new kinds appeared in rock formations assigned to the next period, the Ordovician. But "after this great burst of new constructional themes in the early Ordovician, very few entirely new patterns of organization arose ... trilobites as a whole remained constructed on the same archetypal plan defined in the earliest Cambrian" (Clarkson, 1986, p. 331). All trilobites became extinct, as evidently did many other animals, in what evolutionists call the great Permian extinction.

The Crustaceans

Class Crustacea, phylum Arthropoda, contains over 35,000 species located worldwide, in both freshwater and marine habitats. Crustaceans have the highest diversity of body plans of all Arthropoda and include shrimp, crabs, lobsters, barnacles, wood lice, water fleas such as Daphnia, and copepods (Giribet and Ribera, 2000, p. 220). They have five pairs of locomotion appendages, the first two of which may be pincers for defense or food manipulation. They also have complex, well-developed eyes (Hamilton, 1986). The oldest crustacean fossils date back to the early Cambrian. Anderson notes that, although the

> fossil record is quite abundant for many crustacean groups, it provides no clear evidence on the origin of the Crustacea, and there has been considerable debate regarding the primitive or ancestral body form of the first crustaceans. Current opinion favors a long body with many similar trunk segments, two pairs of biramous [arthropod appendages that have two branches] antennae, and a nauplius [a larva stage characterized by three appendages] larva, but is divided on whether the trunk bore biramous or polyramous [arthropod appendages that have more than two branches] swimming appendages (1998, p. 316, definitions in brackets added).

Other researchers disagree, arguing that crustaceans evolved from a type of spiralian or proto-platyhelminthes worm (Willmer, 1990, pp. 298-299). The phylogenetic relationships of crustaceans are complicated, and little consensus exists (Giribet and Ribera, 2000, p. 220). In short, no clear fossil evidence exists to document crustacean evolution from a common ancestor. An excellent example is a "360 million years old" shrimp that it was "buried rapidly" in what is now Oklahoma and looks exactly like living shrimp (Feldmann, and Schweitzer, 2010).

Arachnida (Chelicerates)

Arachnids (spiders, scorpions, solifuges, mites, and ticks) have four pairs of walking appendages. Spiders are an arachnid group that ranks seventh in number compared to all animal species so far described. Their numbers, estimated between 30,000 and 40,000 species, are found worldwide, from Arctic regions to deserts (Williams and Goette, 1997, p. 3-4).

Many of the fossils in amber that "date from as long as 55 million years ago belong to genera which are still in existence today" (Preston-Mafham, 1996, p. 9). Fully modern-looking scorpions also have been found in amber (1999, pp. 76-78). Leeming concluded that scorpions have existed relatively unchanged since they first appeared in the fossil record—which evolutionists estimate was 450 million years ago (2004).

Recent fossil discoveries date modern arachnid types back to, evolutionists estimate, about 414 million years "forcing scientists to revise their thoughts about ... one of the most important steps in evolutionary history" (Monastersky, 2003, p. 292). The existing examples preserved in amber support the conclusion that no evidence for arachnid macroevolution exists (Shultz, 1994). A common view is that arachnids evolved from some king crab animal type (Preston-Mafham, 1991, pp. 12, 15). As Preston-Mafham admits, however, researchers "can only guess at what the ancestors of spiders and scorpions might have looked like." Although we "as yet have no definite proof, it is believed that all of the arachnids arose from a common ancestor" (1991, pp. 12, 15). A total absence of ancestral links to a common ancestor also exists for scorpions and other arachnids (Poinar et al., 1998; Fortey and Thomas, 1997).

One of the most infamous spiders is the tarantula, a large "hairy" spider, common in horror films, but actually a shy creature whose bites are relatively harmless (Williams and Goette, 1997, pp., 3-4). The tarantula's bite is about as painful as a wasp sting (Foelix, 1982, pp. 45-46). The "earliest" known spiders had a "nearly complete spinneret whose structure is quite advanced" (Preston-Mafham, 1991, p. 13). Even a spider, confirmed to be living in the dinosaur-age, has been found, a putative "165-million-year-old arachnid [is] the oldest known species of the largest web-weaving spiders alive today."[4]

The tough Arachnid exoskeleton aids in both preservation and identification. Many spiders have been extremely well preserved in the fossil record, especially in amber, and their classification is readily identifiable. Amber has effectively preserved even those arthropods that lack tough exoskeletons. Fossil spiders dating to the Tertiary, and some as far back as the Upper Cretaceous or earlier, have been identified from the close to 60 different families found in only one amber location (Penney, 2001, pp. 987-1009; 2002, p. 709; Schawaller, 1983; Poinar, 2000). More than 200 spider species have been identified in Miocene amber from the Dominican Republic alone (Penney, 2001, p. 987).

Evolution of Accessory Organs

The evolution of arachnid accessory organs also must be accounted for by neo-Darwinism. For example, the evolution of the spider silk glands and spinnerets necessary for making webs are explained by assuming that 180 million years ago spider silk was simply "excretory material deposited behind as the spider ran" (Kaston, 1966, p. 27). From this stage the silk evolved into a dragline, next into a trip wire, and, finally, it formed a spider web.

---

[4] April 20, 2011, *Biology Letters*.

Problems with this just-so-story include explaining how the spider survived until the spinneret was fully evolved and the fact that the spinneret silk-producing organ is both irreducibly complex and an organ system separate from the anus.

Another theory of spiderweb evolution is that ancestral spiders used alpha keratin (a component of spider threads) to cover their eggs (Vollrath, 1992). Once the silk glands evolved, the brain program to produce a web also must have evolved simultaneously—the silk is useless to capture food until the spider has the ability to construct a functional web, which requires a brain program (Williams, 1992, pp. 88-89). Furthermore, so-called "...'primitive'webs are not necessarily structurally simpler or less complex than 'advanced' webs" (Williams, 1988, p. 123).

Spider silk is produced in silk glands that open from spigots located on the spinnerets (Donovan, 1994). Many varieties of silk exist—the female garden-cross spider alone can produce at least seven different kinds of silk (Vollrath, 1992). Hydrogen ions from potassium hydrogen phosphate produces an acidic pH protecting the silk from bacterial and fungal attack (Miller and Harley, 2013, p. 248). The silk is proteinaceous and is effectively preserved in the fossil record—threads of spider silk date back to mid-Tertiary, and one spider web dates from the Eocene (Codington, 1992).

The fossil record traces spinnerets all the way back to the Devonian and Carboniferous (Donovan, 1994, p. 211). Evidence indicates that the earliest known spinnerets were fully modern, and no evidence exists of spinneret evolution—the theory that they evolved from a pair of legs is not supported in the fossil record (Vollrath, 1992, p. 72). Arachnida found in amber appear very modern in all respects and even include fully developed web threads (Poinar and Poinar, 1999, pp. 75-76). In conclusion, due to lacking fossil evidence, zoologists can only "believe" that Class Arachnida evolved from the eurypterids (Miller and Harley, 2013, p. 244).

Myriapoda

Class Myriapoda within the Arthropoda phylum includes centipedes and millipedes. Evidence of myriapods exists all the way back to the Cambrian (Budd, 2001; Kraus and Kraus, 1994). These animals have many pairs of walking legs, with either one or two pairs per body segment (Williams, Howe, and White, 1991). Millipedes are effectively preserved in amber, and even in rock, as a result of such events as calcite coating, lining, and the impregnation of the chitinous exoskeletons. Even "delicate structures such as limbs, antennae, gonopods, and eyes" all have been beautifully preserved (Donovan and Veltkamp, 1994, p. 355).

Many Lower Devonian fossils are excellently preserved, revealing the fine detail of the exoskeleton. These fossils even have been found in regions isolated from the major land masses, such as Australia (Edgecombe, 1998, pp. 172-174). The fossils uncovered reveal only evidence of variation, not evolution; many are identical to Myriapoda existing today. The Myriapoda for this reason are one of the most problematic groups to use morphology as a basis for producing phylogenetic trees (Giribet and Ribera, 2000, p. 218).

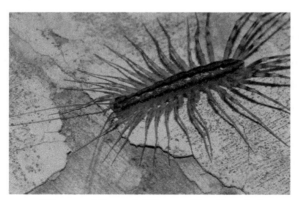

Figure 6.2 — A House Centipede[5]

---

[5] Photo Credit: Jiri Prochazka / Shutterstock.com

Cladogram Analysis

A cladogram is a branching diagram of different life forms arranged according to comparisons of selected characteristics assumed to have been derived from some common ancestor. In a study of 179 published cladograms, Wills concluded, "On several measures, cladograms of arthropods show lower congruence with the fossil record than a large sample of cladograms of various other taxa" (2001, p. 201). The many large gaps in the fossil-record often are given as the reason for this low congruence.

Yet arthropod fossils, such as trilobites, that are most durable, show among the lowest indices of congruence, "and for some trees almost any random range reassignment or random tree topology yields higher congruence" (Wills, 2001, p. 206; see also Weygoldt, 1996). In other words, selection of different traits to make the comparisons produces different cladograms. All of these problems support the belief that many arthropod baramins were separately created. Macro-evolutionism again is shown to be inferior to the concept of special creation.

The practice of overcoming fossil-record problems by using other criteria produces cladograms based solely on morphological traits and totally ignores both biochemical data and the fossil record. None of these methods provide evidence for neo-Darwinism. As Willmer (1990, p. 75) concluded, despite our best efforts, we have "not achieved very much understanding" of invertebrate evolution from our study of the fossil record. New ideas overturning existing once firmly established conclusions are common in the field (Cowen, 2003, p. 292; Doyle, 1996).

Genetic Comparisons

Problems in using the fossil record to trace the origin of arthropods are so major that some researchers have tried to ignore the fossils entirely and have chosen to produce evolutionary trees by using other means, such as DNA sequence data. Biochemical comparisons have so-far not been supportive of neo-Darwinism. For example, Burmester (2002) noted that hemocyanin evolution is strikingly different in each of three arthropoda groups: the Chelicerata, the Myriapoda, and the Crustacea (2002, p. 95). One solution is to place the origin of phyla earlier and hypothesize periods of "speeded-up" molecular evolution (Vermeij, 1996, p. 525). But this solution creates other discrepancies in the fossil record (Schram, and Koenemann, 2001).

Ironically, the most useful nucleotide for studying Metazoan evolution is believed to be the gene that produces ribosomal RNA (rRNA) (Valentine et al., 1996, p. 374). In a study of ribosomal DNA sequences, Giribet and Ribera (2000) found a high level of sequence heterogeneity in the 18s rRNA gene, making it very difficult to do phylogenetic comparisons. Some workers have concluded that this approach is of little or no value. Differences between the data from molecular biology, paleontology, and neontology (the retention of juvenile features in the adult developmental stage) have produced what Giribet and Ribera describe as furious debates (2000, p. 204). They actually conclude that ribosomal DNA sequence data by themselves "may not contain enough information to give a satisfactory explanation for the large and complicated evolutionary history of arthropods" (2000, p. 225).

Because these DNA and RNA data often are contradictory, others such as Meglitsch and Schram (1991, p. 591) ignored both biochemical and DNA data in developing their evolutionary trees. They relied only on the morphology of living animals. Because only a small percentage of arthropods have been examined, it is difficult at this early stage to draw anything but tentative conclusions about the usefulness of genetic comparisons in constructing phylogenies. Also, now we realize that we do not know as much as we thought we did a few years ago about how nucleic acids affect final phenotypes.

Discussion

The whole arthropod fossil record shows what Eldredge found was true of trilobites: that "stability was the norm," although "small" changes (variations within a baramin) occasionally do appear (Eldredge, 2000, p. 84). Eldredge also stated that a century of fossil study by paleontologists has consistently found "the persistence of stable species for millions of years" (2000, p. 85).

After noting that "paleontology has to date contributed almost nothing to evolutionary theory," Eldredge proposed several reasons why this is true. The main reason was that evolution "typically happens so quickly that rarely do we catch it in midstream when we scour the fossil record for insights on how evolution occurs" (2000, p. 85). This conclusion is based on speculation, and this is why Gould concluded that "the basic questions paleontologists have asked about the history of life" have "found no resolution within the Darwinian paradigm" (1977, p. 1).

Even modern symbiotic relationships have been shown to exist in the fossil record of some arthropods. An example is a symbiotic relationship, especially among arthropods and some fishes, in which one organism transports another organism of a different species, commonly called hitchhikers, a phenomenon called a phoresy. Poinar, *et al.*, found that phoresy between pseudoscorpions and many arthropods has a long history and is obligatory in many cases as "demonstrated by its continuance for millions of years, as shown by the fossil record" (1998, p. 79).

Conclusions

If Darwinian evolution had occurred, abundant evidence would exist to support it in the enormously large arthropod fossil record. This review has confirmed invertebrate zoologist Robert Barnes's observation that "the fossil record tells us almost nothing about the evolutionary origin of phyla and classes. Intermediate forms are non-existent" (1980, p. 365). Barnes also noted that the only exception to this generalization may be an animal "which may be on the line leading to the cephalopods" (1980, p. 365). He added, optimistically, that the required intermediate forms exist, but now are undiscovered, or not recognized, and it only requires more searching to reveal them (Barnes, 1980, p. 365).

More than three decades later Barnes's statement still is valid: the needed fossils have not been identified. What the fossil record shows is that the number of marine invertebrate species has been fairly constant for most of what evolutionists conclude is 600 million years of evolutionary "time" (Raup, 1976, 1991; Raup and Boyajian, 1988). One problem is that the proposed lineages were based on charts produced from assumptions based on evolutionary theory, and the charts then were used as evidence of the theory used to produce them, which is circular reasoning (Easton, 1960, p. 34).

Although the fossil record "should be the final arbiter in deciding between opposing theories on major issues of phylogeny" (Willmer, 1990, p. 52), the fossil record is ignored, and whatever method seems to support evolution is selected to support the theory of common descent. Thomas admitted that arthropods rule the world, at least among multicellular animals, and that

> we'd like to think that we understand the basic outlines of their evolutionary relationships. Unfortunately, we don't. The last time experts on all branches of arthropods came together to discuss their phylogeny, back in 1996,

consensus was conspicuously absent. Since then, it is safe to say, virtually everyone accepts that the arthropods are a monophyletic group—that is, their last common ancestor was something we would recognize as an arthropod. Beyond that rather modest point, argument still rages about many of the evolutionary relationships within and between the four major extant arthropod groups.... One of the few points of general agreement has been that the hexapods are monophyletic, that is, they arose just once from a single common six-legged ancestor (Thomas, 2003, p. 1854).

Thomas concluded that, even this consensus on six-legged creatures has now been shattered by DNA research (see Nardi et al., 2003), and this revolution has affected all invertebrates including arthropods (Ruppert et al., 2004).

Further work has made the Darwinistic worldview even more tenuous. As Valentine concluded, "Speculations as to the evolutionary relationships among living animal phyla began shortly after Darwin's seminal publications and have continued to the present time" (1989, p. 2272). This is true even though the fossil record today "extends back more than a hundred million years earlier than that known in Darwin's time" (Valentine, 1989, p. 2272).

References

Aguinaldo, Anna Marie A.; Turbeville, James M.; Linford, Lawrence S.; Rivera, Maria C.; Garey, James R.; Raff, Rudolf A.; Lake, James A. 1997. Evidence for a clade of nematodes, arthropods and other moulting animals. *Nature* 387:489-493.

Alonso, Jesus; Arillo, Antonio; Barron, Eduardo; Corral, J. Carmelo; Grimalt, Joan; Lopez, Jordi F.; Lopez, Rafael; Martinez-Delclos, Xavier; Ortuno, Vicente; Penalver, Enrique; Trincao, Paulo R. 2000. A new fossil resin with biological inclusions in Lower Cretaceous deposits from Alava (northern Spain, Basque-Cantabrian Basin). *Journal of Paleontology*, 74(1):158-178.

Bergman, Jerry. 2004. Insect evolution: a major problem for Darwinism. *Creation ex Nihilo Technical Journal* 18(2):91-97.

Delclos, V. Ortuno, E. Penalver, and P.R. Trincao. 2000. A new fossil resin with biological inclusions in lower cretaceous deposits from alava (northern Spain, Basque-Cantabrian Basin). *Journal of Paleontology* 74:158-178.

Anderson, D.T. (editor). 1998. *Invertebrate Zoology*. Oxford University Press, South Melbourne, Australia.

Barnes, Robert D. 1980. Invertebrate beginnings. *Paleobiology* 6:365-370.

_____. 1987. *Invertebrate Zoology*. Fifth Edition. Saunders, Philadelphia, PA.

Budd, G.E. 1997. Chapter 11: Stem group arthropods from the Lower Cambrian Sirius Passet fauna of North Greenland, pp. 125-136 in *Arthropod Relationships* edited by Fortey and Thomas.

Chapman and Hall, London, UK.

_____. 2001. A myriapod-like arthropod from the Upper Cambrian of East Siberia. *Palaeontologische Zeitschrift* 75:37-41.

Burmester, Thorsten. 2001. Molecular evolution of the arthropod hemocyanin superfamily. *Molecular Biological Evolution*

18:184-195.

_____. 2002. Origin and evolution of arthropod hemocyanins and related proteins. *Journal of Comparative Physiology B: biochemical, systemic, and environmental physiology* 172:95-107.

Chaloner, W.G., A.C. Scott, and J. Stephenson. 1991. Fossil evidence for plant-arthropod interactions in the Palaeozoic and Mesozoic. *Philosophical transactions: Biological sciences* 333:177-185.

Clarkson, Evan Neilson Kerr. 1986. *Invertebrate Palaeontology and Evolution.* Second Edition. Unwin Hyman, London, UK.

_____. 1998. *Invertebrate Palaeontology and Evolution.* Third Edition. Unwin Hyman, London, UK.

Codington, L.A. 1992. "Fossil spider web from the Eocene of Western Colorado". *Geological Society of America Abstracts with Program* 24:A344.

Cook, M.A. 1968. "William J. Meister discovery of human footprint with trilobites in a Cambrian formation of western Utah". *Creation Research Society Quarterly* 5(3):97. December.

Cowen, R. 2003. Genetic trickery probes tropical parasites. *Science News* 138:292.

Davis, L.J. 1968. Rockhound finds puzzling fossil. *Creation Research Society Quarterly* 5(3):102. December.

DeYoung, Don. 2002. Vision. *Creation Research Society Quarterly* 38:190-192.

Donovan, Stephen K. 1994. Chapter 8: Insects and other arthropods as trace-makers in non-marine environments and palaeoenvironments" in *The Palaeobiology of Trace Fossils* edited by S.K. Donovan. The Johns Hopkins University Press, Baltimore, MD.

_____, and C.J. Veltkamp. 1994. Unusual preservation of late Quaternary millipedes from Jamaica. *Lethaia* 27:355-362.

Doyle, Peter. 1996. *Understanding Fossils: an Introduction to Invertebrate Paleontology.* Wiley, New York, NY.

Easton, W.H. 1960. *Invertebrate Paleontology.* Harper, New York, NY.

Edgecombe, Gregory D. (editor). 1998. *Arthropod Fossils and Phylogeny.* Columbia University Press, New York, NY.

———. 1998a. Devonian terrestrial arthropods from Gondwana. *Nature* 394:172-175.

Eldredge, Niles. 1977. Trilobites and evolutionary patterns. Chapter 9 in *Patterns of evolution.* Edited by A. Hallam, pp. 305-332. Elsevier, Amsterdam, The Netherlands.

———. 2000. *The Triumph of Evolution and the Failure of Creationism.* W.H. Freeman, New York, New York.

Feldmann, Rodney, and Carrie Schweitzer. 2010. "The Oldest Shrimp (Devonian: Famennian) and Remarkable Preservation of Soft Tissue." *Journal of Crustacian Biology.* 30(4): 629-635).

Foelix, R. 1982. *Biology of Spiders.* Harvard University Press, Cambridge, MA.

Fortey, Richard A. and R.H. Thomas (editors). 1997. *Anthropod Relationships.* Chapman and Hall, London.

Gayrard-Valy, Yvette. 1994. *Fossils: Evidence of Vanished Worlds.* Abrams, New York.

Giribet, Gonzalo and Carles Ribera. 2000. A review of arthropod phylogeny: New data based on ribosomal DNA sequences and direct character optimization. *Cladistics* 16:204-231.

Gould, Stephen Jay. 1977. Eternal metaphors of palaeontology. Chapter 1 in *Patterns of evolution,* pp. 1-26. Edited by A. Hallam. Amsterdam: Elsevier, Amsterdam, The Netherlands.

Hallam, A. 1977. *Patterns of Evolution as Illustrated by the Fossil Record.* Elsevier Scientific, Oxford, New York, NY.

Hamilton, H.S. 1986. The jumping spider's wondrous eyes. *Creation Research Quarterly* 23:63-64.

Hand, Greg. 2011. Fossil Record Reveals Ancient Migrations, Trilobite Mass Matings. *Science Daily*. March 17.

Harper, David A.T. and Michael J. Benton (editors). 2001. History of biodiversity. *Geological Journal* 36:187-210.

Helder, Margart. 1997. The extra special courtship of horseshoe crabs. *Creation Matters* 2(1):1-3.

Kaston, B.J. 1966. Evolution of the web. *Natural History* 75:27-32.

Kraus, Otto and Margarete Kraus. 1994. "Phylogenetic system of the tracheata (mandibulata): on "myriapoda": insecta interrelationships, phylogenetic age and primary ecological niches" *Verhandlungen des Naturwissenschaftlichen Vereins in Hamburg* 34:5-31.

Kaufmann, David A. 1977. Phylogenetic development of adipose tissue in animals. *Creation Research Quarterly*13:214-215.

Lammerts, Walter.E. 1974. Insect family tree may become a forest. *Creation Research Quarterly*11:124-125.

Le Conte, Joseph. 1908. *Elements of Geology*. D. Appleton and Company, New York, NY.

Leeming, Jonathan. 2004. Book Review: Scorpions of Southern Africa. *Wildwatch — African Wildlife and Conservation*. http://www.wildwatch.com/resources/reviews/scorpionsSA.asp

Levi-Setti, R. 1993. *Trilobites*. The University of Chicago Press, Chicago, IL.

Manning, A. 2003. The Wright brothers' airplane compared to insect flight design. *Creation Research Society Quarterly* 40:1-7.

Manton, S.M. 1973. *Throw Away Your Zoology Textbooks*. Queen Mary College, London, UK.

Margulis, Lynn and Dorlan Sagan. 2002. *Acquiring Genomes; a Theory of the Origins of Species*. Basic Books, New York, NY.

Meglitsch, Paul A. 1967. *Invertebrate zoology*. Oxford University Press, New York, NY.

_____ and F.R. Schram. 1991. *Zoology*. Third Edition. Oxford University Press, New York, NY.

Meister, W.J., Sr. 1968. Discovery of trilobite fossils in shod footprint of human in "trilobite beds" — a Cambrian formation, Antelope Springs, Utah. *Creation Research Quarterly* 5(3): 97-101.

Miller, Stephen and John Harley, 2013, *Zoology*. New York: McGraw Hill.

Monastersky, R. 2003. Fossils push back origin of land animals. *Science News* 138:292.

Morris, Simon Conway. 2000. The Cambrian "explosion": slow-fuse or megatonnage? *Proceedings of the National Academy of Science* 97:4426-4429.

Nardi, Francesco; Giacomo Spinsanti, Jeffrey L. Boore, Antonio Carapelli, Romano Dallai, and Francesco Frati. 2003. Hexapod origins: monophyletic or paraphyletic? *Science* 299:1887-1889.

Penney, David. 2001. Advances in the taxonomy of spiders in Miocene Amber from the Dominican Republic (Arthropoda: Araneae). *Palaeontology* 44:987-1009.

_____. 2002. Spiders in Upper Cretaceous amber from New Jersey (Arthropoda: Araneae). *Palaeontology* 45:709-724.

Poinar, George O., Jr. 2000. Heydenius araneus n.sp. (Nematoda: Mermithidae), a parasite of a fossil spider, with an examination of helminths from extant spiders (arachnida: Araneae). *Invertebrate Biology* 119:388-393.

_____, B.P.M. Curcic, and J.C. Cockendolpher. 1998. Arthropod Phoresy Involving Pseudoscorpions in the Past and Present. *Acta Arachnologica* 47:79-96.

_____ and R. Poinar. 1999. *The Amber Forest*. Princeton University Press, Princeton, NJ.

Preston-Mafham, Rod 1991. *The Book of Spiders*. Chartwell Books, Edison, NJ.

Preston-Mafham, Ken and Rod Preston-Mafham. 1996. *The Natural History of Spiders.* The Crowood Press, Ramsbury, Marlborough Wiltshire, UK.

Prokop, Rudolf. 1995. *Fossils.* Magna, Leicester, England.

Raup, David M. 1976. Species diversity in the phanerozoic: an interpretation. *Paleobiology* 2:289-297.

_____. 1991. A kill curve for Phanerozoic marine species. *Paleobiology* 17:37-48.

_____ and G.E. Boyajian. 1988. Patterns of generic extinction in the fossil record. *Paleobiology* 14:109-125.

Ruppert, Edward E., Richard S. Fox, and Robert D. Barnes. 2004. *Invertebrate Zoology: a Functional Evolutionary Approach.* Seventh Edition. Brooks/Cole, Belmont, CA.

Schawaller, W. 1983. The spider family Hersiliidae in Dominican amber Stuttgart amber collection Arachnida araneae. *Stuttgarter Beitraege zur Naturkunde Serie B (Geologie und Palaeontologie)* 79:1-10.

Schram, Frederic R. and Stefan Koenemann. 2001. Developmental genetics and arthropod evolution: part I, on legs. *Evolution and Development* 3:343-354.

Shear, William A.; Gensel, Patricia A.; Jeram, Andrew J. 1996. Fossils of large terrestrial arthropods from the Lower Devonian of Canada. *Nature* 384:555-557.

Sherwin, F. and M. Armitage. 2003. Trilobites—the eyes have it! *Creation Research Quarterly* 40:172-174.

Sherwin, Frank. 2013. God's Amazing Invertebrates: The Missing Links are Still Missing. *Acts and Facts.* 42(2);12-15

Shultz, Jeffery W. 1994. The limits of stratigraphic evidence in assessing phylogenetic hypotheses of recent arachnids. *Journal of Arachnology* 22:169-172.

Solomon, Eldra, Linda Berg and Diana Martin, 2011. *Biology*, New York: Brooks/Cole.

Springer, J. and Holley, D. 2013. *An Introduction to Zoology*, Boston: Jones & Bartlett.

Thomas, Richard H. 2003. Wingless insects and plucked chickens. *Science* 299:1854-1855.

Tootill, Elizabeth. 1988. *The Facts on File Dictionary of Biology*. *Revised and Expanded Edition*. Facts on File Publications, New York, NY.

Twenhofel, William H. and Robert Rakes Shrock. 1935. *Invertebrate Paleontology*. McGraw Hill, New York, NY.

Valentine, James W. 1989. Bilaterians of the Precambrian-Cambrian transition and the annelid-arthropod relationship. *Proceedings of the National. Academy of Science* 86:2272-2275.

_____,. Douglas H. Erwin, and David Jablonski. 1996. "Developmental Evolution of Metazoan Bodyplans: The Fossil Evidence." *Developmental Biology*, 173:373-381.

Vermeij, Geerat. 1996. Animal Origins. *Science* 274:525.

Vollrath, Fritz. 1992. Spider webs and silks. *Scientific American* 266:70-76.

Weygoldt, P. 1996. Evolutionary morphology of whip spiders: towards a phylogenetic system. *Journal of Zoological Systematics and Evolutionary Research* 34:185-202.

Whittington, H.B. 1992. *Trilobites*. The Boydell Press, Rochester, NY.

Williams, E.L. 1988. Panorama of science. *Creation Research Quarterly* 25:123-124.

_____. 1992. Spiders as engineers. *Creation Research Quarterly* 28:88-89.

_____, and R.L. Goette. 1997. Tarantula goes acourtin', and he does roam. *Creation Research Quarterly* 34:3-4.

_____, G.F. Howe, and R.R. White. 1991. A desert millipede: evolution or design? — an introduction. *Creation Research Quarterly* 28:7-16.

Willmer, Pat. 1990. *Invertebrate relationships* Cambridge University Press, Cambridge.

Wills, Matthew A. 2001. How good is the fossil record of arthropods? an assessment using the stratigraphic congruence of cladograms. *Geological Journal* 36:187-210.

_____, D.E.G. Briggs, and R.A. Fortey. Evolutionary correlates of arthropod tagmosis: scrambled legs, pp. 57-65. In *Arthropod Relationships*, edited by Fortey and Thomas. Chapman and Hall, London, UK.

Chapter 7

Insects — Ancient and Modern

Introduction

Insect evolution rarely is discussed by Darwinists as evidence of macroevolution in spite of the fact that arthropoda (insects, crustaceans, myriapods, and arachnids) should be a major evidence for evolution. This is because fully 80 percent of *all* confirmed animal species—now estimated by many entomologists as close to 1.8 million—are insects, and the grand total of all insect species is currently estimated to be over 5 million (Mayr, 2001, p. 162; Labandeira, 1999, p. 613). Insects currently consist of 33 orders, including one that has over 300,000 members (Pennisi, 2002, p. 447).

Insects—of which almost a million species now are known, and more than five million are believed to exist—are all arthropods. Ninety percent of all arthropods are insects, and the same problem of lack of transitional forms also exists within this group (Gamlin and Vines, 1987, p. 81). Romoser concludes that a lack of consensus exists on the evolutionary relationships of insects are due to the absence of transitional forms in the fossil record.

Furthermore, most insects have short lifecycles and in a century produce far more generations than vertebrates. Consequently, they "should evolve faster than vertebrates," yet "the fossil record indicates that insects have evolved more slowly than vertebrates" if at all (Callahan, 1972, p. 114). Insects are not only bothersome pests, but actually carry out so many critical tasks that civilization "could not survive without them" (Callahan, 1972, p. 20). Two of these many tasks include the pollination of most of our food crops and recycling organic material.

The Fossil Record

A major problem for Darwinism is the "extensive fossil record," not only of insects, but also with few rare exceptions *all* other invertebrates. This extensive fossil record provides no evidence of evolution. If an average of 1,000 transitional forms were required for each species, around 18 billion transitional forms would have existed in the fossil record; yet no clear examples exist (Carpenter, 1953, p. 256; Clarkson, 1986).

In the early 1950s, Harvard entomologist Frank Carpenter estimated that approximately a half-million invertebrate fossil specimens were stored in museums and university collections. These fossils are believed to date back to 340 million years old (myo) when the "forest swarmed with insects, including dragonflies, beetles, and cockroaches" (Wilson, 1992, p. 190). Since the 1950s the number of fossil insects available to researchers has increased enormously. As a result, an extensive insect fossil record exists today. The fossil record is so good that "their diversity exceeds that of preserved vertebrate tetrapods through 91 percent of their evolutionary history" (Labandeira and Sepkoski, 1993, p. 310).

Insect wings are especially common in the fossil record, partly because they "do not readily decay or digest" as readily as most other insect body parts (Grimaldi and Engel, 2005, p. 42). In addition, "wings are a veritable road map to the identification and phylogeny of insects" (Grimaldi and Engel, 2005, p. 42). An example is that an isolated wing alone often allows identification of an insect to the level of family. Because fossil insects often are preserved as organic compressions and inorganic impressions, the insect fossil record often can tell us much more about evolution than terrestrial vertebrate fossils, which are virtually always preserved only as teeth or jaw remains — or as inorganic bone casts. Furthermore, many examples exist of permineralized, charcoalified replicas, as well as inclusions of insects in amber and in certain minerals (Grimaldi and Engel, 2005, p. 42). Paleontologists also often have found what they assume are the trails of ancient insects tunneling through primitive soil; yet no bodies have ever been uncovered (Wilson, 1992, p. 190).

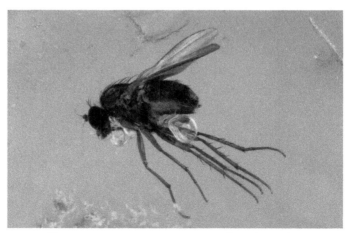

Figure 7.1 — Insect in Fossilized Amber[1]

---

[1] Photo Credit: Matteo Chinellato / Shutterstock.com

Controversy about Insect Evolution

The "diverse, well-preserved" insect fossil record has been summarized in more than 20 major monographs since the 1960s alone (Labandeira, 1999, p. 622). In spite of this abundant fossil record, and the conclusion that the forests swarmed with insects in ancient times, a complete absence of valid fossil evidence exists for insect evolution. Brodsky concluded that the first 20 million years of putative insect evolution "are shrouded in mystery" (1996, p. 79). For this reason "all of the evidence used in the study of [insect] phylogeny is circumstantial" (Boudreaux, 1979a, p. 14). As a result, the evolutionary relationships among three basic branches of arthropods (the trilobites, the chelicerates, and the mandibulates) are

> purely hypothetical. Unfortunately, knowledge of the fossil record is of little help, because each group is distinctly defined in the Cambrian strata, from which the oldest "good" fossils come. This, of course, means that the supposed common ancestor arose in Precambrian times (Romoser and Stoffolano, 1998, p. 326).

The major problem is that, although the study of evolutionary relationships among "animal phyla has occupied the attention of zoologists for more than a century" (Boudeaux, 1979a, p. 15), there still exists little evidence of evolution. Consequently, there exist a wide variety of major theories

> concerning the major lines of evolution in the animal kingdom. Various viewpoints are possible because all the evidence for evolutionary relationships is circumstantial. The fossil record indicates that most of the animal phyla were already in existence in the earliest Paleozoic period at least 600 million years ago. The presumed soft-bodied animals that existed before then

in the Archeozoic (Precambrian) period have left few fossils, which are of no value for indicating possible primitive states. The only record that could indicate possible primitive states is difficult to interpret. This record is coded in the form of genes (Boudeaux, 1979a, p. 15).

The complete lack of fossil evidence for insect evolution arouses much speculation. As a result, the

> evolutionary relationships among the trilobites, chelicerates, and mandibulates are unclear, although there have been a number of opinions expressed. Some investigators argue that the arthropods are a polyphyletic group and that many of their similarities have arisen as a result of convergent evolution. However, others see them as clearly monophyletic, having evolved from a common ancestor. All three subphyla are well represented in the Cambrian strata (Romoser, 1973, p. 295).

The polyphyletic-monophyletic controversy also still is very much alive today (Romoser and Stoffolano, 1998, p. 328) and illustrates the level of speculation in the field of insect evolution. The "number of opinions expressed" includes the speculation that the common ancestor of all insects was an annelid, a soft-bodied, cylindrical, segmented, elongated, bilaterally symmetrical worm, or annelid-like creature that looked like a modern earthworm.

This conclusion is not based on the fossils or other empirical evidence, but on evaluations of living organisms and much guesswork—primarily the observation that insects have a long, segmented body that is superficially similar to modern segmented worms. Because worm-to-insect evolution requires both the addition of many new structures, and the loss of numerous other structures, it would seem that abundant evidence for these many changes would exist in the fossil record.

The most "primitive" of living insects are the bristletail (*Archaeongnatha*) and the silverfish (*Zygentoma*), known in the fossil record at least back to the mid-Devonian (Grimaldi and Engel, 2005, p. 148). These "primitive" insects are very similar to many modern flightless insects. Some so-called "primitive" insects have superior survival skills, and many can live in widely diverse habitats, including elevations as high as 4,800 meters. Silverfish entombed in amber date back only to the Cretaceous, a problem considering that they are considered the sister group of all other dicondylic insects; thus, a "huge gap in their early fossil record" is postulated to exist (Grimaldi and Engel, 2005, p. 152). Another explanation, this one based on evidence, is that these "primitive" insects are neither primitive nor predate more advanced insects.

Yet other entomologists argue that "insects evolved from centipedes in the Silurian" (Busbey et al., 1996, p. 222). Although Class Insecta is assumed by many authorities to have evolved from a Myriapod (millipede) or some type of protomyriapod animal during the Devonian period, this conclusion about insect origins is controversial (Labandeira, 1999, p. 603). Others argue that insects "descended directly from trilobites; others think their immediate ancestors were crustaceans" (Callahan, 1972, p. 102). Much disagreement also exists about Crustacean evolution. For example, Romoser notes that one investigator argued

> that an early crustacean line branched off in the Silurian period and gave rise to the myriapods and insects, which he groups as Atelocerata. Other investigators hypothesize a direct trilobite origin for the myriapods and insects, and still others place the Onychophora in this position (Romoser, 1973, p. 295).

One theory is that the segmented worm class, the Annelida, evolved from the ancient protostomes, which also gave rise to the ancestors of insects. Labandeira (1999, p. 603) discounts this view and instead argues on the basis of biomolecular studies that insects and other hexapods evolved "from an unspecified lineage of crustaceans." He admits that "hexapod origins remains unsettled" and that morphological evaluations still favor a non-crustacean ancestor (1999, p. 603).

Yet other evolutionists argue that "it is reasonable to suppose that" the earliest insects "were similar to silverfish," an animal that appears in the fossil record an estimated 350 million years ago (Lewin, 1982, pp. 130-131). Recent studies also have looked at the role of regulatory genes, such as Homeotic (Hox) genes, in insect evolution (Galant and Carroll, 2002; Ronshaugen, et al., 2002). This research, though, has shown only how mutations in Hox genes could cause the *loss* of structures in history. At least five major theories of the ancestry of insects exist, with one or more leading evolutionists arguing for each (Callahan, 1972, p. 103).

The controversy stems from a complete lack of fossil evidence that might provide support for evolutionary descent. The fact that these conclusions are based heavily on speculation — unconstrained by fossil evidence — results in much disagreement among Darwinists, as is clear from the admission that "there are varying opinions as to the origin of the myriapod and insect groups" (Romoser and Stoffolano, 1998, p. 331).

Although there exists much disagreement about insect origins, currently the most common view is that they evolved from some type of myriapod or protomyriapod prior to the Devonian period. Other Darwinists conclude that it is more likely for myriapods and insects both to have evolved from some unknown common ancestor (Rosomoser and Stoffolano, 1998, p. 329). The sparse (at best) to nonexistent evidence for transitional forms is a major reason why phylogenetic trees vary drastically (Romoser and Stoffolano, 1998, p. 330). Furthermore, the dominant view of insect evolution is not supported by RNA analysis (Ballard, et al., 1992).

This forces researchers to speculate based on both present-day examples and the many fossil insect forms unearthed in the past three centuries, which are little help because, in almost all cases, they are virtually identical to modern forms. To illustrate the wide range of opinions, Romoser recommends that readers "consult the literature on insect evolution" and notes that Sharov (1966) Brues, Melander, and Carpenter (1954) serve as good starting points. (Romoser, 1973, p. 297). Many references totally ignore the problem of insect evolution, only stating that it occurred. In the 1998 edition of his classic text, Romoser stated only that trilobite evolution has "played an important role in the study of arthropod evolution" and gives little other information (1998, p. 326).

Evolutionists date arthropod fossils all the way back to the Cambrian era (Bergström, 1979, p. 3). The origins of each of the millions of insect species has also yet to be documented. Typical is the origin of butterflies. It is "generally agreed today [by evolutionists] that butterflies are descended from moth-like ancestors, and that the separation occurred somewhere between fifty and a hundred million years ago" (Hubbell, 1993, p. 9).

In spite of the abundant fossil record, "little is known" of insect evolution, and only worm-like onychophorans have provided any "real evidence" of insect progenitors (Gamlin and Vines, 1987, p. 81). One reason is that almost all fossils, even those dated by evolutionists to be many millions of years old, are far too similar, often identical, to modern types to support macroevolution. In the words of Bergström, most insect fossils are "too advanced to reveal clear relationships with other groups" (1979, p. 3). Although it is widely recognized that "there has been little evolutionary change in insects" from at least the quaternary era (Callahan, 1972, p. 63). Evidence now exists that this conclusion is true much earlier in the fossil records.

A "fairly accurate picture of the environment that existed

during the life of fossil insects" exists, and from this record it is clear that insect fossils either are close to modern examples or are extinct insects (Callahan, 1972, p. 98). As a result, Darwinists are forced to rely heavily on gross morphology of living animals to develop their theories of evolutionary descent. For example, Gamlin and Vines note that some of the major problems in determining insect evolution include the following:

> One major difference is that the limbs of crustaceans are branched (biramous) whereas those of insects and myriapods are always unbranched, even in their embryonic stages—hence their new name "Uniramia." Chelicerates also have unbranched limbs but they lack antennae and have a different set of mouthparts, in particular a pair of pincer-like structures called chelicerae. Finally there are fundamental differences between the groups in the way the legs and jaws move, which suggest that each developed limbs independently (Gamlin and Vines, 1987, p. 81).

> They concluded that of

> the ancestors themselves, little is known, and only the worm-like onychophorans provide any real evidence. The construction of their body wall and excretory system is distinctly annelid-like, but they also have appendages that could have been the forerunners of the insects' segmented limbs, as well as insect-like antennae, and tracheae for breathing. All this suggests that the Uniramia evolved from annelid stock, but the ancestors of the other groups—the crustaceans and chelicerates—remain a complete mystery (Gamlin and Vines, 1987, p. 81).

In harmony with this assessment, Morris concludes that the

fossil evidence for

> the origin of insects is completely blank. Insects occur in fantastic number and variety, but there is no fossil clue to their development from some kind of evolutionary ancestor (1974, p. 86).

Morris adds that the absence of transitional forms is not due to lack of fossil evidence because insects "have been found fossilized in considerable numbers, preserved in amber, coal, volcanic ash, or such materials. All such deposits must have been formed rapidly ... or the insect fossils could not have endured so long" (1974, p. 86). In one site in Colorado "over 100,000 specimens have been collected" some of which "are perfectly beautiful, almost as if they have been freshly mounted" (Lewin, 1982, p. 130). The Florissant Colorado Shales alone have produced more than 60,000 specimens (Callahan, 1972, p. 67).

Other productive sites include the Burgess Shale in British Columbia, the Elmo Kansas Limestone, and the Hunsrück Shale in Germany. Many arachnids, such as mites and other invertebrates, including insects and even crustaceans (especially ostracods), are extremely well preserved in these sites (Braun, 1997). Russia, North America, and Northern Europe are all rich in insect fossil deposits (Callahan, 1972, p. 68).

Some of the many "exquisitely preserved insect" fossils even have retained their "external color patterns and internal gut contents" (Labandeira, 1999, p. 623). Many of the best fossils are preserved in amber (a tree sap that hardens to a golden yellow). More than 150,000 fossil insects have been collected from Baltic amber alone (Callahan, 1972, p. 70). Amber is an excellent preservative, often retaining small details that allow accurate identification of ancient fossil insects. The preservation quality is so good that specimens commonly include insect wing veins, mouthparts, facets of the compound eye, spines in the legs, and even genitalia, which are preserved in exquisite detail.

One advantage of using insect fossils to study evolution is that most insects have exoskeletons and, consequently, their external morphology usually is well preserved. Conversely, for most vertebrates, frequently only the internal skeleton, or more often, only fragments, are found. Insects also preserve well in viscous tar or asphalt, and in pools of highly mineralized water. Fossil impressions of insects in coal, volcano ash, limestone, and other media also are common.

Clear examples of fully developed dragonflies (specifically protodonatas), cockroaches, and mayfly fossils found in coal and other media have been dated all the way back to the Carboniferous period. It is not unreasonable to conclude that, even though a large sample of fossils have been discovered and although those fossils may not be perfectly representative of insect history, nonetheless, they do not show any evidence of macroevolution. The fossil record so far has revealed only about 20,000 extinct insects (Labandeira, 1999, p. 613), but otherwise

> the insect population of today remains remarkably similar to that of the earlier age. All the major orders of insects now living were represented in the ancient Oligocene forest. Some of the specific types have persisted throughout the 70-million years since then with little or no change (Brues, 1951, pp. 60-61).

Typical is the black fly fossil record, which evolutionists conclude "have been around, in pretty much unchanged form, since the middle of the Jurassic Era, some 180 million years ago" (Hubbell, 1993, p. 77).

Some extinct arthropods, or arthropod-like animals, have been found in the fossil record, but rather than supporting Darwinism, they often complicate insect evolution instead of elucidating it (Bergström, 1973, p. 3). Buchsbaum, et al., in their classic text on arthropods, liken insect evolution to a good novel that contains clues to the mystery as one reads until the "earliest and most important events" are about to be revealed, and then one discovers

> that the rest of the pages in the book are missing. Just this kind of exasperating situation confronts us when we try to relate different phyla of animals to one another in an orderly scheme. Anyone can see that ... spiders are more like lobsters than like clams. But when we attempt to relate groups, especially phyla, which, by definition, are groups of animals with fundamentally different body plans, there is little we can say with certainty. The different groups of arthropods are clearly allied to each other as well as to annelids [phylum Annelida]; but how arthropods are related to each other, or to such utterly different animals as sea stars or vertebrates, remains quite a mystery (Buchsbaum, et al., 1987, p. 533).

They conclude that the insect fossil record, "might be likened to our mystery book" because it

> provides many examples of species that are clearly descended one from another, but it is of practically no use in relating the phyla to each other. For, as we "turn the pages," digging deeper and deeper in the rocks and expecting to find intermediate forms linking different phyla, we instead continue to find fossils of animals that are readily identifiable as members of phyla living today—but few intermediates. In the earliest rocks for which we have good animal fossils, those of the Cambrian period, all the important animal phyla are already represented. Still older rocks contain very few animal fossils, and most of those are difficult to assign even to the phyla represented in the Cambrian (1987, pp.

333-334).

Buchsbaum concludes, "while the fossil record tells us a great deal about what the early forms of most phyla looked like, and the order in which species, or even genera, families, and orders appeared, it has little to say about whether the different phyla are related to each other, and if they are, the sequence in which they appeared" (Buchsbaum, 1987, p. 534). The authors then explain that "despite this, the situation is by no means hopeless," and attempt to outline evidence to show evolutionary relationships. The "most important kind of evidence," they conclude, is comparative morphology (Buchsbaum, 1987, p. 534). Of course, this information cannot provide evidence for macroevolution; nor can the other evidence the authors discuss, such as comparative biochemistry or comparative embryology. All the other evolutionists quoted in this book believe insect evolution from worm-like creatures occurred *in spite* of the lack of evidence. In support of this view, they cite similar evidence as did Buchsbaum.

Minor change is indicated by the fossil record, but does it support Darwinism? Morris concluded that extinct fossil insects are "very similar to those living now," except many insects are "much larger than their modern relatives." Examples include giant dragonflies (some, dated to the Jurassic, had wingspans as long as 30 inches, compared to 3.25 inches today), giant cockroaches, and ants. Although larger, "their form is no different in essence from that of modern insects" (Morris, 1974, p. 86). This assertion can be stated with confidence because examples of the gross morphology "of the insect fossil record are well documented" (Labandeira, 1999, p. 613).

Darwinists have concluded that most of these giant insects have become extinct, or more often evolved into smaller sizes, because their bodies were too large to effectively hide from predators. This contrasts with the alleged major Darwinian trend to produce larger-sized animals, such as the horse and many chordates, including, especially, primates. Darwinists also postulate that large insects originally evolved their gigantic sizes to better compete with other insects. Both conclusions are logical but, aside from being contradictory, lack empirical evidence.

Extinct insects are as complex as those living today, only different (Sanders and Howe, 1985). Occasionally new insects also are discovered that were known only as fossils. One recent discovery was an insect once thought by evolutionists to be extinct 3.5 to 50 million years ago (Trivedi, 2002, p. 4). Another newly identified insect order was found to be identical to a specimen in an estimated 45-million-year-old chunk of golden amber (Pennisi, 2002, p. 447; Trivedi, 2002, p. 2). The fact that insects appear in the fossil record as fully developed non-transitional forms — usually in fully modern forms — often is explained by Darwinists as follows:

> At present we find it hard to trace the causes for such relatively rapid evolutionary changes and widespread radiation, but they are undoubtedly tied to the small size of insects, their rapid generation times, their evolution of winged forms, and their apparently endlessly malleable structures (Strickberger, 2000, p. 382).

The variety of mouth-parts in both extant and extinct insects is enormous — fully 34 fundamental mouth-part systems have been identified in extant insects, and two more in extinct insects (Labandeira, 1999, p. 614). The major fields of insect evolution research include of insect wings, insect flight, the compound eye, and metamorphosis.

Evolution of Insect Wings

The insect wing is a complex, well-designed structure (Pringle, 1983). Made out of an extremely light, but amazingly strong and tough material called cutin, wings are reinforced by a complex set of various "veins" that provide structural support where needed, yet supply the strength to resist bending and twisting (Bishop, 1997, p. 22; Chapman, 1998, p. 186). The 30-odd wing muscles housed in the thorax per square millimeter of cross-sectional area are the most powerful muscles known. Although 200 beats per second is typical in some insects, they can beat as fast as 1,000 times per second (Aberlin, 1995, p. 13). The wings also can be opened up to absorb heat like solar panels do.

The origin of insect wings and insect flight are "one of the most controversial topics in paleoentomology" (Labandeira, 1999, p. 618). The lack of fossil (or other) evidence thus has resulted in enormous speculation about their origin:

> No structure in the Arthropoda, an extensive group of animals, has given rise to such a variety of hypotheses about their origin as have insect wings. Interest in the more than 150-year-old theories of insect flight has not faded ... (Brodsky, 1996, p. 79).

Ancient fossil insects "had fully developed wings," and no evidence of partly developed wings ever has been uncovered, even though insect wings "are usually well preserved" in the fossil record (Callahan, 1972, pp. 73, 96). Because bird wing bones are homologous to animal limbs, it was assumed that bird wings evolved from limbs (Averof and Cohen, 1997). Insect wings, though, are not modified legs, but very different structures added to the insect in addition to legs (Borror, 1976, p. 139). The problem of wing evolution commonly is dealt with by assuming that insects "borrowed" other organs to achieve flight—a process called co-option. The problem in determining how organs could be "appropriated" for wing use as the co-option theory requires is no easy matter.

Figure 7.2 — Fossilized Dragonfly[2]

These problems have forced the development of new theories of insect wing evolution, such as the view that wings evolved from modified fish gills (Averof and Cohen, 1997, p. 627). It widely is accepted that insect wings are not modified legs, but rather arose from flaps located dorsoventrally on the thorax (Borror et al., 1976, p. 138). What function these hypothetical flaps may have served is a subject of much debate—with speculation ranging from sexual displays to gliders (Borror et al., 1976). No fossil (or other) evidence exists to help determine if such flaps ever existed, let alone what function they may have served. Another theory is that they evolved from a novel outgrowth of the insect thorax, and not from preexisting structures.

The problem was discussed by Marden as follows:

> The evolutionary advantages of flight—speed, safety, mobility—would be obvious to any species with an ounce

---

[2] Photo Credit: Marcel Clemens / Shutterstock.com

of foresight. But evolution does not rely on foresight. Step by tedious step, the most sophisticated biological devices must evolve from the meanest parts, without a master plan to guide them. Darwin himself, however, had trouble explaining the origins of complex traits that function only when fully assembled. How could all the machinery of flight–wings, wing articulations, neural circuitry, powerful flight muscles–evolve incrementally? A faulty, half-evolved flying machine could do its owner more harm than good. And if early designs could not carry an insect aloft, what advantages did they confer? As one of Darwin's early critics put it: "What good is a nub of a wing?" (Marden, 1995, p. 26).

One common suggestion is that insects evolved wings from aquatic "pre-insects" that had gill plates used for rowing and skimming across water (Marden and Kramer, 1994). The example used to support this hypothesis is modern stone flies, which flap their wings to obtain thrust without aerodynamic lift. Once wings evolved to obtain thrust,

> stronger and larger water-skimming "wings" could then undergo selection for aerial flight. According to Averof and Cohen, the genetic basis for transforming gill appendages into wings comes from changes in regulatory genes used in developing gill structures in biramous (branched) crustacean legs (Strickberger, 2000, p. 382).

This model is helpful because it indicates what kinds of evidence to look for in the fossil record. Unfortunately for Darwinists, no evidence for this theory has been found in the abundant insect fossil record, even in insects trapped in amber.

The evolution of insect wings is considered a "momentous event" in evolution because, aside from bird wings, insect wings are "the only true wings in the animal world" (Lewin, 1982, p. 131). They are also momentous because "so miraculous a thing is insect flight that nearly all insect biologists believe it could have evolved only once" (Marden, 1995, p. 28). Insects also are the "only group of invertebrates that includes members capable of active flight" (Romoser and Stoffolano, 1998, p. 326).

All Pterygota (winged insects) have two pairs of wings—one pair on their mesothoracic body segments, and the second pair on their metathoracic body segments (Labandeira, 1999, p. 607). Although speculation abounds, and many theories have been postulated, no empirical evidence whatsoever exists for the evolution of insect flight in the abundant insect fossil record. Lewin notes that several theories about how insects evolved flight exist, but there is currently

> no real consensus. As a fraction of a wing would presumably be useless for flight, it is more than likely that wings originated as other structures which then became transformed into wings. Preadaptation once again—not an anticipation of future needs but a fortuitous convergence of different functions on a single structure. One suggestion is that external gills in the young might have provided sufficient lift for an occasional glide to safety after jumping to escape from a predator. Selection for maintaining and enlarging these structures, it is argued, might have eventually given rise to wings (Lewin, 1982, p. 133).

In answer to the question, "Is there any evidence for such a proposal?" Lewin responds:

> Yes and no. Mayfly nymphs, which live in water, do have external gills of the sort envisioned. What is more, they are equipped with muscles which in some

nymphs move the gills at five beats per second, thus increasing the circulation of water around them. In the putative ancestor, these muscles might have evolved into ones that would power flight. But not yet is there good evidence that the young of the early insects had an aquatic stage as in the mayflies (Lewin, 1982, p. 133).

As is also true for bird flight, intermediate forms between the flightless, worm-like animal insect precursors and winged insects are totally absent. Furthermore, many small details of insect wings have been preserved in fossils that have been dated by evolutionists back 325 million years, yet these "wings appear in the fossil record already fully formed" (Marden, 1995, p. 27).

It should be much easier to document insect evolution than bird evolution because of the enormous number of well-preserved insects with wings found in amber, many types of sedimentary rock, and other media. Yet researchers have not been able to locate a single one of the many thousands of intermediate forms that must have existed if a flightless and wingless annelid evolved into winged insects capable of flying (Romoser and Stoffolano, 1998, p. 329). The current state of insect wing evolution was summarized by two of the leading researchers as follows:

When *pterygote* (winged) insects first evolved is a puzzle. Insects with fully-formed, obviously functional wings first appear suddenly in the Carboniferous period. Scientists are confident that these complex structures and the physiological and behavioral requirements associated with them evolved through a long series of intermediate forms. However, what that evolutionary process must have been remains unclear (Romoser and Stoffolano, 1998, p. 332).

Of the many theories of insect wing evolution proposed, only two remain, both of which face major problems (Labaneira, 1999, p. 618). The first, called the **paranotal theory,**

> proposes that wings originated from rigid, lateral projections of thoracic terga that became enlarged, flattened, supplied with a regularized system of veins, and eventually articulated with the thorax to produce flapping flight. However, the paranotal theory suffers from several deficits, including absence of evidence for an articulatory wing hinge characterizing the attachment of paranotal lobes to an associated thorax, thus disallowing flapping flight (Labandeira, 1999, p. 618).

The second theory, called the **epicoxal theory**, speculates that

> serially homologous protowings originated in semiaquatic insects from small appendages located above the leg bases, known as epicoxal exites, initially for purposes other than aerial flight. Subsequently protowings developed laterally on thoracic and abdominal segments from these exites, which were initially articulated to the pleurae, a condition different from the initially rigid attachment proposed by the paranotal theory (Labandeira, 1999, p. 618).

Although this second theory is more consistent with the embryological, genetic, and fossil evidence, "nevertheless, an intermediate stage by which gills or other homologous lateral structures could have been converted to functional aerial wings has always been challenging" (Labandeira, 1999, p. 618). The other proposed hypothesis suffers from major problems (Marden, 1995). Therefore, Marden proposed yet another idea—the view that the first insects skimmed on the water surface by using gills as sails and gradually developed the ability to fly.

A major problem with this theory is that all known insects, both living and extinct, are, and always were, terrestrial and would not have gills, but a lung analog or a means of diffusing oxygen from air. Another problem with this theory is that no evidence exists for it except the fact that a few modern insects, such as winter stoneflies, can skim over water. As Marden admits, "until someone presents direct fossil evidence of the earliest winged insects, there will be room for new viewpoints, interpretations and lively debate" (1995, p. 30).

The oldest full body fossil impression of a flying insect dates back to the Late Carboniferous (Knecht, et al, 2011). As far as can be determined, it has modern wings, thus is labeled a flying insect. Carroll concluded that the fossil record does not support "the nearly continuous spectrum of evolutionary change postulated by Darwin." In fact, the "almost incomprehensible number of species" that inhabit Earth today "do not form a continuous spectrum" but instead

> nearly all species can be recognized as belonging to a relatively limited number of clearly distinct major groups, with very few illustrating intermediate structures or ways of life. All of us can immediately recognize animals as being birds, turtles, insects, or jellyfish, and plants as conifers, ferns, or orchids. Even with millions of living species, there are only a very few that do not fit into readily recognizable taxonomic categories (Carroll, 1997, p. 9).

Carroll adds that nearly all of the hundreds of thousands of recognized insect species can be placed in one

> of the approximately thirty well-characterized orders. One might hypothesize a very different pattern among extinct plants and animals: Fossils would be expected to show a continuous progression of slightly different

forms linking all species and all major groups with one another in a nearly unbroken spectrum. In fact, most well-preserved fossils are as readily classified in a relatively small number of major groups as are living species (Carroll, 1997, p. 9).

Another problem is that insect wings do not function independently, but must articulate appropriately with the body, and also must function as a unit, which requires coordination by a nervous system of great complexity. The energy required for flight is enormous—as much as 100 times that required for resting (Aberlin, 1995, p. 47).

Theories of Folding Wing Evolution

With very few exceptions, such as dragonflies, all insects have a "complicated system of joints" that allow them to compactly fold their wings over their abdomen (Farb, 1962, p. 16). No simple structure, the folding wing is, in the words of a University of Chicago neuroethologist, "the most morphologically complex joint in the animal kingdom" (Dickinson, quoted in Aberlin, 1995, p. 13). A variety of folding systems exists, including longitudinal and transverse, all requiring unique muscle and nerve designs (Chapman, 1998, p. 187).

Yet no evidence for the evolution of wing folding has ever been found in the enormous insect fossil record. The fossil record shows that insects with folding wings have existed as the earliest fossils known until today—and that no evidence exists to indicate that folding wings have evolved from non-folding wings as postulated by Darwinists. The exact opposite is found in the fossil record. For example, cockroaches have folding wings, while dragonflies do not, and both made their debut contemporaneously in the fossil record (Matthews, 1962, p. 113; Sanders and Howe, 1985, p. 168).

Related to wing evolution is halter evolution. Most insects have four wings (a forward and hind pair), and Darwinists assumed that "during the course of their evolution, flies adapted their second pair of wings into balancers, little knobs on their backs called halteres, which help stabilize their flight" (Hubbell, 1993, p. 21). Beetles have "forewings," which is the source of their scientific name: Coleoptera (sheath-winged, from the Greek *koleon*, a sheath). It is "thought that the wing veins became thickened and grew harder until they developed into tough protective covers for the more delicate hind wings, the flying wings that fold underneath the body" (Hubbell, 1993, p. 40). Entomologists have named these wing protector forewings "elytra" from the Greek word for "sheath" or "case." The elytra act as stabilizers when open, but when closed in the resting position produce the hard, armored beetle appearance, thus the word "beetle" implies wing protectors.

The Evolution of the Insect Compound Eye

Another major event that must be explained is the evolution of the insect eye—a complex structure called a compound eye consisting of a large number of closely packed visual elements, each one containing its own separate lens. Many insects, including the fly and honeybee, have about 8,000 "eye" units in its two compound eyes. All terrestrial vertebrates have simple eyes, while most sighted insects have complex, compound eyes called *ommatidia*. The fossil record indicates that the very first insects had compound eyes fully as complex as those today.

Even extinct animals with compound eyes, such as trilobites, also had perfectly developed eyes. Many insects and spiders also have two or three spot-like eyes called **ocelli**. Still another common insect eye type called the *stemmatta* is found on the heads of larvae.

The compound eye can detect the sky's plane of polarization, an ability that helps an insect to navigate. Compound eyes also are very sensitive to movement, and are specially well designed for insect flight. No evidence exists for evolution of the insect eye in the fossil record and, as far as can be determined, the first insect eye was a fully functional eye.

Evolution of Insect Metamorphosis Problem

Metamorphosis, the division of insect life into two distinct stages as illustrated by a caterpillar metamorphosing into a butterfly, is another condition where evidence to support evolution is lacking in the fossil record. The earliest fossil butterfly was dated by evolutionists to be 100 to 140 million years old and it appears so modern that Darwinists postulate that butterflies must have evolved over 200 million years ago (Oceana, 2004, p. 8). Fly larvae look nothing like flies, and major differences in *internal* anatomy also exist.

Many insects undergo complete metamorphosis involving the larva, pupa, and adult stages. Complete metamorphosis is found early in the fossil record, and no evidence of its evolution has ever been found. If "an entomologist were transported by time machine back to the Jurassic period, he would feel right at home among the insects on the earth" (Callahan, 1972, pp. 80-81).

This problem is so difficult that few Darwinists have even attempted to speculate how insect metamorphosis could have evolved. Some entomologists have concluded that, in the field of insect evolution, metamorphism is the most difficult evolutionary advance to explain.

Insect Evolution as Taught in Textbooks and Popular Literature

The popular literature and textbooks often ignore the topic of insect evolution (such as Price, 1996) or present a very different picture of insect evolution than that documented in the professional literature reviewed above. For example, the standard reference text on insects, a 919-page volume published by Harvard University Press, totally avoids the topic of insect evolution (Chapman, 1998). Conversely, many popular articles and books imply that insect evolution is well documented and relate elaborate "just so" stories about how such evolution occurred, as is obvious from the following example:

> The ancestors of the insects (and of other arthropods) probably resembled the marine worms of today. Their bodies were composed of many identical segments. In the insects, the segments gradually changed and fused into three distinct body parts, each of which does a particular job. ...The marine worms had spread-out nerves; nerves in the insects are bunched together into three centers, each serving its own body part. The ancestral worms had a pair of legs on each body segment. (Stein, 1986, pp. 113-114)

The article adds that insects gradually

> developed joints in their legs and rigged them into every sort of appendage a mad inventor could dream up. At the front, they were reshaped into biting and sucking parts as various as the curlable sipping straw of the butterfly, the toothy pincers (called mandibles) of the beetle, and the poison squirter of the soldier termite. Those at the rear became the egg-laying ovipositors of grasshoppers and the stingers of bees. Even the three

limb pairs in the thorax that are used for walking didn't remain primitive. (Stein, 1986, pp. 113-114)

Although this reference implies that the story presented is based on evidence and has been proven, in truth, it is unfounded speculation. Nonetheless, the story helps us to understand that the changes required for worm-to-insect evolution are enormous, requiring a major redesign of the worm. The article continues, noting that insect appendages are

> delicate and very long in the mosquito, come equipped with an elastic spring in the leaping flea, have pouches for carrying pollen in bumblebees, are tipped with suction cups in houseflies, and are bent into fearsomely toothy claws in the preying mantis. That's an example of how ingenious evolution is. New body parts are made by revamping old ones, so that whether what sticks out from an insect walks, bites, or lays an egg, it is only a newfangled leg. Occasionally, mutations undo these transformations and then, like a spell lifted, the appendage is revealed as what it was: The insect grows legs where its mouth parts ought to be, or it grows legs on every segment of its abdomen, where there have been none since bugs began (Stein, 1986, pp. 114-115).

Although no empirical evidence exists for any of these speculations, one would never learn this from reading the chapter. And more study of a specific insect has not helped to reveal its evolutionary history. For example, although

> the Holometabola or endopterygotes are by far the most-studied insects, their origin is completely unknown. It is uncertain where and when the Holometabola originated and why the pupa has evolved. The oldest known undisputed holometabolous insects are lower Permian

in age ... It is likely that particularly old (that is Carboniferous) Holometabola have already been discovered, but that we are unable to recognize them for what they are. We have no idea about the groundplan of the holometabolous insects, and the reason for this is lack of knowledge about the sister group relationships **within** the Holometabola, just as we cannot identify their sister group. Hence, ancient holometabolan remains are of outstanding interest (Willmann, 1998, p. 276).

The same is true of many other insects. How many transitional forms are required can be gleaned by an evaluation of phylogeny charts comparing the actual fossil record with the assumed phylogeny path[3]. Usually the theoretical links are shown as dotted lines, thin lines, or as largely vertical lines.

Actually, DNA research has destroyed at least one putative missing link that once linked termites and roaches. Because they retain so many roach-like features, *Mastotermes* had often been thought of as "missing links." Viewed in this light, termites were seen as highly reduced, myopic, wood eating, social cockroaches. DNA from the extinct termite revealed that it, and all living termite species, are definitely termites, not cockroach "missing links." An evolutionary tree drawn only with the DNA from the living termites and roaches gave one arrangement. With the addition of DNA from the fossil termite, a slightly different arrangement resulted.

The evolutionary tree based on living DNA alone gave an incomplete picture, but was the first glimpse of how incomplete that picture was. Other unexpected results appeared in the DNA of the extinct *Mastotermes*, but enough similarities between it and the living species existed to clearly show that the two species were, in fact, closely related. They did not just share a primitive resemblance.

---

[3]see for instance Grimaldi and Engel, 2005, pp. 108, 145, 154, 163, 169, 180, 191, 194, 460, 466, 469, 519, 528, 553, and 558

Thus, perhaps all fossil *Mastotermes* are closely related.

Conclusions

Insect evolution has been a major problem for evolutionists since Darwin's time, and major disagreement about basic insect evolution still exists today (Boudeaux, 1979). This situation is not due to lack of research. Thousands of articles and several full-length books deal with this subject, including one by Professor Brodsky (1996) and the now-classic text by Pringle (1983). The most recent evidence has supported the conclusions presented in this chapter. Fortey and Thomas, in the preface of their comprehensive review of the evidence, conclude that

> Arthropods — insects, crustaceans, myriapods and arachnids — are the most speciose of all animal groups, and have probably been so for hundreds of millions of years. Their importance in every ecosystem — terrestrial and marine — is not in question. Yet very little has been agreed about how they achieved their pre-eminence. The evolutionary pathways which led to their current diversity are still the subject of controversy, despite the fact that many of the questions of descent have been debated for more than a century (1998, p. xi).

Nor is the "question of descent" problem due to a lack of fossil insect evidence — the fossil record contains many millions of examples. As Grassé notes, evolutionists "are in the dark concerning the origin of insects" (1977, p. 30). Furthermore, in their 150-year-old search, evolutionists are further from a Darwinist explanation than ever before.

One reason is because advancing knowledge in biochemistry and cell biology has shown that insect anatomy and physiology is far more complex than envisioned in Darwin's day, and as we learn more, its complexity no doubt will increase. Actually, as more insects are discovered and named, the problems for Darwinism tend to become even more serious. So little empirical evidence exists that a single new fossil find can change current insect evolution theories so greatly that "every textbook discussing the orders of insects will now need to be rewritten" (Wall, quoted in Trivedi, 2002, p. 2).

Summary

Over one million species of living insects have been identified, requiring an enormous number of insect transitional forms—possibly as many as 18 billion—if macroevolution were true. Not one of these 18 billion insects ever has been confirmed in the abundant fossil record. Yet the abundant fossil record indicates a complete lack of evidence for insect evolution, especially between the genera and above levels, where fossils are critical. Often fairly minor differences divide one species from another. Now it appears likely that the reason they have not been found is because they never existed. Insects consistently appear in the fossil record fully formed, and all such fossil examples found are either of those extant today, or which have become extinct. A summary of the fossils by one of the leading researchers concluded that:

> Insects, which can be traced to the Devonian, have constantly remained numerous and varied. Like the Crustacea, some of their orders and superfamilies have indeed become extinct; however, their antiquity notwithstanding, they have always remained unchanged during the course of their history; they retain as many types as in the past. Despite such "vigor," the history of the insects—the starting point of which is unknown—did not occur in regular sequence. Subclasses succeed each other in a quasilinear fashion: some reached a peak, then declined; some remained as flourishing as when they first

appeared (such as the Collembola, Orthoptera, Odonata, and all the Holometabola) (Grassé, 1977, p. 61).

Furthermore, evidence to explain insect evolution in general is lacking, as does credible evidence for the origin of the many complex structures that are unique to insects, such as their compound eyes, flight, wings that fold, and the complex metamorphosis system that causes development of a worm-like young form to a totally different adult form.

References

Aberlin, Mary Beth. 1995. "Air power: Virtual reality for insects." *The Sciences*, 35(6):13,47.

Averof, Michalis and Stephen M. Cohen. 1997. "Evolutionary origin of insect wings from ancestral gills." *Nature*, 385:627-630.

Ballard, J. William O., Gary J. Olsen, Daniel P. Faith, Wendy A. Odgers, David M. Rowell, and Peter W. Atkinson. 1992. "Evidence from 12S ribosomal RNA sequences that onychophorans are modified arthropods." *Science*, 258:1345-1347.

Bergström, J. 1979. "Morphology of Fossil Arthropods as a Guide to Phylogenetic Relationships." Pages 3-56 in A.P. Gupta (editor) *Arthropod Phylogeny*. New York: Van Nostrand Reinhold.

Bishop, Nic. 1997. *The Secrets of Animal Flight*. Boston: Houghton Mifflin.

Borror, D. J., D. M. Delong and C. A. Tripleton. 1976. *An Introduction to the Study of Insects*. New York: Holt, Rinehart and Winston.

Boudreaux, Bruce. 1979a. Arthropod Phylogeny with Special Reference to Insects. New York: Wiley.

Boudreaux, H. B. 1979b. Chapter 9: "Significance of Intersegmental Tendon System in Arthropod Phylogeny and a Monophyletic Classification of Arthropoda" in *Arthropod Phylogeny*. New York: Van Nostrand Reinhold Company, pp. 551-586, Gupta A. P., editor.

Braun, Andreas. 1997. "Occurrence, Investigation Methods and Significance of Animal Cuticle in Devonian and Carboniferous Coal-Bearing Sedimentary Rocks." *Palaeontographica Abteilung A Palaeozoologie-Stratigraphie*, 245(1-6):83-156.

Brodsky, Andrei K. 1996. *The Evolution of Insect Flight*. New York: Oxford University Press.

Brues, C. T. 1951. "Insects in Amber." *Scientific American* .

185(5):56-61.

Brues, C. T., A. L. Melander and F. M. Carpenter. 1954. *Classification of Insects*. Harvard University Museum of Comparative Zoology, Bulletin, 108.

Buchsbaum, Ralph, Mildred Buchsbaum, John Pearse, and Vicki Pearse. 1987. *Animals Without Backbones*. Third Edition. Chicago, IL: University of Chicago Press.

Busbey, Arthur, Robert Coenraads, David Roots, and Paul Willis. 1996. *Rocks and Fossils*. San Francisco, CA: Weldon Owen.

Callahan, Philip S. 1972. *The Evolution of Insects*. New York: Holiday House.

Carpenter, F. M. 1953. "The geological history and evolution of insects." *American Scientist*. 41(2):256-270.

Carroll, Robert L. 1997. *Patterns and Processes of Vertebrate Evolution*. New York: Cambridge University Press.

Chapman, R. F. 1998. *The Insects; Structure and Function*. 9th edition. Cambridge, MA: Harvard University Press.

Clarkson, E.N.K. 1986. *Invertebrate Palaeontology and Evolution*. Second edition. London: Unwin Hyman.

Farb, Peter. 1962. *The Insects*. New York: Time Incorporated.

Fortey, Richard A. and Richard H. Thomas. 1998. *Arthropod Relationships*. New York: Chapman and Hall.

Galant, Ron and Sean B. Carroll. 2002. "Evolution of a transcriptional repression domain in an insect Hox protein." *Nature*, 415(6874):910-913.

Gamlin, Linda and Gail Vines. 1987. *The Evolution of Life*. New York: Oxford University Press.

Grassé, Pierre-P. 1977. Evolution of Living Organisms; Evidence for a New Theory of Transformation. New York: Academic Press.

Grimaldi, David and Michael Engel. 2005. *Evolution of Insects.* New York: Cambridge University Press.

Gupta, A. P. (editor). 1979. *Arthropod Phylogeny.* New York: Van Nostrand Reinhold Company.

Hardie, R. C. 1984. "Properties of Photo Receptors R-7 and R-8 in Dorsal Marginal Ommatidia in the Compound Eyes of Musca-Domestica and Calliphora-Erythrocephala." *Journal of Comparative Physiology A Sensory Neural and Behavioral Physiology,* 154(2):157-166.

Hubbell, Sue. 1993. Broadsides from the Other Orders: A Book of Bugs. New York: Random House.

Knecht, Richard J, Michael S. Engel and Jacob S. Benner. 2011. "Late Carboniferous Paleoichnology Reveals the Oldest Full-Body Impression of a Flying Insect." *PNAS,* 108(16):6515-6519, April 19.

Labandeira, Conrad. 1999. "Insects and Other Hexapods" in *Encyclopedia of Paleontology.* Chicago, IL: Fitzroy Dearborn, Vol. 1, pp. 603-624.

_____ and J. Sepkoski. 1993. "Insect diversity in the fossil record." *Science,* 261:310-315.

Levine, Mike. 2002. "How insects lose their limbs." *Nature,* 415:848-849.

Lewin, Roger. 1982. *Thread of Life: The Smithsonian Looks at Evolution.* Washington, D.C.: Smithsonian Books.

Marden, James H. 1995. "How insects learned to fly." *The Sciences,* 35(6):26-30.

Marden, James H. and M. G. Kramer. 1994. "Surface-skimming stoneflies: A possible intermediate stage in insect flight evolution." *Science,* 266:427-430.

Matthews, William. 1962. *Fossils.* New York: Barnes and Noble.

Mayr, Ernst. 2001. *What Evolution Is.* New York: Basic Books.

Meglitsch, Paul. A. 1967. *Invertebrate Zoology.* New York:

Oxford University Press.

_____ and Frederick R. Schram. 1991. *Invertebrate Zoology. Third Edition.* Oxford, NY: Oxford University Press.

Morris, Henry. 1974. *Scientific Creationism.* San Diego, CA: Creation Life Publishers.

Oceana Guide to Butterflies, 2004. London: Quantum Publishing.

Olberg, R. M. 1981. "Parallel Encoding of Direction of Wind Head Abdomen and Visual Pattern Movement by Single Inter Neurons in the Dragonfly Anax-Junius." *Journal of Comparative Physiology A Sensory Neural and Behavioral Physiology,* 142(1):27-42.

Pennisi, Elizabeth. 2002. "New Insect Order Speaks to Life's Diversity." *Science,* 296:445-447.

Price, Peter W. 1996. *Biological Evolution.* Fort Worth, TX: Saunders College Publishing.

Pringle, John W. S. 1983. *Insect Flight.* Burlington, NC: Scientific Publications.

Romoser, William. 1973. *The Science of Entomology.* New York: Macmillan.

_____ and John Stoffolano. 1998. *The Science of Entomology.* New York: McGraw-Hill.

Ronshaugen, Matthew, Nadine McGinnis, and William McGinnis. 2002. "Hox protein mutation and macroevolution of the insect body plan." *Nature,* 415:914-917.

Sanders, Robert and George Howe. 1985. "Insects Indicate Creation." *Creation Research Society Quarterly,* 22(4):166-170.

Sharov, Aleksandr G. 1966. *Basic Arthropodan with Special Reference to Insects.* New York: Pergamon Press.

Stein, Sara. 1986. *The Evolution Book.* New York: Workman Publishing.

Strickberger, Monroe. 2000. *Evolution*. Sudbury, MA: Jones and Bartlett.

Trivedi, Bijal P. 2002. "New insect order found in Southern Africa."

http://news. nationalgeographic.com/news/2002/03/ 0328_0328_TVstickinsect.html

National Geographic Today, March 28. National Geographic Today, at 7 p.m. ET/PT in the United States, is a daily news magazine available only on the National Geographic Channel.

Willmann, R. 1998. "Advances in insect phylogeny." Chapter 20 (pp. 269-279) in Fortey and Thomas.

Wilson, Edward O. 1992. *The Diversity of Life*. Cambridge, MA: Belknap (Harvard University Press).

PART III:

The Vertebrates

Chapter 8

Fish — Common Inhabitants of the Fossil Record

Introduction

Over half of all known vertebrate species commonly are classified as fishes (Barton, 2007). The general category of fish usually includes lampreys, sharks, lungfishes, chimaeroids, and teleostomes. Unfortunately, those life forms called fish do not have a unique set of features by which they can be precisely classified (Maisey, 1996, p. 10). Usually, the term *fish* refers to all gill-breathing, cold-blooded, back-boned, finned, non-tetrapod (lack four-legs), aquatic animals. Almost all fish have a built-in system to be able to balance themselves in water to enable them to swim in all six directions (up, down, front, back, left side, and right side) guided by complex undulations controlled by their fin system (Dean, 1987, p. 1).

This chapter focuses only on what traditionally has been called *pisces*, a term no longer used in formal classification systems but commonly used in lay literature. Although organisms in class *pisces* have many similarities, they also are enormously variable.

From an evolutionary standpoint, fish have been "extravagantly successful" (Barton, 2007, p. 19). So far, 25,000 to 30,000 different species in class *pisces* are known, and more are being discovered each year. Basic pisce types include skates, stingrays, lampreys and hag fishes, sharks, saw fish, chimeras and rat fish, catfish deep sea lantern fish, eels, pike, flying fish, flat fish, sailfish, swordfish, sculpins, and hundreds of other types. If macroevolution occurred, then the evolution of most of these fish types should be documented in the fossil record. As Darwin wrote in 1959, "if species have descended from other species by insensibly fine gradations" we should find "innumerable" transitional forms in the fossil record (Darwin, 1859, p. 171). Darwin admitted that this is "the most obvious and gravest objection which can be urged against my theory" (1859, p. 280).

Darwin concluded that the explanation lay in the extreme imperfection of the fossil record (1859, p. 280). As we will document, though, the millions of marine fossils discovered since 1859 have not documented these "innumerable" transitional fossils that evolution requires. The absence of fossil evidence actually is overwhelming.

The variety of fish lifestyles is also enormous. Most lay eggs, while others (e.g., genus *Poeciliopsis*) give birth to their young live using a complex placenta as do mammals (Reznick, *et al.*, 2002). Some fish-like animals, such as the axolotl, have gills like fish but also have arms and legs like tetrapods. Although the axolotl looks very much like a fish, it is classified as an amphibian (Long, 1995, p. 30).

The one trait that best defines fish is their excellent swimming ability, a design feature revealing that their entire body plan specifically is engineered for efficient swimming. The fish fin system is highly integrated into its streamlined body, which, combined with a tail that serves as a rudder, produces a well-designed efficient swimming machine. Most fish also have an "air-bladder" that they use to regulate how deep in the water they travel, a system which forces evolutionists to admit "we still do not entirely understand" how fish could ever have evolved (Curtis, 1961, p. 123).

The "extraordinary evolutionary history" (Barton, 2007, p. 19) of fish extends back to the early Cambrian, dated by evolutionists to be over 500 million years ago (Maisey, 1996, p. 9). The large number of fossil varieties preserved has allowed scientists to conclude that the fossil record is considered a good representation of fish that once lived as far back as the putative Cambrian (Janvier, 1999, p. 21). So many fossils exist that the Devonian period is called the age of fishes.

Furthermore, "large numbers of complete specimens of soft-bodied chordates from the lower Cambrian … have been removed" from the rock layers (Chen et. al., 1999, p. 518). Although the earliest fish remains date back to the Cambrian, fish often are "preserved complete, and with a great deal of fine anatomical detail" from the Ordovician onwards, which Darwinists date from 490 to 443 mya (Benton, 2005, p. 39).

This excellent fossil record allows us to make a valid evaluation of evolutionist's claims. This "great deal of fine detail" would allow researchers to document fish evolution in some detail — if they, in fact, evolved. As early as a half century ago, these anatomical details allowed us to document that "some fishes have survived till today with scarcely a change" (Zim and Shoemaker, 1956, p. 15).

The common theory of the origins of fish is the conclusion that they began "as mud-sucking, armored creatures that wriggled like tadpoles across the bottom of the ancient waters," and that they "slowly evolved jaws and paired fins, which in some cases now function as legs and even wings, to become the most versatile animals of their environment. Today, existing alongside the modern species, there [exist]... holdovers from the past—fishes that are living fossils" (Ommanney, 1971, p. 67). This claim will be examined in the next section.

The Oldest Claimed Fish Ancestor

The putative oldest fish ancestor, and the ancestor of all chordates, is considered by many paleontologists to be a small 5-cm-long worm-like fossil animal called Pikaia (Long, 1995, p. 30). So far, about 60 fragments and whole Pikaia specimens have been discovered, some in an excellent state of preservation. A major reason that Pikaia is considered to be the precursor of all chordates is that they may have possessed a notochord (Long, 1995, p. 30). The Pikaia "dates back" to the Middle Cambrian and first was discovered in 1911 by Charles Walcott.

First classified as a Polychaete worm, in 1979 it was reclassified as a chordate by Simon Conway Morris (1998). Resembling a living lancet, it is believed to have swam like an eel. The most straightforward explanation is that Pikaia is not a primitive evolutionary link, but rather a bottom-dwelling marine chordate similar to an amphioxus that became extinct. Pikaia had a distinct head, a caudal fin, myotomes, and possibly a notochord, all characteristics of chordates. Bond concluded that, although no evidence exists to support the view that fish evolved from a lancelet-like animal, it is "a reasonable model for what the forerunner of the fishlike vertebrates could have been like" (1996, p. 78).

Kyle noted that "if fishes came from the worms, as many suppose, several important changes in structure had to be made before the new arrangement could be attained" (1926, p. 2). One example is that the worm design is far too flabby to achieve the balance required to swim in water. In order to evolve into fish, worms had to evolve sufficient rigidity while retaining the required level of flexibility to swim, which is no easy achievement (Kyle, 1926, p. 3). The enormous gap that exists between fish and worms still is an enigma today. For a muscular body to move through the water on its own accord, "the head and body must be somewhat compressed or flattened; otherwise it [the fish] will roll and twist" (Kyle, 1926, p. 3).

Evolution from a Worm-Like Life Form to Fish

The changes required to evolve small round worms, like nematodes, into fish would have been enormous, because the "worm" that became a fish

> did not look much like a fish. It probably had no paired fins, no real head, brain or advanced sense organs, jaws or teeth. Most likely, its body was cylindrical, with simple digestive organs, a nerve cord running its length from front to back, and below that a sort of stiffening, supporting rod which was its only skeleton, made of a soft material surrounded by a tough sheath. This forerunner of a backbone, or vertebral column, is called a notochord and from it the animals that possessed it, including all the vertebrates, derived their name—the chordates (Ommanney, 1971, p. 60).

Furthermore, to evolve a fish from a worm, the worm nervous and vascular systems would need to be flipped over because the major fish organs are upside-down when compared to the worm organs. Furthermore, although some worms "have tiny eye-spots, ear-stones, and tactile or taste organs," these structures all are relatively simple and microscopic in contrast to the fish's well-developed eyes, rostrum, and a large head with an advanced vertebrate brain (Kyle, 1926, p. 3).

Furthermore, most round and flat worms lack a heart whereas fish have a very well-developed, powerful muscular pump that is located ventrally just behind the head. Each of the aforementioned unique fish features must have evolved, and one of the easiest organs to document should have been the evolution of fins because they appear both "early" in the fossil record and with great clarity.

Professor Bond described the "typical scenario of what could have occurred" to evolve fishlike vertebrates from their hypothesized precursor (1996, p. 78). His model postulates a free-swimming invertebrate with a notochord, a ventral heart, and pharynx clefts that evolved into fish. Bond notes that radical changes in the environment first must have occurred to evolve fish, but the specific changes required for fish evolution are not present in the geological record.

Instead of starting with a worm, Bond's fish evolution scenario began with a creature already very much like a fish. He then speculated that: "One can imagine that there could have been ascidians or related invertebrates that remained in the tadpole larval stage, reproduced, and formed the evolutionary basis for the more complex early vertebrates" (Bond, 1996, p. 78). Bond postulated that a lancelet-like animal is "a reasonable model for what the forerunner of the fishlike vertebrates could have been like" but he cited no evidence, fossil or otherwise, for this admittedly hypothetical scenario (Bond, 1996, p. 78). In conclusion, what is known about postulated fish ancestors is summarized by Ommanney as follows:

> somewhere, either in the oceans or in some fresh-water pond or stream of that far-off Cambrian period, was a creature that would eventually give rise to the fishes .... What this creature looked like, how it functioned and lived, we can only surmise .... Many theories have been advanced for its origin. Some held that it evolved from some form of segmented worm, others that it developed from an arthropod, a phylum that includes spiders, insects and crustaceans. Most likely, however, on the basis of

biochemical and structural evidence, is the hypothesis that this ancestral creature arose from a form similar to the larva of an echinoderm, a group known to us today through the starfishes and sea urchins (1971, p. 60).

Next, we will look at some examples of the supposed evolution of fins.

The Origin of Fins

A major fish trait is their fins that extend out from their flattened sides. They are required to stabilize the animal, thus enabling it to swim. Two basic types of fins exist: vertical fins on top of the fish (the dorsal and caudal fins) and paired fins located on each side. Stanford University ichthyologist, Professor David Starr Jordan (1902, p. 536), wrote that the evolution of fins is one of the most serious problems in evolution, a puzzle still with us over a century later. Jordan wrote that, although several theories of fin evolution exist, all are inadequate, inconclusive, or both. Jordan was hoping that paleontology eventually would provide the answer to the problem of fin evolution, but the fossil record has presented many more problems than solutions (1902, p. 547).

One proposed solution to this fin problem is that the paired horizontal fins evolved from what once was a continuous fold of skin along the lateral line, and the vertical fins from a median skin fold. Other theories include the idea that the paired fins derived from modified gill-arches or septa between the gill-openings. Other experts suggest that fins did not evolve from gill-septa, but from external gills. After extensive study of the evolution of fins in the fossil record, Ommanney concluded that:

> When and how the paired fins originated is a matter of debate—the fossil record provides no clear answer. One theory, now largely discounted, held that they originally

formed as extensions and elaborations of the gill flaps. A more likely explanation seemed for a long time to be that they are the final remnants of a longitudinal fold of skin, with an internal skeleton of parallel bars of bone or cartilage, which originally extended down along each side of the body. The answer now is believed by some to be … paired fins first developed from folds of skin between the spines and the body—and, as they were refined still further in the fishes that followed, according to this theory, the spines from which they originally grew tended to disappear (1971, pp. 61-62).

A major problem largely ignored by evolutionists is the origin of the internal structure of fins, including the required support system, cartilage, muscles, nerves, and bone. All of the aforementioned theories of fish evolution are based on the morphology study of known fish and all evolutionary scenarios of their origins are highly speculative. In fact, no evidence exists for any of the speculative transitions. As paleontologist Janvier admitted, "lacking fossils, paleontologists and anatomists have often tried to imagine the earliest vertebrates," but he added even imagination has not been very helpful in postulating fish evolution (1999, p. 22).

Conodonts

Conodonts are extinct chordates classified in class Conodonta that date back to the late Cambrian. For decades, they were known only from tooth-like fossils, now called conodont elements. Knowledge about their soft tissues still remains relatively sparse but, although they are considered primitive chordates, they possess many advanced features, including large eyes, fin rays, chevron-shaped muscles, and a notochord. The fossil conodont imprints indicate that they were an eel-like creature with 15 to 19 "teeth" that formed a bilaterally symmetrical head array that forms a feeding apparatus radically different from the jaws of modern animals.

Conodonts ranged from about a centimeter long to the 40 cm long giant Promissum. The fossils indicate that they are an extinct chordate and do not provide evidence for evolution from invertebrates into vertebrates such as fish. Speculating that they were transitional forms based only on teeth, and no other hard parts, clearly is extremely difficult. The South China examples of Cambrian conodonts appear to be very complex fully developed fish, not primitive worm-fish transitional forms (Shu et al., 1999, p. 42).

Calcichordates

Calcichordates are putative "primitive" fossils classified in phylum Chordata that have an echinoderm type of alcite skeleton. They are found in Cambrian to Pennsylvanian marine rocks dated by evolutionists at 530 to 300 million years old. They traditionally have been placed in the phylum Echinodermata because of their skeletons, but some experts argued that they are chordates because of their many chordate anatomical features.

The "highly controversial fossils known as the 'calcichordates' … show a puzzling combination of echinoderm and chordate characters" (Morris, 2000, p. 4429). Their calcite skeletons are used to speculate that echinoderms and chordates are closely related. The calcichordate theory of the origin of chordates is the view that each separate lineage of chordate (Cephalochordates, Urochordates, Craniates) evolved from its own lineage of mitrate, and thus the echinoderms and the chordates are sister groups, with the hemichordates as an out-group though. This view is controversial. Lefebvre (2000, p. 359) concluded that a detailed analysis of numerous internal and external structures of stylophora calcichordates has shown that the basic assumptions of the calcichordate theory of fish evolution are invalid. A number of evolutionists have rejected the calcichordate hypothesis based on their various morphological traits when they are compared to fish (Nielsen, 2001, p. 420).

The Agnathans

The first bona fide vertebrates documented in the fossil record are agnathans (Class Agnatha from the Greek "without jaw"), usually small (15 cm or less) "lamprey-like" jawless fish existing in the fossil record all the way back to the lower Cambrian (Shu *et al.*, 1999, p. 42; Chen, *et al.*, 1999; Colbert, et al., 2001, p. 23; Repetski, 1978, p. 529). Thus, the earliest examples of fish date almost to the beginning of the fossil record, specifically as far back as 545 million years ago (Shu et al., 1999, p. 42). Agnathans, sometimes called pre-fish, are the earliest widely recognized direct putative fish ancestor (Bond, 1996). One proposed agnathan example that dates back to the Cambrian is a small (6 mm long) creature that resembles modern hagfishes (Bond, 1996, p. 78).

Except for the lamprey, almost all agnathans now are extinct. All known agnathans, both living and fossil, closely resemble the fish families that began in the Cambrian, and all obtained food by "sucking or scooping up organic matter through their jawless mouths" (Bond, 1996, p. 78). Although many fossils of lampreys exist — some dated by evolutionists back to the Devonian period — and although many were exquisitely preserved, "their evolutionary history is obscure" (Gess, et. al., 2006, p. 981). The earliest known lampreys are anatomically modern. These fossils, often claimed to be the first vertebrates, are placed in an extant class called *cyclostomes*, which fall into two groups — the hagfish and lampreys.

The cyclostome group has "been carefully researched, and many different opinions have been brought forward about the origin and relationship of those animals" (Grzimek, 1973, p. 30).

Because some of these Upper Cambrian fish have "close similarities to modern lampreys" or hagfishes and many "bonelike fragments resembling agnathan dermal armor or scales have been reported from Upper Cambrian," some experts conclude that they are an extinct type of lamprey or hagfish, not an evolutionary ancestor of modern fish (Colbert, et al., 2001, p. 23).

Gregory speculated that "one or another of the ostracoderms gave rise to the modern class of cyclostomes, including the lampreys and hags," but he admitted that "no known gnathostome fishes definitely connect them with the ostracoderms" (Gregory, 1959, p. 76). Professor Romer confessed that the "ostracoderms are primitive vertebrates; but if we seek among the known forms for the ancestors of higher vertebrate groups, we meet with disappointment" (1966, p. 22). Romer concluded that "major evolutionary events must have been occurring in vertebrate history during the Ordovician and Silurian, but we are still in almost complete ignorance regarding them," which agrees with the findings presented in this chapter (1966, p. 16).

Much more is known about a fish called *Sacabambaspis*, "one of the earliest known vertebrates," of which we have "many complete and well-preserved specimens" (Colbert, et al., 2001, p. 23). As far as can be determined, this animal was a fully developed jawless fish and not a transitional form. Rather, it was simply an extinct type of fish.

Other Agnathous Fish

A major conundrum in fish evolution is that many examples of living fish can be found in the fossil record dating back to the Upper Cambrian, a problem explained by hypothesizing that fish evolution originally was extremely rapid, then stabilized very early in history, and remained stable until today (Rapetski, 1978, p. 529). The earliest chordate that paleontologists have comparatively good knowledge about are agnathous fish because they are well-documented in the fossil record and many examples of their close relatives are still living (Colbert, et al., 2001, p. 24). A major reason for the commonality of agnathans in the fossil record is that agnathous heads and chests were covered with fused bony plates and are consequently well preserved. Only about a foot or less in length, they were bottom-dwelling creatures that apparently used their muscular jawless mouths to suck in small slow-moving prey or organic matter. The first clear evidence for the existence of agnathous fish includes a single plate found in the middle Ordovician strata, and many other later finds have enabled us to create an adequate understanding of them (Gregory, 1959, p. 76).

Other Proposed Fish Ancestors

The claim that some ostracoderms were a transitional fish leading to modern jawed fish is falsified by the fact that they co-existed with jawed fish and flourished during the Silurian and Devonian periods (dated by evolutionists at 300 to 400 million years ago). They became extinct sometime at the end of the Devonian period, indicating that they are only an extinct fish type, not an evolutionary link connecting them to Pikaia or any other putative very early fish ancestor. They were evidently a separate fish type more closely related to modern lampreys than to jawed fish. Colbert, et al., concluded that many factors have contributed to the "disappearance of the ostracoderms, acanthodians, and placoderms, but probably the rise and development of the bony fishes and sharks" was a major factor (2001, p. 50).

The Jawed Fish

Jawed fish (Gnathostomes) consist of two monophyletic groups, class chondrichthyes (cartilaginous fish) and class osteichthyans (bony fish) (Botella, et al, 2007). Both have fully developed functional jaws. The evolution of the vertebrate jaw is considered "one of the great evolutionary breakthroughs" in fish evolution (Prothero, 2007, p. 210). One reason why it was thought to be an evolutionary breakthrough is that the diet of jawless fish is extremely limited — most being filter or deposit feeders or parasites, such as lampreys or hagfish. Predator jawed fish are able to consume a diet consisting of much larger prey than jawless fish.

The gnathostomes, which comprise chondrichthyans (cartilaginous fishes), lobe-finned fishes (coelacanths and lungfishes), and actinopterygians (ray-finned fishes), include a wide variety of fish, from the coelacanths to lungfish, including sharks, rays, and chimaeras. Classical evolutionary theorists have maintained that cartilage evolved first and thus cartilage is a more ancient construction material than bone. Conversely, the "paleontological data strongly suggest that bone was a primitive adult skeletal material, [whereas] cartilage [is] an essentially embryonic adaptation which is retained in the adult only as the result of degenerative processes" (Romer, 1966, p. 22). Several major jawed fish are discussed below. The evolutionary relationships of the gnathostomes "have been debated for almost a century" and still are being debated (Venkatesh, et al., 2001, p. 11382).

Acanthodii

Class *Gnathostomata*, Subclass acanthodii (spiny fishes), are small, extinct jawed fish covered with diamond-shaped scales. They possess both dorsal and pectoral fins and numerous irregular dermal bones. The bone-like material was utilized in various places on their epidermis, such as on the top of their head and over the lower shoulder girdle, and some even had a bony flap covering their gill openings. Barton noted that "Widely divergent interpretations have been made of their affinities by paleoichthyologists" (Barton, 2007, pp. 130-131).

Acanthodii were once believed to be transitional between the jawless and jawed fish because the interior skeletons were in many cases constructed out of cartilage. Extensive research, though, has now disproved this theory. Evidences of Acanthodii fossils are found from Lower Silurian to Lower Permian and they indicate little change in their fossil record and no evidence of the transitional claim (Barton, 2007, p. 130).

Placoderms

Placoderm, or armored fish, is a gnathostome which is so ugly that they have often been called armor-plated monsters. The Placoderms were similar to the acanthodii, except that they were more heavily armored. Placoderms now are divided into six clades, including the arthodires, which are the oldest known jawed fish belonging to almost 200 genera. They are relatively common in the fossil record, partly because their armor plates often preserved fairly well. The excellent placoderm fossil record long has caused such great difficulty for evolutionists that Romer's conclusion is still valid today:

> Where to place these curious creatures has been a vexing problem. One or the other of these types has at times been thought allied to the ostracoderms, to the sharks, to the lungfish, to the "ganoids"; but in each case the supposed likenesses have been more than outweighed by the obvious differences. There are few common features uniting these groups other than the fact that they are, without exception, peculiar. All, however, are characterized by the presence of bony skeletal tissues (Romer, 1966, p. 24).

Chondrichthyes

The chondrichthyans (cartilaginous fishes) have a jaw and a skeleton composed of cartilage along with paired appendages. The class includes about 60 families, 185 genera, and about 1,160 species, including sharks, skates, and rays (Barton, 2007, pp. 27-28). Not only is their phylogeny vexing, but they also pose serious problems for evolutionists because, at the Silurian-Devonian boundary, evolutionists

> expect the appearance of proper ancestors for the sharks and higher bony fish groups. We would expect "generalized" forms that would fit neatly into our preconceived evolutionary picture. Do we get them in the placoderms? Not at all. Instead, we find a series of wildly impossible types which do not fit into any proper [evolutionary] pattern (Romer, 1966, p. 33).

Romer concluded chondrichthyans do not appear to have evolved

> from any possible source, or to be appropriate ancestors to any later or more advanced types. In fact, one tends to feel that the presence of these placoderms, making up such an important part of the Devonian fish story, is an incongruous episode; it would have simplified the situation [for evolution] if they had never existed (Romer, 1966, p. 33)!

Then he reasoned that these linking forms must exist in the fossil record. We only need to keep looking for them in an "attempt to fit them into the vertebrate evolutionary story. In our lack of knowledge of antecedent gnathostome types, we cannot even reasonably speculate as to their ancestry among hypothetical agnathous forms" (1966, p. 33).

Osteichthyans

The osteichtyes are the bony-jawed fishes that constitute the vast majority of modern fishes, including both fresh and marine water fishes (Barton, 2007, p. 19). They are divided into the Actinopterygians (sturgeons, gars, teleosts, bichirs, and "bowfins") and the Saropteryians or lobe finned fish (lungfish, some tetrapods, and coelacanths). How these "two osteichthyan lineages evolved their different traits is unknown, as is how their common osteichthyan ancestor arose from non-osteichthyan gnathostome groups" (Zhu, et al., 1999, p. 607). As a result, the elasmobranch (sharks, rays and skates, subclass Elasmobranchii class Chondrichthyes) ancestry for osteichthyans has now largely been abandoned.

The Psarolepis

A putative morphological link, the *Psarolepis*, is based on only one fossil that appears to be a chimeric fish with traits found in two other clades, and not a transitional form (Barton, 2007, p. 131). It was dated by evolutionists to be about 400 million years old. It is considered an evolutionary link because it has an unusual combination of osteichthyan and non-osteichthyan features (Zhu, et al., 1999, p. 607). Thought to be one of the earliest osteichthyans known, this mosaic possesses the fully developed traits of several fish types. It has a huge pectoral spine resembling some placoderms and also a median spine found in sharks.

The Psarolepis are believed by many evolutionists to be a probable missing link because it shows a mix of actinopterygian and sarcoptergian features. The problem with claiming that Psarolepis is a transitional form is that both bony fish clades Actinopterygii and Sarcopterygii first appeared about the same time as Psarolepis in the late Silurian. This precludes Psarolepis from being the ancestor of bony fish (Benton, 2005, p. 62).

In fact, the case for it being any kind of a transitional form is very weak. Two possible positions of *Psarolepis* exist, and the

> conflicts between the two schemes remain unresolved and the exact position of *Psarolepis* remains uncertain. The uncertainty results partly from a lack of information available for *Psarolepis* and other important stem taxa … and partly from the difficulty of selecting and polarizing characters when both osteichthyan and non-osteichthyan groups are used in the same analysis. However, whether *Psarolepis* turns out to be a stem-group sarcopterygian, its unique character combination will have a marked impact on present studies of osteichthyan evolution (Zhu, et al., 1999, pp. 109-110).

This discovery has shaken previous conclusions evolutionists made about Psarolepis because the

> features found in *Psarolepis* (a lower jaw with three infradentary foramina, well-developed internasal cavities and parasymphysial areas carrying tooth whorls) can no longer be used to define porolepiforms and/or dipnomorphs (porolepiforms and lungfishes). The polyplocodont folded teeth and quadrostian skull roof pattern of osteolepiforms should also be regarded as primitive because of their presence in *Psarolepis*. If *Psarolepis* turns out to be a basal osteichthyan, the presence of an intracranial joint and cosmine can no longer serve as defining characters (synapomorphs) for sarcopterygians (Zhu, et al., 1999, pp. 609-610).

The osteichthyans are considered to be advanced fish but have many features thought to be very primitive. A problem is that some members of the osteichthyans are considered very primitive, such as the soft-rayed fishes, which are confounding modern and primitive classification attempts (Barton, 2007, p. 29). Some "highly evolved fish" are found very "early" in the fossil record, all the way back to the Silurian, dated by evolutionists at 423 to 416 mya (Botella, et al., 2007, p. 583).

True Fish

The so-called true fishes are in a superclass that contains an enormous number of species (Zim and Shoemaker, 1956). They all are cold-blooded, jawed, aquatic vertebrates that breathe using gills. They have two-chambered hearts, fins, and streamlined bodies, and most have skin integument covered with scales. The theorized earliest known representation of "true" fish are the Sarcopterygii, the only living members of which are coelacanths and lungfishes (Maisey, 1996, p. 9). As far as can be determined from comparisons of their fossils with modern fish, they are identical to modern fish. Examples include herring, pipefish, sunfish, perch, mooneye fish, lungfish, salmon, garfish, trout, and sand fish, all of which have been dated by evolutionists as being about 50 to over 100 million years old (Oktar, 2007).

Fish Phylogeny

Fish phylogeny is very difficult to construct for several reasons. A major puzzle in determining their phylogeny is that fish are very different both in anatomy and physiology from all proposed fish ancestors. There exists so much variety in fish compared to almost all other life-forms. So it is concluded fish must not represent a single "lineage of creatures that evolved from a common ancestor" but rather requires several separate lineages, requiring a large number of fossils to support separate lineages, evidence that does not exist (Maisey, 1996, p. 10).

Disagreement over phylogeny exist all the way back to the base of the proposed fish lineage. For example, "Depending on one's perspective, the jawless fishes—the hagfishes and lampreys—constitute a single, monophyletic taxon or two taxa of disparate origins" but others argue for a polyphyletic taxon (Barton, 2007, p. 19). One proposed fish ancestor is the craniate, a marine animal with a skull that largely encloses the brain. The craniates are theorized to have branched into multiple lineages of saurischians, including the lungfishes, coelacanths, ray-finned fishes, acanthodians, and placoderms—a theory that requires a large number of fossil transitions which don't exist (Maisey, 1996, p. 10).

In contrast to evolutionary assumptions, the fossil record of all basic classes of fish, including Agnatha, Placodermi, Acanthodii, Osteichthyes, and Chondrichthyes began at close to the same evolutionary time, mostly during the Devonian or before (Botella, et al., 2007, p. 585). Thus, they existed contemporaneously, or close, with no evidence of transitional forms. For this reason only a very tentative phylogeny is possible. Nelson concluded over 40 years ago that the phylogenetic interrelationships of many animals, including turtles, frogs, salamanders, lungfishes, and coelacanths, are "hardly established at all," a conclusion that still is valid today (1969, p. 18). He added that the perplexities in devising phylogenies for fish are serious:

> There is little justification for selecting a particular recent fish, e.g., a minnow, herring or trout, and assuming that it is some primitive teleost from which another has evolved … no recent species or higher taxonomic group ultimately can be said to have given rise to any other. It is probably true that in some ways a minnow is more primitive than a perch, but in others, it is more advanced. Such matters are worthy of investigation, but we don't progress much by making a teleostean morphotype out of a minnow, or for

that matter a vertebrate morphotype out of a lamprey or any other single, recent vertebrate or vertebrate group (1969, p. 27).

Another evolutionary difficulty is that the supposed ancestors of modern fish, the teleostians, are not "more evolved" than most putative ancient primitive fish, just different: "Fishes did not become more complicated as they evolved; if anything, the tendency was for them to simplify themselves" (Ommanney, 1971, p. 61).

Discussion of the Fish Fossil Record and Evolution Problem

As discussed, fish are divided into two major divisions: jawless and jawed fish. Jawless fish comprise only sixty species compared to 51,000 species of jawed vertebrates (Janvier, 2006, p. 921). Some evolutionists hypothesize that jawless fish evolved into jawed fish, an idea that is greatly disputed among the experts. Nor do we know how cartilaginous fish evolved as even the "origin of sharks is still a mystery" (Long, 1995, p. 69). There even exists a "lot of debate over the origins and diversity of the first fishes" (Long, quoted in Werner, 2007, p. 98).

This is true despite the excellent fossil record that exists for jawed fish, cartilaginous fish, bony fish, and sharks. It is not even clear "how much of early fish evolution took place in the sea, and how much in fresh waters" and, for this reason, "one of the great mysteries and problems to be solved in vertebrate evolution" is the "origins and the interrelationships of these jawed fishes" (Long, as quoted in Werner, 2007, p. 98).

The fossil record also reveals that "evolution is usually slow, sometimes reversible, and highly dependent on ecological conditions" (Bond, 1996, p. 74). This is an indication that what the fossil record shows is not macroevolution but normal genetic fluctuation, such as recently documented to occur with the famous Darwin's finches of the Galapagos Islands, and is likely partly the result of some epigenetic influence. Stahl concluded that the "higher fishes, when they appear in the Devonian period, already have acquired the characteristics that identify them as belonging to one of the major assemblages of bony or cartilaginous forms," which illustrates the fact that fish, like many other life forms, abruptly appear in the fossil record (Stahl, 1974, p. 126). Romer's conclusion that the "common ancestor of the bony fish groups is unknown" is still true (1966, p. 53).

Figure 8.1 — Fossil Fish[1] [2]

---

[1] Photo Credit (top): I love photo / Shutterstock.com
[2] Photo Credit (bottom): In Green / Shutterstock.com

Lancelet-like fish commonly are believed to be modern fish precursors, but no evidence of this lancelet-like precursor animal has been found in the fossil record, nor has any evidence been found of these species that is considered intermediate between the lancelets and the earliest known vertebrates (Bond, 1996, p. 78). The paucity of fossil evidence for fish evolution allows speculation about fish origins to abound. For example, Colbert wrote that the bony and cartilaginous fish

> appeared in the late Silurian period, and it is possible that they may have originated at some earlier time, although there is no fossil evidence to prove this. Some paleontologists have proposed that different groups of sharklike fishes evolved from different placoderms, and that the Chondrichthyes are therefore polyphyletic. At present, there is insufficient evidence to resolve this issue (Colbert, et al., 2001, p. 53).

The most common explanation for the total lack of fossil evidence for fish evolution is that very few, if any, transitional fossils have been preserved. This is an invalid conclusion because every major fish kind known today has been found in the fossil record, evidence that the existing known fossil record is a fairly complete representation of all fish that have ever existed (Benton, 2005, p. 62). New fossil finds are virtually always more of the same and occasionally new species are discovered which, instead of filling in existing gaps, only create more gaps in the fossil record. Most of the known 34 orders and 418 fish families are represented in the fish fossil record, as well as 29 orders of cartilaginous and bony fish (Grzimek, 1973, p. 45).

A detailed comparison of all known fossil examples shows they consist of extinct fish, fish once thought to be extinct such as the coelacanth, or fully modern fish that easily can be identified as such. All major groups of fish have appeared in strata labeled by evolutionists as far back as the Ordovician and Silurian eras (443–417 Myr) and are abundant during the Devonian (Benton, 2005, p. 39).

This abundant fossil record provides little evidence for the evolution of fish and, for this reason, the "actual ancestral group of fishes has not yet been identified" (Grzimek, 1973, pp. 45–46). It is clear from the fossil record that "from the beginning of their evolutionary history," sharks and bony fishes possessed the morphology required to effectively travel in water (Colbert et al., 2001, p. 50). Their "superior design for swimming" is mostly due to their fin design. Examples include the ostracoderms, acanthodians, and placoderms (Colbert et al., 2001, p. 50). Although microevolution has been observed in both living and fossil fish, "exactly how natural selection makes species is not well understood" (Bond, 1996, p. 66).

Bond concluded that in only a "few fortunate cases, we can actually study the *likely* ancestors and observe primitive characters and observe their descent and modification in their own ecological context" (1996, p. 74, emphasis added). This review supports Ommanney's conclusion about the fish fossil record penned over 40 years ago. He wrote that it is not known

> "what stages of development it went through to eventually give rise to truly fishlike creatures …. Between the Cambrian when it probably originated, and the Ordovician when the first fossils of animals with really fishlike characteristics appeared, there is a gap of perhaps 100 million years which we will probably never be able to fill" (1971, p. 60).

Implications of the Fish Fossil Record

The absence of fossil evidence for evolution is significant because fish are one of the most common fossil types with close to one half-million specimens in museums alone. So many fossil fish have been found that the Devonian period, dated by evolutionists as 350 million years ago, is called "the Age of Fishes." Many fossil fish have been exquisitely preserved, including their bones, fins, and even their scales. It is estimated that there could be more extinct than extant fish species, indicating that there should be no shortage of potential links if fish arose by evolution, yet "significant gaps in the fossil record" is the norm (Maisey, 1996, p. 10).

Dean wrote that fish are critically important evidence for evolution because "Fish hold an important place in the history of back-boned animals: their group is the largest and most widely distributed: its fossil members are by far the earliest of known chordates; and among its living representatives are forms which are believed to closely resemble the ancestral vertebrate" (1987, p. 10).

The lack of evidence for fish evolution in the fossil record includes not only the absence of evidence for fish origins, but also the absence of evidence for the evolution of the many fish types *within* all major fish classes. As a result of a lack of transitional forms, Long concluded that the "transition from spineless invertebrates to the first backboned fishes is still shrouded in mystery, and many theories abound as to how the changes took place" (1995, p. 30). Thus, Long wrote that the "remarkable permanence of the different types of fishes seems a striking proof of how unchanging" aquatic living conditions must have been (1995, p. 64). Dean attempted to explain this fact by noting that dating back to the Devonian

> have been living members of the four sub-classes of existing fishes — Sharks, Chimaeroids, Dipnoans, and Teleostomes. Even their ancient sub-groups (orders and

sub-orders) usually present surviving members; while, on the other hand, there is but a single group of any structural importance that has been evolved during the lapse of ages—the sub-order of Bony Fishes. There are many instances in which even the very types of living fishes are known to be of remarkable antiquity: thus the genus of the Port Jackson Shark, *Cestracion*, is known to have been represented early in the Mesozoic; the Australian Lung-fish, *Ceratodus*, dates back to Jurassic times; the Frilled Shark, *Chlamydoselache*, though not of a Paleozoic genus, as formerly supposed (Cope), must at least be regarded as closely akin to the Sharks of the Silurian (1987, p. 10).

One characteristic that typifies the fossil record is stasis. For example, the lamprey, although a very "primitive" life-form, evolutionists conclude has not changed in the past 360 million years except that it is now slightly longer (Gess, Coates and Rubidge, 2006). A problem with all fossils, as explained by Nelson, is the common mistaken belief that "even one fossil species or fossil "group" can be demonstrated to have been ancestral to another. The ancestor-descendant relationship may only be assumed to have existed in the absence of evidence indicating otherwise" (1969, p. 22).

It also is of much interest to compare the past speculation of paleontologists with far more complete knowledge. Another difficulty is that new discoveries often overthrow old ideas, especially the finding of new fossils that date contemporaneously with a putative fossil ancestor. For example, it once was concluded "that lampreys evolved from armored jawless vertebrates. But a recently discovered lamprey fossil dates from the twilight age of their supposed ancestors, and looks surprisingly modern" (Janvier, 2006, p. 921).

Sometimes a single discovery can move the earliest known example of a vertebrate back by as much as forty million years, forcing a major re-evaluation of the fossil record (Repetski, 1978, p. 529; Jablonski, et al., 2003). A major problem for evolution is that new findings tend to push the origin of fish farther and farther back in time. This makes it even harder to explain fish origins because much less time exists for them to evolve. It also creates a longer period of stasis without evolutionary changes (Wieland, 2000; Brown, 1996).

Conclusions

Much research has been completed on the microevolution of fish (e.g., see Echelle and Kornfield, 1984), but only speculation exists about their macroevolution from a common ancestor. Since paleontologists have no evidence of the evolution of fish from non-fish, nor any evidence of the evolution of the many basic kinds of fish from other fish, Long noted there still exist "many different opinions as to which invertebrate group may have given rise to the vertebrates or first fishes" (quoted in Werner, 2007, p. 98).

Not only is the origin of cartilaginous fish unknown, but "The origin of bony fish is also shrouded in mystery" (Long, quoted in Werner, 2007, p. 98). One major current theory is that all bony fish evolved from spiny-finned acanthodian fishes, sharks, or placoderms. However, this controversial view is not supported by the fossil record. We do know that what is believed by paleontologists to be the earliest known fossil fish have all of the basic characteristics of modern fish. Many fish species have become extinct, but in spite of almost two centuries of searching, no evidence of gradual macroevolution has been found in the abundant fossil record so far uncovered.

The fact is no justification exists

> for selecting even a particular fossil species or group,
> and assuming that it was some primitive animal from
> which another has evolved. How, after all, can we hope
> to demonstrate that ostracoderms ever gave rise to
> anything else but other ostracoderms? This particular
> point cannot be overemphasized in view of past
> practices of vertebrate zoologists, who all too often have
> been willing to make facile assumptions about what is
> or is not primitive, and to derive one species or group
> from another. ... we have no ancestors alive today, that
> in all probability such ancestors have been dead for
> many tens or hundreds of millions of years, and that
> even in the fossil record they are not accessible to us
> (Nelson, 1969, p. 27).

Thus, "the evolution of fish is still very much debated amongst paleontologists" (Long, quoted in Werner, 2007, p. 98) because of the scarcity of evidence that includes not only the evolutionary origins of fish, but also the evolution of the many very different kinds of fish. The conclusion of fish biologist Kyle that fishes "occupy a peculiar position in the hierarchy of animal life" and that we "cannot be sure whence they came" is still very true today (1926, p. vii).

The claim made by Gregory in 1959, that "there are still many gaps" in the fossil record among fish, is also still true today (1959, p. 123). Not much has changed since the seminal meeting on fish paleontology that highlighted the controversies in the field of fish evolution in 1967 (White, 1978).

Conclusions of fish evolution that are almost a century old are still largely current, as Strahler's evaluation of Dr. Duane Gish's book on the fossil record documents:

mainstream paleontologists have found no fossil record of transitional chordates leading up to the appearance of the first class of fishes, the Agnatha, or of transitional forms between the primitive, jawless agnaths and the jaw-bearing class Placodermi, or of transition from the placoderms (which were poorly structured for swimming) to the class Chondrichthyes, or from those cartilaginous-skeleton sharklike fishes to the class Osteichthyes, or bony fishes .... Neither ... is there any record of transitional forms leading to the rise of the lungfishes and the crossopterygians from the lobe-finned bony fishes, an evolutionary step that is supposed to have led to the rise of amphibians and ultimately to the conquest of the lands by air-breathing vertebrates (Strahler, 1987, p. 408).

Strahler concluded that "Gish finds all the confessions he needs" in the writings of paleontologists to support the conclusion that each fish class "appears suddenly and with no trace of ancestors" in the fossil record, adding the fact that the

absence of the transitional fossils in the gaps between each group of fishes and its ancestor is repeated in standard treatises on vertebrate evolution. Even Chris McGowan's 1984 anticreationist work ... makes no mention of Gish's four pages of text on the origin of the fish classes. Knowing that McGowan is an authority on vertebrate paleontology, keen on faulting the creationists at every opportunity, I must assume that I haven't missed anything important in this area. This is one count in the creationists' charge that can only evoke in unison from the paleontologists a plea of *nolo contendere* (Strahler, 1987, p. 408).

The results of this review document a complete lack of fossil evidence for fish evolution in spite of an abundance of fossils. Darwin's claim has been falsified, supporting the creation account recorded in Genesis 1:21 that reads "God created the great creatures of the sea and every living and moving thing with which the water teems according to their kinds" (New International Version).

References

Anonymous. 1999. "First Fish." *New Scientist.* No 2211. November 6.

Barton, Michael. 2007. *Bond's Biology of Fishes.* Third Edition, Thomson Brooks/Cole.

Benton, Michael. 2005. *Vertebrate Palaeontology.* Malden, MA: Blackwell.

Bond, Carl E. 1996. *Biology of Fishes.* Second Edition. Ft. Worth, TX: Harcourt Brace College Publishers/Saunders College Publishing.

Brown, Robert. 1880. *Science for All.* Volume 6. London: Cassell and Company.

Botella, Hector and Henning Blom, Markus Dorda, Per Erik Ahlberg and Philippe Janvier. 2007. "Jaws and Teeth of the Earliest Bony Fishes." *Nature,* 448(2):583-586, August.

Brown, Colin. 1996. "Devonian Fish and Amphibians and the Gene-Theme Model." *CRSQ,* 33(1):13-15. June.

Chen, Jun-Yuan, Di-Ying Huang and Chia-Wei Li. 1999. "An Early Cambrian Craniate-like Chordate." *Nature* 402: 518-522. December 2.

Cleland, Herdman. 1925. *Geology: Physical and Historical.* New York: American Book Company.

Colbert, Edwin H., Michael Morales, and Eli C. Minkoff. 2001. *Evolution of the Vertebrates: A History of the Backboned Animals Through Time,* 5th ed. New York: Wiley-Liss, Inc.

Curtis, Brian. 1961. *The Life Story of the Fish: His Morals and Manners.* New York: Dover Publications, Inc.

Dean, Bashford. 1987. *Fishes: Living and Fossil.* Maliwara, Delhi: Narendra Publishing House.

Dana, James. 1863. *A Textbook of Geology for Schools and Academies.* New York: Ivison, Blakeman, Taylor, & Company.

Darwin, Charles. 1859. *The Origin of Species*, London: John Murray.

Echelle, Anthony A. and Irv Kornfield (Editors). 1984. *Evolution of Fish Species Flocks*. Orono ME: University of Maine at Orono Press.

Gess, Robert W., Michael I. Coates and Bruce S. Rubidge. 2006. "A Lamprey from the Devonian Period of South Africa." *Nature,* 443(26):981-984, October.

Gish, Duane 1986. *Evolution; The Fossil Record.* El Cajon, CA: Creation-Life Publishers.

Gould, Stephen Jay. 1989. *Wonderful Life: The Burgess Shale and the Nature of History.* New York, NY: W.W. Norton.

Gregory, William K. 1959. *Fish Skulls: A Study of the Evolution of Natural Mechanisms.* Laurel, FL: Eric Lundberg (reprint of the original 1933 edition).

Grzimek, Bernhard. 1973. Grzimek's Animal Life Encyclopedia. New York: Van Nostrand. Volume 4 Fishes I.

Jablonski, David, Kaustuv Roy, James W. Valentine, Rebecca M. Price, and Philip S. Anderson. 2003. "The Impact of the Pull of the Recent on the History of Marine Diversity." *Science*, 300:1133-1135.

Janvier, Philippe. 1999. "Catching the First Fish." *Nature,* 402: 21-22.

_____. 2006. "Modern Look for Ancient Lamprey." *Nature,* 443(26):921-924, October.

Jordan, David Starr. 1902. "Origin of the Fins of Fishes." *Popular Science Monthly,* 61:536-547. October.

Kyle, Harry M. 1926. *The Biology of Fishes.* New York, NY: The Macmillan Company.

Lefebvre, Bertrand. 2000. Homologies in Stylophora: A Test of the 'Calcichordate Theory'
Geobios 33(3):359-364.

204 | Chapter 8: Fish – Common Inhabitants of the Fossil Record

Long, John. 1995. *The Rise of Fishes: 500 Million Years of Evolution*. Baltimore, MD: Johns Hopkins University.

Maisey, John G. 1996. *Discovering Fossil Fishes*. New York, NY: Henry Holt.

Morris, Simon Conway. 1998. *The Crucible of Creation: The Burgess Shale and the Rise of Animals*. New York, NY: Oxford University Press.

_____. 2000. The Cambrian "explosion": Slow-fuse or megatonnage? *Proceedings of the National Academy of Science*. 97(9): 4426–4429. April 25.

Nielsen, Claus. 2001. *Animal evolution - Interrelationships of the living phyla*. New York: Oxford University Press.

Nelson, Gareth J. 1969. "Origin and Diversification of Teleostean Fishes." *Annals of the New York Academy of Sciences*. 167(1): 18-30.

Oktar, Adnan. 2007. *Atlas of Creation*. Vol I. Istanbul, Turkey; Global Publishing.

Ommanney, F.D. 1971. *The Fishes*. New York: Time Life Nature Library.

Patterson, Colin and P. H. Greenwood (editors). 1967. *Fossil Vertebrates: Papers Presented to Dr. Errol I. White.* New York: Linnaean Society by Academic Press.

Prothero, Donald. 2007. *Evolution: What the Fossils Say and Why it Matters.* New York: Columbia University Press.

Repetski, John E. 1978. "A Fish from the Upper Cambrian of North America." *Science,* 200:529-531.

Reznick, David, Mariana Mateos, and Mark S. Springer. 2002. "Independent Origins and Rapid Evolution of the Placenta in the Fish Genus Poeciliopsis." *Science,* 298:1018-1020.

Romer, Alfred. 1966. *Vertebrate Paleontology*. Chicago: The University of Chicago Press.

Shu, D-G, S. Conway Morris, X-L. Zhang, L. Chen, J. Han, M. Zhu and L-Z. Chen. 1999. "Lower Cambrian Vertebrates from South China." *Nature* 402: 42-46.

Stahl, Barbara. 1974. *Vertebrate History: Problems in Evolution.* New York: Dover.

Strahler, Arthur N. 1987. *Science and Earth History — The Evolution/Creation Controversy.* Buffalo, N.Y.: Prometheus Books.

Venkatesh, Byrappa and Mark V. Erdmann, and Sydney Brenner. 2001. "Molecular synapomorphies resolve evolutionary relationships of extant jawed vertebrates." *Proceedings of the National Academy of Science.* 98(20): 11382–11387. September 25.

Werner, Carl. 2007. *Evolution: The Grand Experiment.* Green Forrest, AR: New Leaf Press.

White, Errol. 1978. "The Larger Arthrodiran Fishes from the Area of the Burrinjuck Dam, NSW" *Transactions of the Zoology Society of London.* 43:149-262

Wieland, Carl. 2000. "Fish Origins Scaled Back." *Creation,* 22(2): 9.

Zhu, Min, Xiaobo Yu, and Philippe Janvier. 1999. "A Primitive Fossil Fish Sheds Light on the Origin of Bony Fishes" *Nature.* 397, 607-610.

Zim, Herbert and Hurst Shoemaker. 1956. *Fishes.* New York: Simon and Schuster.

Chapter 9

Amphibians—Persistence in the Fossil Record

Introduction

Amphibians are ectothermic (cold-blooded) vertebrates consisting of frogs (Anura), salamanders (Caudata), and wormlike caecilians (Gymnophiona) (Marent, 2008, p. 20). The term amphibian means double life, named because many amphibians spend their entire early life in the water. As they mature, most amphibians develop lungs and other structures that allow them to live on land. The classic example is a tadpole's development into a frog (see Figure 9.1).

Exceptions to this classification trait include the few animal kinds classified as amphibians that develop on land without water, and others that live their *entire* lives in the water. All amphibians lack feathers, hair, and large reptile-like scales; instead their integument is soft smooth "skin" that must be kept moist by glands (Noble, 1931, p. 1). Most adult amphibians have lungs but also can breathe through their skin (Johnson, 2010, p. 8). As adults, some amphibians usually never travel very far from the water; others live their entire life under rocks and logs on high ground or even in forests. Detailed research has confirmed that "frogs, salamanders, and caecilians are very different from one another in skeletal structure and ways of life, both now and throughout their known fossil" history (Carroll, 1988, p. 181). Furthermore, paleontologists

> have found no fossil evidence of any possible antecedents that possessed the specialized features common to all three modern [amphibian] orders. ...In the absence of fossil evidence that frogs, salamanders, and caecilians evolved from a close common ancestor, we must consider the possibility that each of the modern orders evolved from a distinct group of Paleozoic amphibians" (Carroll, 1988, pp. 182, 184).

For this reason, according to Northeastern Illinois University herpetologist Ellin Beltz, one of the "big scientific issues now is whether the three groups of amphibians—the salamanders, the caecilians, and the frogs and toads—are all descended from one common fish-like ancestor called 'Lissamphibia'" (Beltz, 2005, p. 19), or, as speculated by Noble, some other "more or less aquatic tetrapod" (Noble, 1931, p. 2).

Lissamphibia actually is a very unlikely common ancestor candidate because it is a living fossil that includes all recent amphibians. The problem is that the "origin of the Lissamphibia is the subject of continuing debate, and there is no current consensus" (Schoch and Milner, 2004, 345). Darwin speculated that all the amphibians descended from a fish "like the Lepidosiren," a South American lungfish (Darwin, 1871, pp. 212-213). Since Darwin, a fish origin of amphibians has been the dominate view.

FROG life cycle

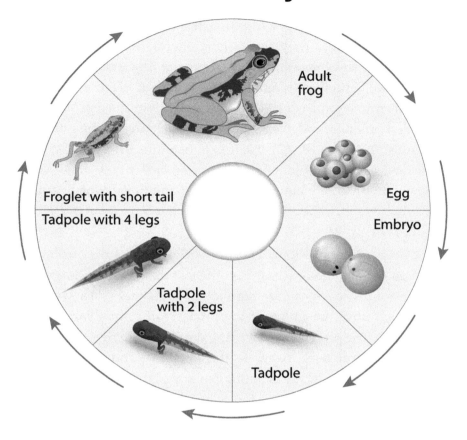

Figure 9.1 — Frog Life Cycle[1]

A common claim is that some fish species developed the ability to climb out of the water, to survive on land, and simultaneously evolve the amphibian reproductive system and other common amphibian features. We will show that many hypothetical ancestors of amphibians have been proposed, but specific evidence for any one ancestor is non-existent.

---

[1] Image Credit: Designua / Shutterstock.com

The Origin of Amphibians from Fish

Most paleontologists agree that the earliest amphibian must have been fish-like. They assume that "tetrapods evolved from a fish ancestor and that amphibians were the first tetrapods" (Gish, 1995, p. 83). Specifically, many evolutionists believe amphibians evolved from a group of fleshly-finned carnivorous fish about 350 million years ago and were the first vertebrates to live on land (Johnson, 2010, pp. 8, 12). No fossil fish species yet have been identified as *ancestral* to amphibians; nor has any evidence of an animal "intermediate between the finned and limbed forms" of life been discovered, although many possibilities have been postulated (Stahl, 1974, pp. 194-195).

One possible ancestor is a crossopterygian fish, a conclusion that relies on bone homology based on the fact that the crossopterygian fish pectoral fin bones "are similar to, or homologous with, the humerus, radius, and ulna of the forelimb of amphibians" (Gish, 1995, p. 87). The problem is "there the similarity of either the pectoral or pelvic fins of these fishes to the forelimbs and hind limbs of amphibians ceases. There is nothing in any of these fish to equate to or homologize with hand and feet of amphibians" (Gish, 1995, p. 87). A more recent reference arrived at the same conclusion: "Even in the earliest known tetrapods, the pelvic girdle had become far different in structure from that of a fish" (Clack, 2012 p. 51).

The Rhipidistia are traditionally a suborder or order of crossopterygians or tassel-finned fish that lived from the Devonian to the Permian Periods, becoming extinct by the end of the Paleozoic. They were related indirectly to the living coelacanth. With the discovery of recent fossils, the most recent cladistic analysis recommends placing traditional rhipidistians and lungfishes in the Sarcopterygii along with tetrapods. The proposed rhipidistian ancestor, claimed to have skeletal features resembling amphibians, also is problematic. For example, the function of the thick, lobate-paired extinct rhipidistian fin

> was very different from the function of the feet and legs
> of the amphibians. In the rhipidistian fish the humerus
> (of the front paired fins) and the femur (of the rear
> paired fins) were held close to the body, which restricted
> lateral or rotational movement. Thus their fins point in a
> posterior direction. In the "primitive" tetrapods,
> however, the limbs are extended forward and away
> from the trunk during locomotion. The mode of
> locomotion of amphibians, including the "earliest" or
> most "primitive" amphibians, was thus drastically
> different from that of any fish (Carroll, 1988, p. 145).

To evolve from a fish that spends most of its time in the water, to a tetrapod that spends most of its time as an adult on land, required a radical new respiration system, from a gill system to an air breathing lung system, and from a finned fish to a four-legged tetrapod that effectively could walk on land. Even the lungless salamanders require an entirely new respiratory system that effectively could take in enough oxygen through their skin to allow the animal to live (Johnson, 2010, p. 39).

Yet another set of radical changes includes maintaining proper internal water balance. When moving from water to dry land, the proto-amphibians would suffer serious levels of water loss through their mouth, lungs and body surfaces. Significant changes would be required in these, and many other organs and structures, to minimize water losses. Furthermore: "tetrapods and fish move in exactly opposite ways. In fish, locomotion is provided by the body, with the tail propelling the fish through the water. In tetrapods, the legs are used for propulsion; the longer tetrapod tail is only for balance" (Beltz, 2005, p. 20).

The major evolutionary gap between fish and both frogs and salamanders long has been recognized. Noble notes that by comparing

> a frog sitting on the edge of a pond with the perches,
> catfish, or eels in the water, the difference between a
> tetrapod and a fish seems tremendous. A scrutiny of
> their detailed structure brings forth such a series of
> differences in skull, appendages, and breathing
> apparatus that the change from fish to frog would seem
> to be one of the most radical steps in the evolution of the
> vertebrates. This step does not seem less tremendous
> when we compare the aquatic newt with the fish, for
> the former is a typical tetrapod which has secondarily
> taken up a life in the water. It is no wonder that
> anatomists were puzzled for many years as to how the
> first tetrapod arose, and even today there is no
> agreement (1931, p. 2).

The same problem is still with us today. Benton notes the "major problems" that exist "in moving from water onto the land" include "weight and structural support ... new ways of feeding, of sensing prey and predators, of water balance and of reproduction" (2005, p. 75). He then documents each of these problems in detail. Nonetheless, in spite of these problems, paleoanthropologists continue to speculate on the identity of the possible ancestors of amphibians.

Darwinists often describe the extinct fish order *Rhipidistian* as an "ancestral group" to amphibians. Rhipidistians have some skeletal features resembling early amphibians, including skeletal features that may have evolved into legs. The rhipidistians are known by only a "relatively small number of fossils, many of which show little more than dermal bones and scales" (Stahl, 1974, p. 146). Stahl added that "none of the known fishes is thought to be directly ancestral to the earliest land vertebrates. Most of them lived after the first amphibians appeared, and those that came before show no evidence of developing the stout limbs and ribs that characterized the primitive tetrapods" (Stahl, 1974, p. 148).

In addition, the "question of where tetrapods evolved is even more difficult to answer than that of when (Clack 2012, p. 128). Even the transitional path between the fin structural elements in fish and those in tetrapods limbs remains elusive (Woltering, *et al.*, 2013). This is true in spite of the fact that the path remains elusive in contrast to evolutionist Mark Ridley's claim in his evolution text that there exists "a good fossil record from fish to amphibian" (Ridley, (2004 p. 540).

Many paleontologists considered the coelacanth to be closely related to the rhipidistians until a living coelacanth specimen was discovered in 1938. This discovery was expected to shed light on the soft body parts of the putative immediate ancestors of amphibians. When

> dissected, however, its internal organs showed no signs of being preadapted for a land environment and gave no indication of how it might be possible for a fish to become an amphibian. The experience suggests that a rhipidistian fish might be equally disappointing to Darwinists if its soft body parts could be examined (Johnson, 1993, p. 77).

The three groups - tetrapods, coelacanths and lungfish — all have a past history as distinct *separate* animals. Other amphibian ancestor candidates include three fish: Ganoidei fish, a group of mostly extinct bony fishes characterized by armor-like bony scales; dipnoan fish, fish that can respire by lungs as well as gills (Dziewa, 1980) and Labyrinthodontia. All of these claims are so problematic that Benton only briefly covers the problems of amphibian evolution without speculating on any possible resolution (Benton, 2005, p. 79). Order Ganoidei is named after their scale type, ganoid scales, that are thick non-overlapping and composed of bone overlaid with an enamel-like substance called ganoin. This scale type most commonly is found on the lobed-finned coelacanth.

All of these proposals are based on certain specific similarities of fish and reptiles or mammals. All that is required to document amphibian evolution is a few transitional forms to "reveal what was ancestral to amphibians and what the evolutionary pathway was. Lacking that, all suggestions are mere scenarios and empty rhetoric" (Gish, 1995, p. 85). Thus Gish concludes that when one carefully reads

> the massive amount of literature on the origin of major groups, such as the origin of tetrapods ... one soon becomes overwhelmed and confused by the many controversial and contradictory notions of evolutionists. Each espouses his supposedly logical argument based on a comparison of the many characteristics that the theorist assumes to be the most important in selecting the creature believed to be the probable ancestor (Gish, 1995, p. 84).

As we will show, the same problem still exists today. While Carroll argues for a rhipidistian fish ancestor, other experts advocate for a much earlier ancestor such as a coelacanth-like animal, and still others for some lung-fish as Darwin did. Of all the known extinct amphibians, all clearly are amphibians, although some are much larger than their modern amphibian relatives, a few as long as 1.5 meters. The aquatic tetrapod ancestors, as well as the whole process by which land colonization occurred, although an active area of research and debate among paleontologists, the "interrelationships of early tetrapods constitute a problem that for the time being is unsatisfactorily resolved (Clack, 2012, p. 267).

Frogs and Toads

Frogs and toads are amphibians in the order Anura (meaning "tail-less," Greek *an-*, without, plus *oura* (tail)). Over 6,000 amphibian species have been identified so-far, and Anurans make up about 90 percent of the class Amphibia. Most frogs are designed to enable them to jump long distances, a movement mode called saltatorial locomotion.

This design includes long powerful hind legs, a short body, webbed fingers and toes, and the absence of a tail—which would interfere with jumping. Large protruding eyes allow frogs to accurately land on designated targets. Many other frog anatomical characteristics, such as their nervous system and brain, specifically were designed to improve jumping ability, both their length and their accuracy.

Frog habitats range from tropic to subarctic regions, but most species live in tropical rainforests. Some frog species synthesize an antifreeze substance that gives them the "amazing ability to freeze solidly in the winter and thaw out in the spring with no harm done" (Holman, 2003, p. 206). Their permeable skin enables most frogs to be semi-aquatic, meaning they inhabit humid regions, but can easily move about on land.

Toads are Anurans that have wart-like dry skin, short legs, parotid glands, and other adaptations enabling them to be well-adapted to dry environments. The only family exclusively referred to by the common name "toad" is the genus *Anaxyrus*, the North American toads classified as *Bufonidae*, or *Bufo* in Europe, but spade foot frogs also are classified as toads.

Frogs	Toads
long and skinny	short and stubby
long legs and arms	short legs and arms
long faces	blunt faces
eyes that see up and over to their butts periphery	eyes that see mainly forward with a little
smooth skin	warty skin
not too many wrinkles at joints	sometimes very saggy, baggy, skin
not as successful at tongue hunting	extremely successful at tongue hunting—implies better brain power and better eyesight resolution.
"dignified" mating, lay mostly egg masses	massive frothy free-for-alls ending in amplexed pairs stuck for days laying eggs in strings
slower-developing tadpoles	very fast-developing tadpoles
lives in lower temperatures and moister	lives in higher temperatures and drier places
most frog species have five toes,	some true toads (and a few frogs) have
jointed 2-2-3-4-3	only four toes on their hind feet (from Beltz, 2005, p. 41)

Table 9.1 - General Differences Between Frogs and Toads

Frogs typically lay their eggs in mud puddles and ponds. As they mature they lose their tail and gills, and also develop lungs needed for land living. Frogs tend to be carnivorous, consuming mostly arthropods, annelids, and gastropods. These small creatures are distinguished by their night calls during mating seasons.

Frogs are among the most diverse groups of vertebrates known, and the approximately 6,000 known species are arranged into 30 families (Marent, 2008, p. 20). Unfortunately, populations of certain frog species are declining significantly. The North American green frog is the most familiar type, but frogs come in an amazing variety of vibrant colors, from bright blue to red and even dark or solid black coloration. Many are multi-colored, such as black and orange, red and blue, or yellow and red, and commonly their skin is poisonous.

Evidence of Frog Evolution

Frog fossils have been found on all continents except Antarctica. Biogeographic data indicates that they once inhabited Antarctica when it had a *warmer* climate. Extinct frog species exist in the fossil record, but the first frog clearly was a frog. Modern frogs actually are in two major ways less complex than so-called primitive frogs — "primitive frogs had up to eight rib bones; modern frogs have few or none" and, secondly, modern frogs have lost their once short tails (Beltz, 2005, p. 20). They were labeled primitive because they possessed character traits found in their presumed ancestors and not necessarily because these traits were "simple" or "inferior."

Figure 9.2 — Fossilized Frog[2]

---

[2] Photo Credit: Marcel Clemens / Shutterstock.com

Modern frogs are speculated to have evolved from early temnospondyls, such as the *Eryops*, an animal similar to an overweight alligator and very unlike a frog (Colbert and Minkoff, 2001, p. 96). *Eryops* was as long as almost two meters, as large as many reptiles of the time, and was well adapted to land (Colbert and Minkoff, 2001, p. 108). It had a "large" bony head, strong limbs, a long tail, and rows of sharp teeth in a large mouth. This frog-salmander fossil is speculated to be an amphibian missing link, but lived a life very much like modern day alligators, which it strongly resembled (Beltz, 2005, p. 21).

Marjanovic and Laurin concluded that a "review of the paleontological literature shows that the early dates of the appearance of Lissamphibia recently inferred from molecular data do not favor an origin of extant amphibians from temnospondyls, contrary to recent claims" (2007, p. 369). The choice of this unlikely animal as the frog ancestor was partly due to the fact that a more plausible frog ancestor does not exist. Molecular analyses has also cast a cloud over the frog-salamander divergence. Anderson *et al.*, concluded "Recent molecular analyses are also controversial, with estimations for the batrachian (frog-salamander) divergence significantly older that the paleontological evidence supports." (Anderson, *et al.* 2008, p. 515).

The problem is the first putative frog ancestors left no trace that we have been able to find "in spite of paleontologists searching the globe" looking for fossil frogs in ancient rocks likely to preserve animals and plants contemporary to when frog ancestors were theorized to have first evolved (Beltz, 2005, pp. 24-25). The first frog in the fossil record clearly was a frog.

Paleontologists have found a few extinct frog-like animals, such as the Early Permian *Gerobatrachus hottoni*, (meaning Hotton's elder frog) a frog with salamander-like traits discovered in Texas in 1995 by a Smithsonian field researcher. Only one known specimen of the 12 cm-long animal exists, and this example is very incomplete.

One of the earliest known frog-like animals was *Triadobatrachus massinoti*, an early Triassic animal that evolutionists conclude lived in Madagascar 250 million years ago. Its broad skull with large eye sockets and "a nearly modern configuration of the jumping apparatus" are all very frog-like (Carroll, 1998, p. 284). The fossils possess several features that are different from most modern amphibians, including their ileum, a longer body with more vertebrae, and separate tail vertebra (modern frogs have fused tail vertebrae). The tibia and fibula bones also are unfused and separate, thus *Triadobatrachus* probably was not an efficient leaper.

Evaluation of its restored skeleton reveals that many "characters (e.g., orbit size, fusion of frontoparietals, morphology of pterygoids and squamosals, etc.) are developed to the same degree as in modern anurans, but other features, mainly in its postcranial skeleton, are very different than modern frogs" (Rage and Rocek, 1989, p. 15). It was likely merely an extinct frog because its restored skeleton looks almost identical to a modern frog skeleton (Rage and Rocek, 1989, p. 15).

Of the two anuran families known to have lived during the Paleocene (The earliest epoch of the Tertiary Period, dated by evolutionists from about 65 to 58 million years ago), one is extinct and the other is a "modern type" still alive today (Holman, 1998, p. 12). Another example is the "frogamander," a fossil dated by evolutionists to be 290 million-years-old that some claim to be the fish to amphibian missing link (Caselman, 2008).

Another fossil frog, *Prosalirus bitis*, called the earliest known anuran, was discovered in 1995 in Arizona's Kayenta Formation (Jenkins and Shubin, 1998, p. 495). It was dated by evolutionists as the Early Jurassic epoch (190 million years ago). This is somewhat younger than *Triadobatrachus*, documenting that *Triadobatrachus* could not be a transitional form but merely an extinct frog. Like *Triadobatrachus*, *Prosalirus* effectively used saltatorial locomotion, but had the typical three-pronged pelvic structure. *Prosalirus bitis* was so modern that Jenkins and Shubin concluded that it "demonstrates that many of the distinctive anatomical features of modern anurans were established by Early Jurassic time" (Jenkins and Shubin, 1998, p. 505).

Unlike *Triadobatrachus*, *Prosalirus* had a small stub-like tail and was well adapted for jumping. Likely it was an extinct frog. Artists' drawings show that it was unmistakably a frog, as does an evaluation of the skeleton (Jenkins and Shubin, 1998, p. 505). All fossil frogs dated after this example are recognized by paleontologists as fully modern frogs. One paleo-herpetologist pointed to the problem that these frogs are only extinct varieties of frogs and, as has been argued "before and will be again, you need a comparative anuran skeleton collection to be able to make reliable identifications of fossil frogs because of the osteological variations that occur within species. But limitations exist, as seldom do you get an adequate sample of fossil amphibian species" (Holman, 2003, p. 207).

The earliest well-documented fully modern frog, *Vieraella herbsti*, has been dated by evolutionists back to the early Jurassic (188–213 million years ago) when dinosaurs were believed to have populated vast land regions. It is known only from the dorsal and ventral impressions of a single animal estimated to be only 33 mm (1.3 in) from snout to vent.

Another modern frog, *Notobatrachus degiustoi*, was dated from the Middle Jurassic, about 155–170 million years ago. Compared to early extinct frogs, the only morphological differences seen in modern frogs are a slightly shorter body and total loss of the tail. The earliest *complete* fossil of a fully modern frog is the *Sanyanlichan*, which evolutionists claim lived 125 million years ago and possessed all modern frog features. Thus, the fossil evidence has documented that the first modern frog, dated by evolutionists as living about 190 million years ago, was fully a frog.

The most accurate method of determining frog evolution is to evaluate the frogs entombed in amber. One example is a frog and a mushroom that were found in Dominican Republic amber dated at 40 million years (Poinar and Poinar, 1994, p. 178). This excellently preserved frog looks identical to a modern frog (Poinar, 1992, p. 216). Also, what looks like a modern tadpole was discovered entombed in amber (Poinar and Poinar, 1999, p. 155).

The conclusion of these many fossil studies is that frog fauna in North America, British Isles and Europe "existed in a state of evolutionary stasis during the entire Pleistocene epoch" (Holman, 2003, p. 206). Furthermore, the evidence reveals that, "other than large tortoises or unique island taxa ... all Pleistocene amphibian and reptile species ... belong to modern species" (Holman, 2003, p. 207). This conclusion is based on the fact that all of the "Pleistocene herpetofaunas that have been documented at numerous sites in continental North America have been strikingly more stable than the mammalian and avian faunas" (Holman, 2003, p. 208).

Duffett concluded from a detailed study of ancient frogs that "fossils of allegedly ancient frogs show that adult frogs have always resembled frogs" (Duffett, 1984, p. 199). Romer's 1966 conclusion still is valid today in spite of numerous new well-preserved fossil frog finds since then:

> Records of late Cretaceous and Tertiary frogs are not uncommon; most are fragmentary and poorly preserved, and hence often difficult to assign to their proper... classification. It seems clear, however, that most of the modern families have been in existence since the early part of the Cretaceous. In recent years several good specimens of frogs have been found in the Jurassic of South America and Europe ... Although these finds carry the frog story far back in time, they do not tell us much of frog evolutionary history, for even the "primitive" frog families differ only in

relatively minor features from the more "advanced" ones (Romer, 1966, p. 100).

He concludes that the "basic pattern of anuran structure was already established by the early Jurassic and exemplified by the South American *Vieraella*—essentially a modern frog in its general adaptation, despite its great age" (Romer, 1966, p. 100). Romer adds that the fossil history of frogs goes back as far as the

> Triassic, overlapping the history of the older groups in time, but without closing the morphological gap. In the early Triassic of Madagascar has been found the skeleton of a small animal, *Triadobatrachus* [*Protobatrachus*]. The specimen displays a skull which, although incomplete, appears to be basically similar to that of modern frogs and toads (Romer, 1966, p. 100).

Furthermore, although enormous variety of color, body size and other features exist, "the adult frog shows remarkable constancy of body plan and general morphology, indicating they all belong to one baramin" (Duffett, 1984, p. 199).

Salamanders and Newts

Salamanders and newts (both family Salamandridae order Urodela) are the second largest group of amphibians (Johnson, 2010). Salamander is the common name for more than 535 amphibian species that are characterized by long slender bodies, short noses, and long tails (Min, *et al.*, 2005). Salamanders never have more than five toes, and some have large feet, others, such as the Olm, have thin, short feet. More than 70 percent are classified in a single family, the *Plethodontidae* or lungless salamanders (Min, *et al.*, 2005, p. 87). All known fossils and extinct salamander species are grouped in the order Caudata.

Most salamanders lay their eggs in water. When the eggs hatch they look more like tadpoles than salamanders, and are referred to as "salamander nymphs." The nymphs have feathery gills that extend outward from the sides of their necks to help the young salamanders absorb oxygen from the water. Their moist skin requirement forces them to live in habitats in or near water, or in wetlands. Some have lungs, others feathery gills; yet others, such as the mudpuppy, have larger external bushy gills (Johnson, 2010, p. 43).

Some salamander species are fully aquatic throughout their life; other types take to the water intermittently, and many are entirely terrestrial. Salamanders are unique among all vertebrates because many species can regenerate lost limbs and certain other body parts. The strange looking Axolotl has a long dorsal and ventral fin like a tadpole, and is a popular animal used to research limb regeneration.

Salamander Evolution

Researchers have only a small "sample of fossil amphibian species — an obvious exception is the hundreds of specimens of *Ambystoma tigrinum* that J. A. Tihen was able to study in Kansas." From these "hundreds of specimens" some conclusions about evolution can be made (Holman, 2003, p. 204). Since Holman's work, many more discoveries have been made.

Evolutionists have traced the salamander's genetic lineage back to more than 110 million years. David Wake of U.C. Berkeley's Department of Integrative Biology, a specialist on the diversity of amphibians, has studied salamander species for nearly 50 years. A team of researchers he led found that no significant changes in salamanders have occurred for 110 million years (Wake and Vredenburg, 2008). Another unsolved puzzle is Asian species of salamanders which "have only four toes on their feet, while the salamanders of Europe and the Americas all have five. And none of us can think of any reason why four toes would make a salamander species better adapted for survival than five" (Perlman, 2006, p. 1

Neil Shubin and his colleagues have been collecting thousands of salamander fossils from seven excavation sites in China that evolutionists date back to 161 million years, many of which have preserved the entire skeleton and even impressions of soft tissues. The fossils closely resemble the North American hellbender, a common salamander found in Asia as well as the Allegheny Mountains (Gianaro, 2003, p. 2).

Most of the changes in modern salamanders compared to fossil salamanders involve minor differences in the shape of their front skull bones and minor finger, toe, and rib variations. One unique feature is that its "unicapitate" ribs have only one facet or head where they connect to the vertebra—most modern salamanders have two-headed ribs, otherwise they were identical to modern salamanders. Because scientists claim that salamanders have had the same body morphology for millions of years, they are called living fossils:

> Despite its Bathonian age, the new cryptobranchid shows extraordinary morphological similarity to its living relatives. This similarity underscores the stasis within salamander anatomical evolution. Indeed, extant cryptobranchid salamanders can be regarded as living fossils whose structures have remained little changed for over 160 million years (Gao and Shubin, 2003, p. 428).

These research conclusions were based on "200 specimens ... many of which preserve evidence of soft tissues" (Gao and Shubin, 2003, p. 426). Shubin adds that:

> Whether you look at a salamander you find under a rock in the local forest preserve or in a rock in China dating back 165 million years, they look alike. In fact, they look alike in

great detail–the bones in their wrists are the same, the way their skulls are formed–intricate details are the same" (Shubin, quoted in Gianaro, 2003, p. 3).

This finding is based on "thousands of salamander fossils— many of which preserve the entire skeleton and impressions of soft tissues" (Gianaro, 2003, p. 1). One reason for the

> apparent stasis of Pleistocene amphibians may be gleaned from additional studies of modern as well as fossil amphibians. … ectothermic (cold-blooded) animals, such as amphibians, that have very low metabolic rates and are able to hibernate (in winter) or estivate (in summer) during inclement conditions would have many advantages over endothermic (warm-blooded) birds and mammals during intervals of climatic fluctuations (Holman, 2006, p. 204).

He concluded that the fact that many amphibians can

> freeze solid in the winter, sometimes several times, without dying … certainly must have been adaptive during the glacial periods of the Pleistocene. In some species of amphibians glycogen from the liver is converted to glucose, which acts as an antifreeze. In others, such as the Old World salamander *Salamandrella keyserlingii*, converted glycerol is used (Holman, 2006, p. 204).

Of course, this only explains how they survived so well in extreme conditions, not how they evolved from non-salamanders by descent with modification as a result of the accumulation of mutations. The problem of "evolutionary stasis in North American Pleistocene Amphibians" also applies to salamanders: "Despite all the Pleistocene stresses that had to be coped with, North American salamanders appeared to exist in a state of evolutionary stasis during" this epoch (Holman, 2006, p. 203). The first salamanders were modern salamanders.

Caecilians

Caecilians (order *Gymnophiona*) are poorly known snakelike tropical amphibians that are long, legless, and tailless. Externally, they strongly resemble earthworms, but have several clear vertebrate characteristics, including teeth and a unique jaw-closing system (Mauro, et al., 2004). Caecilians commonly are found around swampy locations in most tropical regions, but seldom are seen because of their underground habitat. Their compact skulls contain recessed mouths and small eyes (Measey and Herrel, 2006, p. 485). A few species remain aquatic as adults and resemble eels. The approximately 50 known species range in size from 18 cm to 140 cm long and most are about 30 cm long.

Their bodies are ringed with grooves, and some species have small thin scales embedded in their skin, a feature that evolutionists label a primitive amphibian trait. Grooves on both sides of their head contain retractable sensory tentacles. Their eyes are nearly functionless, and some species lack eyes. Caecilians live in the ground and consume small invertebrates including termites and earthworms.

The phylogeny of the Gymnophiona is poorly understood and received little attention until recently (Nussbaum and Wilkinson, 1989, p. 1). The prevailing theory is that they evolved from a four-legged animal "in response to their specialized head-first burrowing lifestyle" (Measey and Herrel, 2006, p. 485). No fossil or other evidence exists for this view, but it is accepted because it is the most plausible theory of the many unlikely evolutionary scenarios (Measey and Herrel, 2006, p. 485). Nussbaum and Wilkinson concluded that "present knowledge does not allow establishment of a robust, phylogenetic classification of Caecilians" (1989, p. 1).

The first caecilians in the fossil record are found in the Lower Jurassic, and they are very similar to modern forms, thus have not changed since this time (Beltz, 2005, p. 22). Savage and Wake noted several theories about their origin, at least the origins of certain species, which they admitted were not based on relevant empirical evidence (2001, p. 60).

Hybridization Research

Many new hybridization studies are required to determine monobaramins (Hennigan, 2010). One hybridization study established that Linguaelapsus, Ambystoma-2 and Mexican ambystomatids are all part of a Salamander Monobaramin (Brophy and Kramer, 2007).

Conclusions

All three groups – the caecilians, urodeles and anurans – appear fully differentiated as far back as Jurassic sediments. Furthermore, many contrasts exist between the early tetropods and the amphibians. One of many examples is early tetrapods had a single bone in their middle ear, while modern amphibians have two bones.

As predicted by creationists, when amphibians first appeared in the fossil record, they were modern and very diverse in structure, as is also true today (Caldwell, 2003; Channing, 2001). This is true of frogs, salamanders, newts, and caecilians. Carroll observed that when they first appeared in the fossil record during the Jurassic

> both frogs and salamanders appear essentially modern in their skeletal anatomy. The described fossil record of Gymnophionans (caecilians) is limited to isolated vertebrae from the Upper Cretaceous and Paleocene that are very similar to those of modern genera (1988, p. 180).

According to Colbert, although logical explanations of frog evolution exist due to total lack of empirical evidence for their evolution, scientists "can only speculate about" amphibians' putative "change from an aquatic to a terrestrial mode of life" (Colbert and Morales, 2001, pp. 84-85). The evolutionary origins of frogs lack clear support in the fossil record, and because "the fossil material provides no evidence of ... the transformation from fish to tetrapod, paleontologists have had to speculate how legs and aerial breathing evolved" (Stahl, 1974, p. 195).

Enormous gaps exist in the Amphibia fossil record, and the largest gap is the origin of amphibians (Benton, 2005). Furthermore, most of the amphibians identified in the ancient fossil record are based on a few isolated bone fragments, thus are subject to revision as more fossils are discovered (Carroll, 1998, p. 116). Three evolutionists in a report on *amphibamid temnospondyl* from the Early Permian that supposedly "bridges the gap" stated in *Nature* that the "origin of extant amphibians (Lissamphibia: frogs, salamanders, and caecilians) is one of the most controversial questions in vertebrate evolution, owing to the large morphological and temporal gaps in the fossil record." (Anderson, et al. 2008.p. 515).

Because the first known frogs are extinct, but are clearly frogs, evolutionists conclude that the evolution of modern Anura had ceased during the Jurassic period. All frogs dated after this time clearly are modern frogs. In other words, the evidence shows that frogs have not changed during what evolutionists claim was over 200 million years! In conclusion, Colbert and Morales stated that "there is no evidence of any Paleozoic amphibians combining the characteristics that would be expected in a single common ancestor. The oldest known frogs, salamanders, and caecilians are very similar to their living descendants" (1991, p. 99).

The most recent careful evaluation of amphibians has determined that "herptofauna appears to have been in remarkable stasis since the onset of the Pleistocene, in other words, virtually unchanged for the last 1.64 million years" (Holman, 1998, p. 221). Holman concluded that there is

> no doubt that the herpetofaunas of the British Islands, the European continent, and North America have been strikingly more stable since the beginning of the Pleistocene than the endothermic faunas there. Moreover, this has been documented by hundreds of Pleistocene sites (Holman, 1998, pp. 221-222).

Why "Pleistocene herpetofaunal stasis" exists has not been explained by evolutionists, but they have faith that additional fossil studies may hold the answer (Holman, 1998, p. 222). In view of the existing large herpetofaunal fossil record, though, this appears very unlikely. A more recent study concluded

> The relationships of the three extant groups of amphibians (Anura, Urodela, Apoda) to each other, and the identification of their closest Palaeozoic relatives, have been subjects of controversy over the last century. The interrelationship of the modern groups continues to be controversial because neither morphological nor molecular cladistic analyses give a consistent pattern of relationships between the frogs, salamanders, and caecilians (Schoch and Milner, 2004, pp. 345-346).

This is true in spite of the wealth of evidence obtained (including new fossils and new nucleotide sequences) allowing for a revision of the current evolutionary theories (Kupriyanova, 2009, p. 819). As evolutionist Jennifer Clack recently concluded, one result of all of the attempts

> to unravel the origin or origins of modern amphibians is that the authors of the various ideas and analyses do not seem to be swayed by anyone else. Rather, they continue to retrieve their preferred hypotheses regardless of how

many characters or how many taxa they include in their attempts. This probably says as much about the methods of cladistic analysis and the way they are used as about the intractability of the problem (Clack, 2012, p. 385).

Creationism in general predicts variation within the created kinds, but stasis of the created kinds. Further research is required to better document the discontinuity between amphibians and their putative ancestors and the continuity within the amphibian kinds, which likely involves the frog, salamander, and caecilian kinds. The discontinuity in the amphibian fossil record is consistent with the creationary predictions of the creation of separate Genesis kinds.

References

Anderson, Jason S., Robert R. Reisz, Diane Scott, Nadia B. Fro"bisch and Stuart S. Sumida. 2008.. A stem batrachian from the Early Permian of Texas and the origin of frogs and salamanders. *Nature* v. 453:515-519. May 22.

Beltz, E. 2005. *Frogs: Inside Their Remarkable World*. Firefly Books, Buffalo, NY.

Benton, M. 2005. *Vertebrate Palaeontology*. Malden, MA: Blackwell.

Brophy, Timothy R. and Peter Kramer. 2007. Preliminary results from a baraminological analysis of the mole salamanders (Caudata: Ambystomatidae). *Occasional Papers of the BSG*, 10:10-11.

Brown, Robert. 1880. *Science for all*. Cassell, Peter, Galpin & Co. New York. Vol 3.

Caldwell, M. 2003. 'Without a leg to stand on:' On the evolution and development of axial elongation and limblessness in tetrapods. *Canadian Journal of Earth Science*, 40:573-588.

Carroll, Robert. 1988. *Vertebrate Paleontology and Evolution*. New York: W. H. Freeman.

_____. 1998. *Patterns and Processes of Vertebrate Evolution*. Cambridge University Press, Cambridge, United Kingdom.

Casselman, A. 2008. 'Frog-amander' Fossil may be amphibian missing link. *National Geographic News*. http://news.nationalgeographic.com/news/pf/3063026.html. May 21.

Channing, A. 2001. *Amphibians of Central and Southern Africa*. Cornell University Press, Ithaca, NY.

Clack, Jennifer. 2012 *Gaining Ground*, Indiana University Press, Second edition.

Colbert, E.H. and M. Morales. 1991. *Evolution of the Vertebrates*. John Wiley and Sons, New York, NY.

_____, and E. C. Minkoff. 2001. *Evolution of the Vertebrates: A History of the Backboned Animals Through Time,* 5th edition Wiley-Liss, New York, NY.

Darwin, Charles. 1871. *The Descent of Man and Selection in Relation to Sex.* London, John Murray.

Duffett, G. H. 1984. The adult common frog *Rana temporaria* L.: a linkological evaluation. *Creation Research Society Quarterly,* 20(4):199-211.

Dziewa, Thomas. 1980. Note on a Dipnoan Fish from the Triassic of Antarctica. *Journal of Paleontology.* 54(2):488-490.

Gao, K. and N. Shubin. 2003. Earliest Known Crown-Group Salamanders. *Nature,* 422:424-428.

Gianaro, C. 2003. New salamander species provide new answers to old questions in evolution. *The University of Chicago Chronicle* 22:1-3.

Gish, Duane. 1995. *The Fossils Still say No.* Institute for Creation Research, El Cajon, CA.

Hennigan, Tom. 2010. *Reproductive Thievery in Salamanders.* http://www.answersingenesis.org/articles/aid/v5/n1/reproductive-thievery-in-salamanders.

Holman, A. 1998. *Pleistocene amphibians and reptiles in Britain and Europe.* Oxford University Press, New York, NY.

_____. 2003. *Fossil Frogs and Toads of North America.* Indiana University Press, Bloomington, IN.

_____. 2006. *Fossil Salamanders of North America.* Indiana University Press, Bloomington, IN.

Jenkins, F. Jr. and N. Shubin. 1998. *Prosalirus* Bitis and the Anuran Caudopelvic Mechanism. *Journal of Vertebrate Paleontology.* 18:495-510. September.

Johnson, J. 2010. *The complete guide to reptiles and amphibians.* London: Burlington.

Johnson, Phillip. 1993. *Darwin on Trial*. Regnery Gateway, Washington, DC.

Kupriyanova, N.S. 2009. Current views of the origin and diversification of tetrapods. *Molecular Biology*. 42(5):819-833.

Marent, T. 2008. *The Frog*. DK Publishing, New York, NY.

Marjanovic, D., and M. Laurin. 2007. Fossils, molecules, divergence times, and the origin of lissamphibians. *Systematic Biology*. 56:369-388.

Mauro, D., D. Gower, O. Oommen, M. Wilkinson, and R. Zardoya. 2004. Phylogeny of Caecilian Amphibians (Gymnophiona) based on complete mitochondrial genomes and nuclear RAG1. *Molecular Phylogenetics and Evolution*, 33:413-427.

Measey, G. J. and A. Herrel. 2006. Rotational feeding in Caecilians: putting a spin on the evolution of cranial design. *Biology Letters* 2:485-487.

Min, M. S., S. Y. Yang, R. M. Bonett, D. R. Vieites, R. A. Brandon, and D. B. Wake. 2005. Discovery of the first Asian Plethodontid Salamander. *Nature* 435:87-90.

Noble, G. K. 1931. *The Biology of the Amphibia*. McGraw Hill, New York.

Nussbaum, R. A. and M. Wilkinson. 1989. On the Classification and Phylogeny of Caecilians (Amphibia: Gymnophiona), A Critical Review. *Herpetological Monographs*, 3:1-42.

Perlman, D. 2006. Salamanders' evolution traced. Berkeley, Chinese scientists say geologic movement is reason. May 19, 2006, *Chronicle Science*.

Poinar, G. 1992. *Life in Amber*. Stanford University Press, Stanford, CA.

_____ and R. Poinar. 1994. *The Quest for Life in Amber*. Reading, MA: Addison-Wesley /Helix Books.

_____ and R. Poinar. 1999. *The Amber Forest: A Reconstruction of a Vanished World.* Princeton University Press, Princeton, NJ.

Rage, J. and Z. Rocek. 1989. Redescription of *Triadobatrachus Massinoti* (Piveteau, 1936): An anuran amphibian from the early Triassic. *Palaeobotany/Palaeophytology,* 206:1-16.

Romer, A. 1966. *Vertebrate Paleontology.* Chicago, Il. The University of Chicago Press.

Savage, J. M. and M. H. Wake. 2001. Reevaluation of the Status of Taxa of Central American Caecilians (Amphibia: Gymnophiona), with Comments on Their Origin and Evolution. *Copeia* 1: 52-64.

Schoch, R. and A. Milner. 2004. Structure and implications of theories on the origin of lissamphibians. *Recent Advances in the Origin and Early Radiation of Vertebrates.* Pfeil, München, Germany pp. 345-377.

Stahl, Barbara. 1974. *Vertebrate History: Problems in Evolution.* Dover, New York, NY.

Wake, D. and V. Vredenburg. 2008. Are we in the midst of the sixth mass extinction? A view from the world of amphibians. *Proceedings of the National Academy of Sciences.* 105:11466-11473.

Woltering, Joost M., Daan Noordermeer, Marion Leleu, Denis Duboule. 2014. "Conservation and Divergence of Regulatory Strategies at Hox Loci and the Origin of Tetrapod Digits." *PLOS Biology.* 12(1):1-14. e1001773.

Chapter 10

Dinosaurs — Separating Conjecture from Confirmation

Introduction

Dinosaurs are "astonishing animals" that are a major topic of both popular interest and scientific study (Weishampel, *et al.*, 2007, p. 7). The discovery of dinosaurs in the early 1800s radically challenged our worldview and, especially, our view of the past (Croft, 1982, p. 12). Their study is an ideal area to evaluate evolution because an enormous amount of excellent fossil evidence exists. One reason for the excellent dinosaur fossil record is that their fossils are preserved better than those of most all other animals, such as the smaller hollow-boned birds, due to the dinosaur's large size and thick bones.

A large collection of dinosaur teeth, and even some soft tissues, have been preserved (Hwang, 2005; Lingham-Soliar, 2008). Since

235

abundant fossil evidence exists, if dinosaurs evolved from some primitive precursor, good fossil evidence for their evolution from their earlier ancestors should have been uncovered by now. However, the fossil evidence does not support their evolution from some lower forms of life.

The popular meaning of the term dinosaur is *terrible lizard* because of their size and assumed ferociousness. They were all terrestrial reptiles—members of the archosauria clade that had scaly skin and hatched their young from eggs. A few dinosaur species were enormous in size, but most were around the size of bulls, and a few were as small as chickens. Dinosaurs were not only huge, they "were the first land animals … designed for speed and agility" (Haines, 1999, p. 14). Most were excellent terrestrial runners, usually running on their toes due to their hip and ankle construction.

A problem is, in spite of the abundant fossil record, our "knowledge of dinosaurs is very fragmentary and much that has been written remains speculation" and "many authors have failed to differentiate between speculation and fact" (Croft, 1982, p. 9). Although much has been learned since this was written, it is still true that we know comparatively little about dinosaurs, partly because most of our knowledge is based on footprints, bones, teeth and a few body parts such as scales.

These parts make up only about ten percent of the animal (Croft, 1982, p. 9). The many major unknowns include their specific diet, although, judging by structures such as teeth, most types are classified either as herbivores or carnivores. Another controversy is if they were cold blooded (ectotherms), the common view in the past, or warm blooded (endotherms), a view which much evidence has accumulated to support (DeYoung, 2000, pp. 94-98).

Dinosaur Taxonomy

Dinosaurs are part of the archosauria (ancient lizard) clade that includes thecodontians saurischians, ornithschians, crocodilians, and flying pterosaurs (Weishampel et. al, 2007, p. 8). The only members of the archosauria clade still known to be alive today are crocodiles and alligators (Parker, 2000, p. 18). Dinosauria is divided up into two significantly distinct dinosaur families, those with bird-like hips that point downwards and towards the tail, the *ornithischians*, and those with lizard-like hips that point downwards and to the front, the *saurischians*. The saurischians include some small, slightly built reptiles and others that are large fierce animals believed to have evolved before dinosaurs. So far, all "attempts to relate these two types of dinosaurs to the Triassic pseudosuchians" have been problematic because "there appears to be a puzzling overlap in time between the two groups," and "possible evolutionary links between them obstinately refuse to appear" in spite of intense fossil research and the large existing fossil record (Cox, 1976, p. 314).

The saurischia are divided into the *theropods* (beast feet) that walked on two three-toed bird-like feet with sharp claws, and the *sauropods* (lizard feet), that walked on four feet, and had small heads, long necks, and bulky bodies such as *apatosaurs* (Cranfield, 2002). The ornithischians were a very large and varied group (Parker, 2000, p. 44). Even this basic classification has come under fire. Forster wrote that "most paleontologists now feel that we simply need to stop considering the Dinosauria as being composed of only the Saurischia and Ornithischia" (Forster, 2000, p. 46).

Paleontologists know almost nothing "about the early evolution of these creatures, and in particular, the evolution of the dinosaurs before the [putative] saurishian-ornithischian split" (2000, p. 46). The paleontology taxonomy system that formed the basis of modern taxonomy was problematic from the beginning of the discovery of dinosaurs to today. An example is when E.D. Cope and O.C. Marsh were competing

> for the glory of finding spectacular dinosaurs and
> mammals in the American West, they fell into a pattern
> of rush and superficiality born of their intense
> competition and mutual dislike. Both wanted to bag as
> many names as possible, so they published too quickly,
> often with inadequate descriptions, careless study, and
> poor illustrations. In this unseemly rush, they frequently
> gave names to fragmentary material that could not be
> well characterized and sometimes described the same
> creature twice by failing to make proper distinctions
> among the fragments … both Cope and Marsh often
> described and officially named a species when only a
> few bones had been excavated and most of the skeleton
> remained in the ground (Gould, 1991, p. 87).

So far, based on the 2500 fairly articulated specimens (most are only of a few species) , plus multi-thousands of partially complete skeletons, and, depending on what authority you consult, around 400 to 700 different dinosaur species have been identified (Novacek, 1996). Some estimate as many as around 1,000 species exist; but, as we find more fossils, the number tends to become reduced due to the fact that it becomes clear that fossils thought to be a separate species are part of an existing species. Some authorities estimate the current number could be reduced as much as 40 percent. Another problem is that about half of all putative species are known only by "a few teeth or bone scraps" (Horner and Lessem, 1993, p. 128).

In spite of decades of intensive effort by paleontologists, major disagreement about dinosaur classification still exists, which is one reason why determining their phylogeny is so difficult. The problems in dinosaur evolution are so severe that the most recent taxonomy proposal is not evolution or fossil tree based, but cladistic analysis using 107 anatomical traits (Weishampel et. al, 2007). The fact is, how "closely related one fossil animal is to another is very much a matter of opinion," and this is one reason why so much disagreement exists about their phylogeny.

The Origin of Dinosaurs

By the late Triassic, dinosaurs were abundant in number and variety around the world (Forster, 2000, p. 49). Their variety and abundance, coupled with a lack of any empirical evidence for their evolution, has resulted in many phylogeny proposals. One of the most common phylogeny theories today is that dinosaurs evolved from an alligator-like reptile. Haines wrote there is still a great deal of "controversy about how and when dinosaurs evolved. But the most popular current theory has dinosaurs first appearing as small, two-legged carnivores in the mid-Triassic, around 235 million years ago with a combination of features that marked them as different" (1999, p. 14).

The Archosaura reptiles (i.e., from which some believe the dinosaurs have descended) are thecodonts that first appeared in the fossil record during the Triassic (Benton, 1984, p. 144). Thecodont, a term meaning "socket toothed," were large heavy crocodile-like animals that crawled on all four legs low to the ground. They had long jaws and tails similar to crocodiles and, some argue, for these reasons they were only a type of primitive crocodile.

Other experts argue that thecodonts were an offshoot or branch of the line that led to the dinosaurs. This theory postulates that a thecodont's (or some other Archosaur's) limb position evolved to allow the dinosaur precursors to walk in a more upright position until they eventually could walk on their back legs, eventually becoming the dinosaurs that we know today from the fossil record. This speculation is not directly based on evidence but is the most plausible conjecture postulated for dinosaur evolution because all other possibilities are even less tenable. No fossil evidence exists for this widely accepted theory, or for any of the other less accepted theories.

Another candidate for the earliest direct dinosaur ancestor is a house-cat-sized animal named *Lagosuchus* that is believed by evolutionists to have lived in Argentina 235 million years ago (Horner and Lessem, 1993, p. 124). Some paleontologists speculate that "Lagosuchus or one of its relatives may have been the ancestor of the dinosaurs" because they possessed "many of the features thought to be present in [the] oldest dinosaurs" (Forster, 2000, p. 44). Unfortunately, so far only fragmentary remains of *Lagosuchus* and its kin have been discovered, so its status as the ancestor of the dinosaurs is highly speculative (Forster, 2000, pp. 44-45). Forster concluded, from the fragmentary *Lagosuchus* remains recovered so far that it is "probably not the ancestor" of dinosaurs, but "is at least closely related to the ancestors of the dinosaurs" (2000, p. 45). Others argue yet some other Archosaur that appeared in the late Permian, many of which strongly resemble crocodiles, were their ancestor (Richardson, 2003, pp. 40-41).

The "first dinosaurs are known from a small number of mostly incomplete specimens that so far have been found in only two locations in South America" (Forster, 2000, p. 42). Many other fossils are very incomplete, and/or badly damaged, requiring what is assumed to be a closely related animal called an analogy to fill in the missing parts (Shipman, 1986, p. 94). Analogies are problematic because they require the assumption that two similar fossils can be compared in detail. If two fossils have certain bone similarities, the analogue method assumes that they are also similar in ways that cannot be compared due to lack of physical evidence.

One popular theory is that some amphibians crawled out of the water, adapted to land, and eventually evolved into the *Crocodylotarsi* (crocodile ankle) that later evolved into the dinosaurs and the *Ornithosuchia* (bird-crocodile), which became the crocodilians (Forster, 2000, p. 44). Furthermore, the Thecodontians are theorized to have given rise to Theropods, which gave rise to the Saurischians, then to the Sauropods, Camosaurs, and Coelurosaurs (Croft, 1982, p. 19). Others speculate the Thecodontians also gave rise to the ornithischians, which gave rise to both the ornithopods and stegosaurs. From these groups evolved pachycephalosaurs, hadrosaurs, ceratopsians, and ankylosaurs (Croft, 1982, p. 9).

In the 1990s three widely accepted hypotheses of carnosauria (meat eating dinosaurs) origins existed. One hypothesis was that prosauropods were direct descendants from certain thecodontians. Another hypothesis is that carnosaurs were one monophyletic group called theropoda that evolved from Podokesauridae (Weishampel, 1990, p. 192). Another theory is that carnosaurs evolved from a primitive coelurosaur-like animal, a group of bird-like dinosaurs. These many theories all are unconstrained by fossil evidence; rather they rely on morphological comparisons and a great deal of conjecture. Consequently, the imaginations of Darwinists are allowed great freedom in developing a hypothesis. Some evolutionists reject all of these theories, concluding that dinosaurs evolved from some "unspecified quadrupeds" (Weishampel, 1990, p. 193).

The earliest known ornithischian dinosaur is *Pisanosaurus*, known by only one poorly preserved, badly weathered fragmentary skeleton discovered by Galileo Scaglia in Argentina (Forster, 2000, p. 46). Only some jaw parts, a shoulder blade fragment, parts of the hind leg, and a few vertebrae were found. Based on the small blunt teeth that lie side by side in the jaw, it was first judged to be a very early ornithischian (Forster, 2000, p. 46).

Although their teeth are characteristic of ornithischians, and not either herrerasaurids or saurischian dinosaurs, some paleontologists are not convinced that *Pisanosaurus* is even an ornithischian dinosaur. The fact that it was a small, lightly built animal only as large as a medium-sized dog indicates that it may not be a dinosaur at all, but rather an extinct animal of some type.

It is not known if it walked on two or four legs, but evidence suggests that it may have been bipedal (Forster, 2000, p. 47).

So much controversy exists about dinosaur origins that some argue for diphyletic (having two separate) dinosaur origins, others for three or four or more separate origins from different stem archosaurs (Fastovsky and Weishampel, 2005, p. 90). In the 1970s a revolution in dinosaur origins occurred, uniting not only saurischians and ornithischians, two very different animals, but also birds, into one clade, an idea widely accepted by the mid 1980s.

The group Class Thecodontia has now been abandoned by many paleontologists. Although the monophyletic view now dominates, evidence for "multiple roots of Dinosauria might still exist and in fact may be more obvious now that the cover of 'Thecodontia' has been blown" (Fastovsky and Weishampel, 2005, p. 91). The reason for these disagreements is because these theories are based largely on speculation, not fossil or genetic evidence (2005, p. 92).

The First Dinosaurs — Prosauropods

Darwinists postulate that one of the first group of dinosaurs to evolve was Prosauropoda, a group of which 17 genera are now known (Forster, 2000, pp. 18-50). The problem with the Prosauropoda origins theory is that they were common at the end of the Late Triassic, both contemporaneously with, as well as *after*, the dinosaurs that they supposedly evolved into (Forster, 2000, p. 50). The herbivorous monsters with long necks, bodies, and tails appeared in large numbers around the world, causing paleontologists to conclude that "they must have evolved and spread very rapidly around the ancient world" (Forster, 2000, p. 50). Forster concludes:

> Exactly what the ancestors of prosauropods were, what they looked like, and where the prosauropods evolved is still a mystery. Although the name prosauropod,

meaning "before-sauropods," implies they were the ancestors of the enormous sauropods, paleontologists now believe they did not give rise to the sauropods. They were already too specialized to have developed into the sauropods. The prosauropods and sauropods instead shared a common, yet unknown, ancestor, giving them a first cousin relationship (2000, p. 50).

Herrerasaurus

One of the earliest known well-documented animals described as early pre-dinosaurs are rather small bipedal theropods called Herrerasaurus that evolutionists date back to the Late Triassic about 245 million years ago. Herrerasaurus were usually four or five feet tall but may have grown as large as ten feet long and up to 500 pounds in weight, ran on their hind legs, and had huge teeth. So far only one complete skeleton has been found, allowing paleontologists to create a reasonably good picture of the animal (Forster, 2000, p. 47). The lone complete skeleton found in Argentina in 1988 is the earliest whole dinosaur skeleton known.

Because Herrerasaurus possess many dinosaur features shared by both Saurischia and Ornithischia, Herrerasaurus is considered their common ancestor by some, or at least related to their common ancestor. Others conclude that Herrerasaurus "wasn't a direct ancestor" of dinosaurs, "but it's the best we've got from that time" (Horner and Lessem, 1993, p. 125). Because it lacks many dinosaurian features, other paleontologists have concluded that Herrerasaurus was not even a dinosaur (Forster, 2000, p. 46) but another extinct reptile that happened to have some traits common with both Saurischia and Ornithischia. This confusion "shows how little we know about the early evolution of the dinosaurs" (Forster, 2000, p. 46). Novacek summarized another theory of dinosaur evolution that argues

> Dinosaurs are part of a whole range of forms called archosaurs, where familiar lineages like crocodiles also eventually branched off. But the details of this story — namely which kinds of other archosaurs are clearly the closest kin of the dinosaurs — are not decisively known. It has been suggested that the nearest relatives of dinosaurs may have been some early forms of the winged "flying reptiles," the pterosaurs. Thus dinosaurs might be rooted in the unknown ancestor that also gave rise to the pterosaurs (1996, p. 81).

In other words, some bird-like flying reptile evolved into a dinosaur, and dinosaurs in turn later evolved into birds. This claim illustrates the major problems that exist for determining even a tentative hypothetical dinosaur evolutionary phylogeny.

Dinosaur Phylogeny

Because Dinosauria appear in large numbers in many parts of the world, and the fossil record does not document their evolution, the whole dinosaur phylogeny field is rife with speculation. One of the most heated proposals involved a major rethinking in paleontology, which removed dinosaurs from class Reptilia and placing them in a new class called *Dinosauria* (Weishampel, 1990).

A major problem is, as so many dinosaurs are known only from fossil fragments, it is difficult to determine what species that many dinosaurs belong to. Determining if they are phylogenetic ancestors of some other animal is even more difficult (Forster, 2000, p. 47). An example is the discovery of three species that some paleontologists concluded were not three *separate* species (Herrerasaurus, Isehisaurus, and Frenguellisaurus) but one species, namely Herrerasaurus. Furthermore, many paleontologists consider another putative primitive early dinosaur, the staurikosaurus, to be a herrerasaurid as well. As Fastovsky and Weishampel conclude "so far, we haven't yet identified who within Archosauria might have the closest relationship to Dinosauria" (2005, p. 92).

Constructing phylogenic trees is another major problem. It has proved so difficult that parallel evolution has been proposed to explain the existing conflicting tree hypothesis:

> Many similarities in structural features among end forms of different archosaurian lines have not been inherited as such from a common ancestor but have been independently acquired by members of the different groups. This, however, does not debar such characters from consideration as indications of relationship. Study of fossil forms increasingly indicates that there has been an enormous amount of parallelism in evolution (Romer, 1966, p. 136).

Much confusion exists about the dinosaur's phylogeny for other reasons as well. An example is a dinosaur discovered in 1822 called Iguanodon. The find consisted of a few large teeth that were similar to iguana teeth, only much larger. For this reason, the creature was named Iguanodon, meaning Iguana-tooth, and was believed to be a giant iguana. Later, a partial skeleton was discovered and a new reconstruction resulted in a ponderous heavy creature with a large horn, indicating that the animal was a reptilian, a rhino, or a pachyderm equivalent. More fossil finds indicated its limbs were closer to a kangaroo than a pachyderm, producing a type of chimera. Next, research by T.H. Huxley discovered the creature had a pelvis and hind limbs like a ground-dwelling bird similar to an emu. With more discoveries it looked more like the picture we have of a type of duck-billed dinosaur. Clearly, basing phylogeny on a few specific traits is very problematic.

The Fossil Record

The fossil record indicates that dinosaurs were "extremely rare in the early part of the Late Triassic," but by the end of the Triassic, entirely "new groups of dinosaurs" had rapidly "spread worldwide in an ever-increasing array of species" without leaving a trace of fossil evidence for their evolution (Forster, 2000, p. 49). The fact is, no one knows the reason for this "ever-increasing array" of new species, nor do we have any fossil evidence to document their evolution—abrupt appearance is the only term that can describe what the fossil record reveals.

Based on an extensive study of the fossil record, Fastovsky and Weishampel concluded that the likelihood of determining the progenitor of any one lineage being fossilized is nil (2005, p. 92). This is true in spite of the fact that dinosaur bones usually are very easy to identify because many dinosaur species have several unique physical traits, such as an extra hole in their skull, grasping hands, and specialized ankle-bones

> but it is dinosaurs' hips that are most distinctive. They had five fused sacral vertebrae that helped to create a very strong hip. Together with a specialized socket for the thigh bone, this gave dinosaurs their powerful upright posture. A long tail put their center of balance firmly over the pelvis, allowing them to run on two legs. This also freed their front limbs for catching food. All this was helped by a highly specialized skeleton. Many of their bones contained air sacs, like birds, and in the course of evolution they reduced many bones that were not absolutely necessary for structural strength. For their size, dinosaurs were probably surprisingly light (Haines, 1999, p. 14).

One process employed to help determine a dinosaur's ancestry is to use a hierarchy of characters in a cladogram to determine what features should exist in an ancestor. The next step is to find evidence of

> an organism that most closely matches the expected combinations of characters and character states. As we have seen, the likelihood of the very progenitor of lineage being fossilized is nil; however, we can commonly find representatives of closely related lineages that embody most of the features of the hypothetical ancestor (Fastovsky and Weishampel, 2005, p. 92).

The next section looks at some specific examples.

Tyrannosaurus Rex

The most well-known dinosaur is *Tyrannosaurus rex*, an 18 foot tall, 42 foot long, 14,000 pound monster, the largest carnivore that has ever lived. It was classified as a theropod, a meat-eating hollow thin-walled boned animal that can range in size from the Placodus to the ichthyosaur *Cymbospondylus*. All dinosaurs are postulated to have evolved from an animal the size of a chicken. So far 32 *T. rex* specimens have been located, half of which are close to complete (Weishampel, 2004). Horner and Lessem wrote "*T. rex* was the last and most spectacular product of dinosaur evolution. It was an experiment that can't be repeated" (1993, p. 124).

Darwinists estimate that dinosaurs first evolved 235 million years ago, the *T. rex* ancestors 190 million years ago, and the first *T. rex* about 70. How they know this from only 32 specimens is unknown. So far not a single direct *T. rex* ancestor has been located. Potential ancestors, including Coelophysis, Herrerasaurus, Eoraptor, and Allosaurus, all have been eliminated by most experts as possible *T. rex* ancestors.

Two fossil specimens considered by some paleontologists to be the most primitive *T. rex* fossils are a dinosaur called Guanlong Wucaii (Xu, et al., 2006). This dinosaur, identified as a *T. rex* ancestral link from the teeth and pelvic structures, is a nine-foot-long adult that had a crested head about 2.5 inches tall that was as thin as a tortilla. The crest is assumed to be an ornamental feature used to attract mates.

The leading *T. rex* experts, Horner and Lessem, admit the animal that the *T. rex* and the tyrannosaurids evolved from is unknown, "maybe they came from the allosaur line of big predators, maybe they came from a common ancestor, along with the Troodontids, a man-sized group of dinosaurs with many birdlike features" (Horner and Lessem, 1993, p. 127). Horner and Lessem admit that, although "you can imagine a hypothetical ancestral tyrannosaurid," no evidence of this hypothetical ancestor has ever been found. They conclude that a logical *T. rex* dinosaur ancestor is a meat-eating creature, but "which one we can't say yet" (1993, p. 127).

Another problem is that dinosaurs were not primitive as the word normally is defined. An example is the intelligent design of the *T. rex* eye. It has been assumed that they had very poor, fuzzy vision, but recent research has shown that they were able to achieve very detailed images similar to that of many modern animals (DeYoung, 2000, pp. 120-121). Many other examples exist to show that dinosaurs were very well designed for their environments.

Figure 10.1 – A Reconstructed Fossil Tyrannosaurus[1]

---

[1] Photo Credit: David Herraez Calzada / Shutterstock.com

Horned Dinosaurs

Horned dinosaurs (ceratopsids) were very successful animals that lived throughout the Northern Nemisphere (Norman and Wellnhofer, 2000, p. 134). The ceratopsians (horned face) had shelf-like ridges or expanded areas around their skull edges and a sharp, narrow parrot-like beak (Parker, 2003, p. 353). They ranged from the size of a pig to twice the size of large rhinoceroses, which they resembled. The best known horned dinosaur, and one of the largest, was the Triceratops. Triceratops, meaning "three horned face," is an ornithischian dinosaur that has a pelvis shape similar to that of birds, a crown like a hat, plus three large horns, two on its head and one on its snout.

Since their horns preserve well and "literally hundreds of remains (including complete skeletons) of these dinosaurs" have been uncovered, horned dinosaurs as a group are excellent examples to determine the limits of evolution. Although hundreds of Triceratop skeletons, many very complete, have been found since the first one was uncovered in 1855, no evidence of their evolution has ever been uncovered. This is especially problematic for Darwinists because *Triceratops* are the largest horned dinosaur known and easily identified by its very unique skeletal traits, especially its distinctive skull and horns. In one fossil location alone, thirty-two triceratops skulls were recovered.

One theory is that *Triceratops* evolved from "bipedal ancestors not unlike *Psitta*cosaurus or *Microceratops*," but the only evidence for this theory is their morphological similarity. Since no fossil evidence exists to support any evolution theory, this speculation remains an assumption (Norman and Wellnhofer, 2000, p. 136). Parker concluded that horned dinosaurs "were, in general, a group that underwent relatively little evolution, as is evident from the many thousands of specimens that have been found in hundreds of sites" (2003, p. 373).

The fossil record shows that "the horned dinosaurs were relatively "conservative," a term used to describe a group that does not change very much from its original basic shape and form, despite a long time for evolution to occur" (Parker, 2003, p. 373). In other words, as is true of all dinosaurs, they appeared suddenly in the fossil record as fully developed horned dinosaurs and did not change until they became extinct. They have been dated all the way back to the very end of the dinosaur age. Norman and Wellnhofer wrote the evolutionary "relations of the so-called short-frilled ceratopids are not clear. Each is so distinct that [their] kinship is not at all obvious" (2000, p. 134).

Another very early dinosaur, *Ornithodesmus*, was first identified as a terrestrial pterosaur (Parker, 2003, p. 159). Further studies concluded it was not a pterosaur, but rather a small dinosaur. Many examples of dinosaur reclassification could be cited, such as fossils first identified as ornithodesmus that have been regrouped back in with the pterosaurs! Eight named and one unnamed species of Troodontidae exist, and four phylogenetic hypotheses have been proposed to explain their origins (Weishampel *et al.*, 2007, p. 93).

Clearly, the "evidence is limited and there continue to be many disagreements" in the field of dinosaur phylogeny that often are so serious that they call into question the whole basis of dinosaur macroevolution (Parker, 2003, p. 159). The enormous differences between pterosaurs and ornithodesmus illustrate the difficulty of even determining the type that a set of dinosaur bone fragments belongs to, even if a complete skeleton, which is only five percent or less of the whole animal. Identifying evolutionary transitional forms is even more difficult.

Conclusions

Over 30 million dinosaur bones and parts, some in excellent states of preservation, have been identified and, although much speculation exists, not a single documented plausible direct ancestor has yet been located. All known dinosaurs appear fully formed in the fossil record. As Forster admits "much mystery remains about the origin of the dinosaurs" (2000, p. 42). Several possible evolutionary candidates have been suggested, but difficulties exist with all of them, and most are likely only extinct reptiles and not evolutionary links. Furthermore, confusion about dinosaurian phylogeny has reigned for more than a century in spite of the discovery of enormous fossil evidence.

For this reason, other methods have been utilized to determine their phylogeny. Since 1980, cladistic methods have revolutionized our views of their phylogeny. Computer algorithms have also been used to produce similarity comparisons, often using contemporaneously existing species that are limited in helping us to determine their evolutionary history.

Benton concludes that so "many riddles remain unsolved" that "a single fossil find can sometimes provide us with exciting new evidence and provide all new theory" (1984, p. 142). How dinosaurs "came to be" are "questions pondered since the creation of the name by Sir Richard Owen just over 150 years ago" and are still being pondered (Fastovsky and Weishampel, 2005, p. 87). We can conclude with the following observation, which is still true today:

> Although many pages have been written discussing the mystery of the extinction of the dinosaurs, almost as much uncertainty surrounds their origin — or origins. …
> the poor paleontologist searching for answers is therefore, in the origin of the dinosaurs, confronted with

complexity where he hoped for simplicity, while in the replacement of the pseudosuchians by their varied offspring he meets a sudden (if delayed) simple event where he expected complexity (Cox, 1976, p. 314).

The more paleontological discoveries that are made, the more that we realize our knowledge of dinosaur types is fairly complete, and no ancestral forms ever will be found because they do not exist. As a result, paleontologists are forced to conjecture about their ancestors based on very little physical evidence and a lot of speculation. In conclusion, no credible evidence exists for dinosaur evolution from a primitive precursor animal, supporting the creation model. Dinosaurs appear suddenly and, evidently, also went extinct rather suddenly.

References

Bakker, Robert T., and Peter M. Galton. 1974. "Dinosaur Monophyly and a New Class of Vertebrates." *Nature*, 248:168-172.

Benton, Michael. 1984. *The Dinosaur Encyclopedia*. New York, NY: Aladdin.

Cox, Barry. 1976. "Mysteries of Early Dinosaur Evolution." *Nature*. 264: 314.

Cranfield, Ingrid. 2002. *The Illustrated Dictionary of Dinosaurs*. London, U.K.: Salamander Books.

Croft, L.R. 1982. *The Last Dinosaurs: A New Look at the Extinction of the Dinosaurs*. Haslam Printers Ltd, Chorley, Lancashire, UK.

DeYoung, Don. 2000. *Dinosaurs and Creation*, Grand Rapids, MI: Baker.

Dixon, Dougal. 2004. *The Pocket Book of Dinosaurs*. Salamander Books, London, U.K.

Fastovsky, David E. and David B. Weishampel. 2005. *The Evolution and Extinction of the Dinosaurs,* 2nd Edition. Cambridge University Press, New York, NY.

Forster, Catherine. 2000. "The First Dinosaurs" chapter 2 pp. 41-52 in R. Silverberg. editor, *The Ultimate Dinosaur*. Ibooks, New York, NY a division of Simon and Schuster.

Gould, Stephen. 1991. *Bully for Brontosaurus*. New York, NY: Norton.

Haines, Tim. 1999. *Walking with Dinosaurs*. BBC Worldwide Ltd, London, UK.

Horner, John R. and Don Lessem. 1993. *The Complete T. Rex*. Simon and Schuster, New York, NY.

Hwang, Sunny H. 2005. Phylogenetic Patterns of Enamel Microstructure in Dinosaur Teeth. *Journal of Morphology* 266: 208-240.

Lingham-Soliar, Theagarten. 2008. "A Unique Cross Section Through the Skin of the Dinosaur *Psittacosaurus* from China

Showing a Complex Fibre Architecture." *Proceedings of the Royal Society B.* 275(1636):775-780.

Norman, David, and Peter Wellnhofer. 2000. *The Illustrated Encyclopedia of Dinosaurs: An Original and Compelling Insight into Life in the Dinosaur Kingdom.* Salamander Books, London, U.K.

Novacek, Michael. 1996. *Dinosaurs of the Flaming Cliffs.* New York, NY: Doubleday Anchor.

Parker, Steve. 2000. *The Encyclopedia of the Age of the Dinosaurs.* Surry, Great Britain: Pegasus.

Parker, Steve. 2003. *Dinosaurs: The Complete Guide to Dinosaurs.* Crescent Richmond Hill, Ontario, Canada: Firefly Books.

Richardson, Hazel. 2003. *Dinosaurs and Prehistoric Life.* New York, NY: Dorling Kindersley.

Romer, Alfred. 1966. *Vertebrate Paleontology.* Chicago, IL: University of Chicago Press.

Shipman, Pat. 1986. "How a 125 Million-Year-Dinosaur Evolved in 160 Years." *Discover.* 7(10):94-102.

Weishampel, David (editor). 1990. *The Dinosauria.* University of California Press, Berkeley, CA.

Weishampel, David, Peter Dodson, and Halszka Osmolska (Editors). 2007. *The Dinosauria. Second Edition.* Berkeley, CA: University of California Press.

Xu, Xing, James M. Clark, Catherine A. Forster, Mark Norell, Gregory M. Erickson, David A. Eberth, Chengkai Jia and Qi Zhao. 2002. A basal Tyrannosauroid Dinosaur from the Late Jurassic of China. *Nature.* 439: 715-718.

Chapter 11

Birds — Sky Creatures in the Rocks

Introduction

After carefully reviewing the literature on the evolution of birds, the authors discovered most of these theories could be refuted. Evolutionary science's most recent theory is that birds evolved from dinosaurs. We briefly discuss this idea, noting that a number of leading paleontologists are critical of the theory. It would take a book to fully detail the problems with birds evolving from dinosaurs. This chapter is a brief discussion of its most glaring flaws.

The Wonder of Birds

Birds (Class Aves/Avis) are winged, feathered, bipedal, and endothermic (warm-blooded). They are hard-shelled egg-laying vertebrates that have horny bills instead of the teeth that are typically found in many reptiles (Witmer, 1995, p. 9). They are programmed to achieve complex activities, such as building intricate nests and singing elaborate songs. Of all the higher life forms except humans and dogs, birds are the most beautiful, melodious, admired, studied, and defended (Peterson, 1963, p. 9, Snow 2006, p 7).

All living bird species possess wings, except the now extinct flightless Moa of New Zealand. With the exception of ratites (Ostrich etc.), penguins, and several diverse endemic island species, all are excellent flyers. The entire anatomy and physiology of birds is uniquely designed around their flight capabilities. Other designs unique to birds include an elegant locking mechanism in their toes which insures they don't fall off their perches while sleeping. Their navigational skills are unsurpassed in the animal world:

> The amazing navigational skills shown by migratory birds are believed to result from tiny magnetic crystals set in the upper beak, creating a compass, combined with an astounding ability to memorize features of land and sky, such as star patterns. Most long distance movements occur at night but some birds may set out on complex migratory paths following specific foods by day, without actually leaving their country (Cusack, 2008, p. 64).

Their flying feats are astounding — peregrine falcons can fly as fast as 180 miles per hour and have been clocked diving at circa 245 mph.[1] Bar-head geese can fly at over 5 ½ miles altitude, which is higher than Mt. Everest. Many bird species undertake annual long-distance flights. These are often grueling and little short of miraculous, like the Arctic Terns yearly average of 44,000 miles

---

[1] *The Falcon that Flew with Man*, Leo Dickinson Films

from pole to pole migrations. Many others fly shorter annual migrations. Birds truly stand far apart from all other animals (Witmer, 1995, p. 10).

The Enormous Variety of Birds

Birds are among the most successful of all land animals—an estimated 300 billion birds are living at any one time (Witmer, 1995, p. 10). They are also the most varied of all known chordates (O'Donoghue, 2010, p. 36). There exist about twice as many kinds of birds as mammals.

An estimated 10,000 living bird species inhabit every known ecosystem from the Arctic to the Antarctic. This includes desert, temperate and tropical lands, and even open sea and ice. Significantly, this enormous variety extends all the way back to the origin of birds (Chiappe, 1995, p. 248).

Extant birds range in size from the 5-cm (2-in)-long Bee Hummingbird to the 2.75-m (9-ft)-long ostrich. Close to 130 species have become extinct as a result of human activity since the 17th century, and hundreds more before then. An estimated 1,200 bird species are currently threatened with extinction. Efforts now are underway to try to insure that this does not happen (Steele, 1991; Gurevitch and Padilla, 2004).

Birds are social animals that communicate using visual signals, calls, and songs, which are often very rich, individual, and beautiful. These vary hugely, according to the species. Their social behaviors include cooperative breeding, hunting, flocking, migrating, and mobbing of predators. Some birds, including parrots and corvids, are among the most intelligent animal species known. A number of bird species have been observed using—and even making—tools. Many social animals, including birds and bees, exhibit the transmission of cultural knowledge, which includes bird songs, feeding, and nest sites, across generations.

The vast majority of bird species are monogamous, usually for one breeding season, but sometimes for years, and some, as Mute Swans, for a lifetime. Furthermore, both parents (and sometimes even sub adults) in more than 90 percent of all bird species share in the care of the young. Eggs are usually laid in a nest built by the parents and then incubated by both. After hatching it is normal for them to provide their offspring with an extended period of parental care.

Evidence for Bird Evolution

Birds actually are ideal animals for studying evolution because their fossils preserve very well in certain environments. Over 9,000 living species are now known, all which have a very unique skeletal morphology, yet only 45 extinct bird taxa have ever been identified (Davis and Dyke, 1999, p. 162), thus providing strong evidence that relatively few types of non-modern birds have existed throughout history. This conclusion is supported by the fact that, of 329 living families of terrestrial vertebrates, fully 79 percent have been found as fossils, as have 97.7 percent of the 43 living terrestrial vertebrate orders (Denton, 1986, p. 189).

The most common theory of bird evolution is they evolved from "the culmination of a long process of development. For millions of years this process has been going on, building up in the race for perfect mastery of the air which we so easily take for granted" (Aymar, 1935, p. 1).

Thomas Henry Huxley first proposed in the 1800s that birds evolved from some dinosaur-like creature. He noted the bone structure of a small rooster-sized dinosaur called *compsognathus* and *Archaeopteryx lithographica* were very bird-like, and the skeleton of certain modern birds, such as ostriches, looked remarkably similar to many dinosaur skeletons (Stone, 2010).

In spite of skeletal similarities, the entire field of the "origin of birds and avian flight … has been among the most contentious issues in paleobiology" (Feduccia et al., 2005, p. 125). In 2010, O'Donoghue, states on pg. 36: "the evolutionary history of birds has long been an enigma. Ever since a single fossil feather was dug up 150 years ago the origin of birds has been one of biology's most contentious issues."

The origin of birds is one of the most problematic fields in evolution for many reasons. They include a complete lack of uncontested fossil evidence, excepting the very controversial Archaeopteryx , and "Protoavis" (meaning "first bird") discovered in 1948 by Sankar Chatterjee (1997) of Texas Tech University. Chatterjee described Protoavis as a modern, 35-cm-tall crow-like bird. It is regarded by its supporters as "much more closely related to modern neornithine (the latest common ancestors of all extant birds) birds than is Archaeopteryx" (Chiappe, 1995, p. 349). Protoavis fragmentary remains are from Late Triassic deposits near Post, Texas. Chatterjee concluded his specimen was from a single species that lived, according to his estimates, 210 million years ago in what is now Texas. When first described, the fossils were believed to be a primitive bird. If the identification is valid, it would push avian origins, according to evolutionists, back some 60-75 million years. Hence, many have rejected the validity of this find!

Though it existed far earlier than Archaeopteryx, as presented by Chatterjee, its skeletal structure appears to be more bird-like. The animal had teeth on the tip of its jaws and eyes located at the front of its skull, indicating a nocturnal or crepuscular lifestyle. A recent re-evaluation of the fossil material has convinced most paleontologists that Protoavis is not a bird and that all the remains did not come from a single species. Its fossils were found in a jumbled cache of disarticulated bones that indicate mass mortality following a 'flash flood.' As a result, Archaeopteryx "stands alone in the fossil record of birds of the end of the Jurassic period"

(Chiappe, 2009, p. 253). Archaeopteryx origin theory is also problematic because "Archaeopteryx has always been considered to be the most primitive as well as the most ancient bird. Yet its strange mix of traits—the teeth, legs, claws, and tail of a dinosaur but the wings and feathers of a bird—continues to raise doubts about its true affinities. Recent discoveries have only added to the enigma" (O'Donoghue, 2010, p. 36).

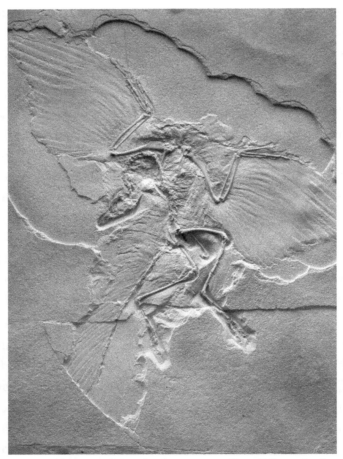

Figure 11.1—*Archaeopteryx* Fossil Imprint[2]

---

[2] Photo Credit: MikhailSh / Shutterstock.com

After the "discovery of *Archaeopteryx*, no other reptile-bird intermediates were found for many years, leaving a gaping hole between modern birds and their ancestors" (Coyne, 2009, p. 40). Although Coyne claims that a "spate of astonishing discoveries from China began to fill in the gap" none of these discoveries actually even begins to fill this enormous void. Almost all of the examples that Coyne lists of so-called proto-feathered dinosaurs, or putative feathered dinosaurs, have been refuted because of questionable research; furthermore, they are all far 'younger' than Archaeopteryx.

> ...findings show no evidence for the existence of protofeathers and consequently no evidence in support of the follicular theory of the morphogenesis of the feather. Rather, based on histological studies of the integument of modern reptiles, which show complex patterns of the collagen fibers of the dermis, we conclude that "protofeathers" are probably the remains of collagenous fiber "meshworks" that reinforced the dinosaur integument. These "meshworks" of the skin frequently formed aberrant patterns resembling feathers as a consequence of decomposition. Our findings also draw support from new paleontological evidence (Feduccia, et al., 2005, p. 125).

Alan Feduccia (1999, p. 404) laments the huge gap (c. 90 million years ago) between the archetypal "First Bird," *Archaeopteryx lithographica,* and modern fossil discoveries, such as the Chinese, so-called "proto-feathered" dinosaurs. Benton added that "it has become clear that ... 30 or more characteristics ... distinguish the small flying Archaeopteryx from ground-dwelling carnivorous dinosaurs (theropods)" (Benton, 2014, p. 508). The contrast between cold-blooded and "massive ground-dwelling theropod dinosaurs" and warm-blooded, often small, "light, volant birds," meaning those capable of flying, is enormous (Lee, et al., 2014).

The Fossil Record

The major problem for evolutionists is "of all the classes of vertebrates, the birds are least known from their fossil record" (Colbert, 2001, p. 236). Actually, bird fossils are very common, but not usually of the "correct" sort or age! For, of the many bird and other fossils discovered so far, none help to bridge the enormous gap between birds and any of their theorized ancestors. Many bird fossils are extinct birds, some rather different from modern birds, but all that appear in the fossil record are fully formed birds. A large chronological and phylogenetic gap even exists between the so-called "First Bird," Archaeopteryx, and the life forms postulated to be the key to avian origins. This gap cannot be explained away by the putative "Feathered Dinosaurs" (Chiappe, 1995, p. 349).

Another problem is that not much weight "can be placed in single fossil elements or bone fragments that have so frequently been described from both the Cretaceous and early Tertiary: regretfully, many must simply be ignored" (Feduccia, 1996, p. 165). Unfortunately, many ancient birds, like many other fossil life-forms, consist only of fragmentary evidence.

The lack of fossil evidence for bird evolution is often explained by postulating an extraordinarily explosive evolution of birds, one that produced all living orders within a "short time frame like the Cambrian explosion" (Feduccia, 1996, p. 167). In other words, the "tremendous diversity of early avian" animals documents an avian evolutionary explosion similar to the Cambrian explosion. For this reason, the origin of birds has stirred "intense, nearly century-long, controversies" (Ruben, 2010, p. 2733).

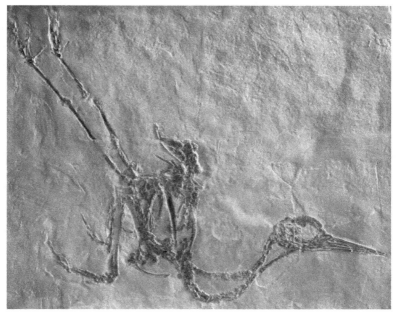

Figure 11.2—Bird Fossil from Green River, Wyoming[3]

One very early theory postulated birds evolved from an early species of dinosaur. It fell out of favor when Professor Heilmann published a "hugely influential book" in 1926. He argued the now carefully refuted theory that birds "evolved from a primitive archosaur reptilian group which also gave rise to dinosaurs, pterosaurs, and crocodiles" (O'Donoghue, 2010, p. 38).

In a classic 1935 book on birds (Aymar, 1935, p. 1), an entire chapter was devoted to their evolution. It concluded that it is "among the reptiles that we must look for the origin of" birds in the fossil record. It is for this and other reasons that for the past century and a half, evolutionists have continued to look among the reptiles for bird evolution. Although no valid evidence for bird origins has been discovered, there have been some hotly debated discoveries,

_____

[3] Photo Credit: Mark Higgins / Shutterstock.com

including the dinosaur "proto feathers" noted above.

The Aymar text includes sections on Archaeopteryx, Archaeornis, the Dodo, and others, but admits there is still no good evidence for bird evolution. Actually, no significant progress has been made on bird evolution since 1935, although Whetstone and Martin claim that a recent upheaval in bird evolution theory has occurred:

> During the period 1926-73 most ornithologists and vertebrate palaeontologists supported Heilmann's theory of avian origins. Heilmann argued that all dinosaurs and pterosaurs were too specialized to have been ancestral to birds. Instead he chose to derive birds directly from a primitive group of Triassic archosaurs, the Pseudosuchia. Heilmann's theory has recently been challenged by Walker, who has suggested that birds evolved from an early crocodilian, and by Ostrom, who argued that birds descended from theropod dinosaurs (1979, p. 234).

Currently, the most popular theory is the evolution of birds evolved from a theropod dinosaur during the Jurassic period, about 150 to 200 million years ago. Many paleontologists regard birds as the only dinosaur clade to have survived the Cretaceous–Tertiary extinction event, approximately 65.5 million years ago. Colbert writes that it "has long been evident that birds are descended from archosaurian reptiles, and for many years it was thought that they had a theocodont ancestry ... Thus, in one sense, dinosaurs did not become completely extinct because one line of theropods evolved into all the birds alive today." (Colbert, et al., 2001, p. 230).

Colbert adds that, although the "majority of workers today hold the view that birds are descendants of theropods," a small group of paleontologists have concluded that

...the similarities between birds, especially Archaeopteryx, and small theropods are the result of convergent evolution in the two lineages from a common ancestor that was an advanced ornithosuchian thecodont. In this minority view, theropods and birds are not ancestor and descendant, respectively, but rather are sister groups that evolved from the same ancestor group (Colbert, 2001, p. 230).

The main evidence for the conventional view of dinosaur-to-bird evolution are the commonalities between birds and certain dinosaurs, similarities in bone structures existing at both macroscopic and microscopic levels. The largest problems include the many anatomical and size differences and the fact that both dinosaur and bird fossils are commonly found together in the fossil record. But, no set of existing fossils shows that vital set of intermediate transitional forms.

From Which Dinosaur Did Birds Evolve?

The controversy about bird origins includes the question of whether they evolved from dinosaurs or from more primitive archosaurs. Dinosaur origins researchers disagree about whether ornithischian or theropod dinosaurs were more likely to be the ancestors of birds. The controversy results from the fact that little or no evidence of fossil transitions exists to support either theory. Although Ornithischian (bird-hipped) dinosaurs share the basic hip structure of modern birds, confusingly for evolutionists, it is the Saurischian (lizard-hipped) dinosaurs that have more similarities to birds. As a result they are more widely accepted as the ancestor of birds.

For this reason, some evolutionists argue that birds must have evolved their ornithischian hip structure independently of dinosaurs, always keeping in mind the massive problems with

Neo-Darwinian evolution's only mechanisms, genetic mutation, which is overwhelmingly retrograde or neutral, and 'Natural Selection,' that is only able to winnow existing structures, not create new ones. A bird-like hip structure is postulated to have evolved at least three separate times, the third time among a group of theropods known as the Therizinosauridae. Other ornithologists argue, based on fossil and other evidence, that birds are not dinosaurs at all, but actually evolved from some early archosaur such as Longisquama, which appears to be some sort of flying lizard.

The 1913 discovery of the small carnivorous animal Euparkeria, the best-known member of the pseudosuchians (false crocodiles), seemed to have solved the mystery of the origin of birds. It had a collarbone and could run either bipedally or on all fours. Best of all, it appeared to have lived earlier than any known fossil bird (Witmer, 1995, p. 32). The Euparkeria origins theory became so well accepted that "for over fifty years the problem of the origin of birds was thought to be solved" (Witmer, 1995, p. 32).

The theory hypothesized that pseudosuchians were the ancestors of not only birds, but also pterosaurs, dinosaurs, and, later, Archosaurs, egg-laying ancestors of both crocodilians and birds (Witmer, 1995, p. 32). The Euparkeria theory was not seriously questioned until the 1970s. Since then at least a dozen theories of bird origins have been advanced, several of which will be reviewed here, and all of which have their critics who have articulated good reasons why each theory cannot be scientifically valid. Feduccia, *et al.* (2005), writes that before

> ... the 1970s birds and dinosaurs were thought to have shared a common ancestry through Triassic basal archosaurs, often collectively termed thecondonts, characterized by the Triassic *Euparkeria*. But with John Ostrom's discovery of the bird-like Early Cretaceous

Deinonychus, the dinosaurian origin of birds gained ascendancy as the reigning dogma, based on overall similarity of this newly discovered dromaeosaur to birds and *Archaeopteryx* (Witmer, 2005, 125).

One theory challenging the Euparkeria hypothesis was proposed in 1972, and suggested that birds evolved from crocodylomorphs, an animal similar to crocodiles. This idea was based on comparisons of the ear region of living birds and crocodiles and comparisons between fossil reptiles and dinosaurs. Whetstone and Martin rejected the dinosaurian ancestry for birds, concluding "advanced features in the ear region support a common ancestry for crocodiles and birds, independent of both saurischian and ornithischian dinosaurs" (1979, p. 236). Another supportive study is by Hedges who found strong backing for a bird-crocodilian relationship when he analyzed comparisons of molecular sequence data. He concluded the data pointed to birds evolving not from dinosaurs but crocodiles[4] (Hedges, 1994)!

The crocodylomorph that birds were considered to be most closely related to was the sphenosuchus, a bizarre, quadrupedic "leggy, doc-croc"! Although the external morphology of crocodylomorphs and birds is very different, they possess a number of critical skull similarities, including their teeth shapes, their ear region details, jawbone attachment system and skull cavity design (Witmer, 1995, p. 33). The theory soon lost favor mostly because there are too many major differences in external morphology, and a new discovery, the *deinonychus*, came along that appeared more plausible. So, as can be seen, theories frequently clash and reverse almost as fast as fashions!

---

[4] In personal correspondence, dated June 10, 2016, Professor Jon Ahlquist noted in their DNA hybridization research done at Yale, crocodilians were closet to birds.

Deinonychus as the Link to Birds

A fourth theory is that birds evolved from Coelurosaurs (Greek, meaning "hollow tailed lizards"), then into Ornithurines (meaning short, bird tails, which include Ichthyornis, Hesperornis, Hongshanornis, and Gansus), and finally into modern birds, a theory that Cusack admitted has "great gaps" (Cusack, 2008, pp. 24, 44). Other paleontologists concluded birds evolved from pterosaurs (leathery-winged, flying reptiles), due to the many structural similarities they share with birds (Witmer, 1995, p. 30).

Still other paleontologists concluded birds could not have evolved from any type of dinosaur because dinosaurs were "too specialized to have been the ancestors of birds" (Witmer, 1995, p. 30). Additional problems with dinosaur-to-bird theory include the many major structural differences that exist between birds and dinosaurs—birds have wishbones and, with the exception of very few dinosaurs and pterosaurs, do not possess a collarbone. This controversy illustrates the clear limitations of using morphology as a basis for postulating evolutionary ancestry. The observation that many creatures share similar structures or blueprints, known as Homology, far better illustrates the reality of a master Creator rather than random evolution.

Another theory postulates birds evolved from a small upright, bipedal, carnivorous theropod coelurosaurian dinosaur called *Compsognathus* (Ostrom, 1973, p. 136). *Compsognathus* are not Ornithischian (bird-hipped) but Saurischian (lizard-hipped) dinosaurs. Ornithurines both were judged to be "more advanced in design than their contemporary 'cousins'" and also had some "primitive" traits like those found on Archaeopteryx, such as claws on their wings. In truth, the fossil record shows most birds have a combination of so-called primitive and modern traits. This is true also of several modern birds with wing-claws and longish tails (Snow, 2006, p. 156). As a result, a term that is now consistently and conveniently used by researchers to describe the evolution of birds "is "mosaicism," which largely negates the "long held dream of finding a direct ancestral line, since progress over many tens of millions of years seems to have come in tiny spurts across a huge variety of experiments. It may be that identifying sister groups is as close as can ever be achieved." (Cusack, 2008, p. 32).

As already noted, another of the more commonly cited bird ancestors is *Compsognathus*, a small rooster-sized theropod saurischian dinosaur first discussed by Huxley. Although bipedal with bird-like legs, it definitely was lizard-like. Compsognathus was selected, not due to evidence, but largely because it is physically the closest known extinct animal to birds. In other words, it is the only known ancient creature that with imagination could slightly resemble a bird.

As Witmer noted, some of the theories about bird evolution "came and went quickly," and the next to come into vogue was a small theropod saurischian called *Deinonychus*, which was the ancestor of birds (Witmer, 1995, p. 33). This animal was "very closely related to Velociraptor" (Witmer, 1995, p. 36). Support for this theory included the fact that Deinonychus is very different from most modern birds and possessed a number of critical similarities to Archaeopteryx, including number and shape of the snout openings, position of the teeth, number of fingers, comparative sizes and shape of the wrist bones and phalanges, hip bone arrangement, and foot and ankle structure similarities (Witmer, 1995, p. 38).

Although *Deinonychus* is more similar to birds than to other dinosaurs, it is still very different from birds (Witmer, 1995, p. 39). Other candidates are even more dissimilar! Nevertheless, the *Deinonychus*, theropod-like dinosaur ancestor of birds theory is now the most widely accepted view despite its many problems and despite the fact that much disagreement still exists.

One valid reason for disagreement is evidence that other theropod dinosaurs, such as *Troodon*, are more similar to birds than the *Deinonychus*. Confusingly, although the arguments for *Troodon* includes that *Deinonychus* has "certain skull traits closer to birds, and *Troodon* lacks many bird-like features that *Deinonychus* possesses" (Witmer, 1995, p. 42). The largest problem with the *Deinonychus* theory of bird origins is "nearly all of the birdlike theropod dinosaurs appeared later in time than the first bird, Archaeopteryx" (Witmer, 1995, p. 42). The "oldest" example of an animal cannot be younger than its putative descendent, although evolutionists argue, with their usual elasticity, that a "successful" form could persist way past its descendants. This incidentally is how they explain why both apes and humans still exist!

Therefore, evolutionists deal with the problem by assuming Troodon and Deinonychus, or both, are descendants of the common ancestor of Deinonychus, Troodon, and birds. However, there is no evidence in the fossil record to support this view. A second theory is that both Troodon and Deinonychus evolved from birds, this is discussed in more detail below. A third theory is both the Troodon and Deinonychus theories are wrong. All of the birdlike traits in these animals evolved separately and do not provide evidence for any systematic evolution of reptiles into birds, or vice-versa.

Another current evolutionary theory is dinosaurs such as the famous *T. rex* must have been warm-blooded because of the evidence for so-called "proto-feathers" on other dinosaurs, although this is circular thinking, even tautology. Yet another theory is that some "proto-feathered" creatures may actually be fossilized true flightless birds resembling the present day Rhea. Some fossils like *Protoavis* or *Caudipteryx zoui* superficially resemble it, at least in their evolutionary reconstructions (illustrated by Snow, 2006, p. 156-160).

Problems with the Dinosaur-Bird Theory

Although many paleontologists accept the view that birds descended from dinosaurs, a wide variety of bird forms were discovered to have lived during the Cretaceous Period. This caused severe problems for the dinosaur-to-bird evolution theory. John Ruben, Professor of Zoology at Oregon State University, wrote, "When interpreting the Paleobiology of long extinct taxa, new fossils, and reinterpretations of well-known fossils, sharply at odds with conventional wisdom never seem to cease popping up" (Ruben, 2010, p. 2733). He added that "an affinity between theropod dinosaurs and birds has long been recognized, 'nonetheless' paleontologists generally accepted that an ancestor-descendant relationship between these two groups was unlikely" (Ruben, 2010, p. 2733).

Turning the most popular interpretation completely on its head, Ruben added, "The weight of evidence is now suggesting that not only did birds not descend from dinosaurs, *but that some species now believed to be dinosaurs may have descended from birds*" (emphasis added). There are just too many inconsistencies with the idea that birds had dinosaur ancestors (Oregon State University, 2010, p.1).

As if that is not enough of a problem for Darwinism, thousands of fossilized bird tracks have been found alongside dinosaur foot tracks in many parts of the world, creating problems for their evolution from dinosaurs (Snow, 2006, p. 155). Evolutionists, surprisingly, argue that this is compelling evidence that both birds and dinosaurs must have a common ancestor.

The analysis of an unusual fossil discovered in 2003, called "Microraptor," has resulted in challenging questions for dinosaur-to-bird evolution theory. Three-dimensional models were used to study the flight potential of the Microraptor. They concluded this small-feathered species must have been a "glider" that jumped from trees. A 1915 drawing by naturalist William Beebe shows one view of what evolutionists theorize early birds may have looked like. It bears a striking similarity to the fossil discovered in 2003, raising serious doubts about the theory of birds descended from ground-dwelling theropod dinosaurs (Stevens, 2009).

University of Kansas scientists recently examined a fossil bird that had feathers on all four limbs, thus somewhat resembling a biplane (Alexandera, et al., 2010). Glide tests based on its structure have determined that it would have been impractical for it to have flown from the ground up, but it could have glided down from trees somewhat like modern-day gliding reptiles, or flying squirrels. This is the Arboreal versus Cursorial theory, that some wing-developing reptile helped evolve flight by jumping out of trees, rather than madly flapping along the ground seeking eventual take-off.

Many researchers have long believed that some type of glider, and not a tetrapod dinosaur, was the ancestor of birds. In contrast, if birds descended from theropod dinosaurs, a great lineage of ground-dwelling meat-eaters with strong hind legs and short forelimbs must have existed to support the ancestors of modern birds, a lineage for which no evidence has been found.

The level of speculation involved in bird evolution is indicated by the words of one expert who noted that the dinosaur bird "model was not consistent with successful flight from the ground up, and that makes it pretty difficult to make a case for a ground-dwelling theropod dinosaur to have developed wings and flown away." The new research

> ...is consistent with a string of recent studies that increasingly challenge the birds-from-dinosaurs theory ... The weight of the evidence is now suggesting that not only birds did not descend from dinosaurs, but that some dinosaur species may have descended from birds.

We're finally breaking out of the conventional wisdom of the last 20 years, which insisted that birds evolved from dinosaurs. This issue isn't resolved at all (Oregon State University, 2010, p.1).

The new theory raises the question, if dinosaurs evolved from birds, where did birds come from? The conclusions of almost 20 years of research at Oregon State University comparing birds and dinosaurs is much more consistent with the view that birds had an ancient common ancestor with dinosaurs, but evolved separately along their own path and not from dinosaurs.

This view postulates that, after millions of years of separate evolution, raptors evolved from birds. Support for this theory comes mainly from the fact that raptors "look quite a bit like dinosaurs but they have much more in common with birds than they do with other theropod dinosaurs such as Tyrannosaurus [rex]," (Oregon State University, 2010, p. 1). ("Raptors" here refers to dinosaurian "bird-like predators." This is not the same definition that many ornithologists give to raptors, which they define as modern predatory birds of prey like eagles, hawks, and falcons.)

The researchers concluded that raptors, which are considered dinosaurs, were "actually descended from birds, not the other way around. Small animals such as velociraptor that have generally been thought to be dinosaurs are more likely flightless birds" (Oregon State University, 2010 p. 1). A Florida State University study raised similar doubts.

Anatomical Differences between Birds and Non-birds

The greatest difficulty with determining what animal birds evolved from is the chasm that exists between birds and all other animals. Just one example is birds are very highly adapted for flight. This includes a bird's unique digestive and respiratory systems, their high metabolic rate, and lightweight, but very strong skeleton. In some ways birds are more similar to mammals than reptiles. An example is that in contrast to reptiles, birds have a four-chambered heart like mammals.

Among the other radical changes required to convert a reptile into a bird is the reptile's bellows-type lung, which is far more similar to a mammal lung, including ours. To convert a bellows-type lung into a bird's long, one-way and tube-like lung would be highly problematic! Birds have a unique and elaborately complicated system of air sacs involving the head and neck sinuses and air sacs in the thorax. Their design insures that air always flows in one direction through special tubes in the lung system called parabronchi. Blood moves through the lung's blood vessels in the opposite direction, allowing very efficient oxygen uptake. This superior engineering design allows birds to conserve the energy normally used for breathing. In contrast, mammal lungs draw air into tiny sacs called alveoli where red blood cells extract oxygen and allow carbon dioxide to be exhaled out of the same pathway that the air traveled into the lungs.

How the "bellows" lung system of mammals and reptiles could have gradually evolved into avian lungs has baffled evolutionists for generations. Research has shown that all hypothetical intermediate stages were nonfunctional, the animal would not have been able to breathe. "Natural Selection" would preserve the existing reptile arrangement and eliminate any intermediates required to evolve into the modern respiratory bird system. The fact that the design of the avian respiratory system is extremely similar in all birds, as well as being highly sophisticated and individual, is evidence that bird-reptile transitions are not even remotely feasible (Snow, 2006, p. 159).

Assuming that a highly theoretical series of functional intermediate stages could be constructed, "Natural Selection" alone would not drive the bird gas exchange evolution because bats manage very well with bellows-style mammal lungs. This fact indicates that flying birds could also function fairly well with bellows-style lungs—thus there would have been no major selective advantage in replacing the reptilian lung design with a new radically different respiratory system.

Although the avian lung's highly efficient design is especially advantageous at very high altitudes where low oxygen levels exist—some species can hunt at altitudes of over two miles (three km)- the fact that bats do very well at low altitudes indicates that only a minor, if any, selective advantage exists for the bird system, at least at lower altitudes.

Another major and fatal difference between reptiles and birds is that reptiles are cold-blooded and birds are warm-blooded. Aymar speculates that this evolution occurred as follows: "From the cold-blooded, sluggish reptile this increased activity of climbing, gliding and finally flapping, changed it into a warm-blooded animal. The feathers acted as insulation to protect it from the cold." (1935, p. 2).

Although feathers themselves are "lightweight miracles of engineering", as even evolutionists admit, imagining they could accidentally evolve from a fraying reptilian scale is far-fetched. The scales would need to not only fray into thousands of very fine equidistant strands, but accidentally 'evolve' the many 'hooks and eyes' that zip them so precisely together. Oil glands and strong hollow shafts also needed to 'evolve' and somehow migrate deep into the skin. Amazingly, genetic research has determined that these many incredibly complex changes all have occurred at different DNA sites! Then, there's the pigments and microscopic 'Photonic crystal structures' that turn white light into the dazzling color that gives bird feathers such brilliance and variety (Snow, 2006, p 54-95)!

Other challenges to a theory of bird-from-dinosaur evolution include the vast differences between their bones. One example notes theropods lacked collarbones (clavicles) that fuse together to become the wishbone (furcula) in birds. Heilmann (1926) argued that, if this feature were lost, it would have to have re-evolved at a later date. This is highly unlikely; therefore theropods could not be the ancestor of birds. Yet another contrast between bird and dinosaur bones is the enormous size difference. The average modern bird is about the size of the average dinosaur heart. Learning to fly is yet another significant problem for the bird to dinosaur evolution theory (Stevens, 2009; Snow, 2006).

Baraminology Research

Research comparing birds with dinosaurs has produced mixed results. Baraminology (from the Hebrew Bara – Create, Min - Kind) is technique that uses comparisons of select molecular, genetic, morphological, and physiological traits. To estimate the relative similarity of two animal groups, Baraminology theorists then analyze their data by multidimensional scaling and Pearson correlation coefficient calculations. Use of this technique on birds and dinosaurs was completed by Wood (2011, p. 915). Comparing 187 characters of 42 taxa, Wood found a positive correlation between all birds in the sample and deinonychosaurians. In addition, no bird was found to share a positive distance correlation with any nondeinonychosaurians coelurosaur (Wood, 2011, p. 916).

The greatest difficulty with this type of analysis is the researcher must select the traits to compare, each trait is given equal weight, and the researcher must also select the birds and dinosaur taxa to compare. This requires subjective judgments that could produce either positive or negative correlations, depending on the animal taxa and traits selected (Yoon, 2009). Using another set of traits, Senter found results very different than creationist Wood's

(Senter, 2010, p. 1732-1743). Wood responded to this study as follows: "using Senter's set of taxa and characters supports his conclusions of morphological continuity, but other sets with more characters do not" (Wood, 2011, 914). Wood added that baraminology compairsons "can be disputed, and none can be considered truly definitive" (Wood, 2011, p. 917). In a review of the history, problems, and promise of baraminology research, Wood admitted that "bias in group and character selection prevents firm conclusions." He felt that further research may resolve some of the problems, especially trait selection, with the technique (2006, pp. 149, 156). A main problem is "it is unlikely that all members of a potentiality region can be known, [therefore] the baramin is a purely theoretical construct" (Wood et al., 2003, p. 8).

The basis for comparisons of dinosaurs with birds is largely limited to teeth and bones, thus very limited conclusions are possible. If dogs were long extinct, in view of the drastic differences between their skeletons, they likely would be classified as several difference species today. As one biology text wrote:

> The skeletons of lions and tigers are so near identical that they would be classified as the same species. Yet the living animals are classified as different species [this classification turned out to be wrong; a liger is a hybrid cross between a male lion (*Panthera* leo) and a female tiger (*Panthera* tigris)]. If the skeletons of dogs, such as Chihuahuas, dachshunds, collies, and bulldogs were examined as fossils, they no doubt would be considered different species; but they are the same species (MacKenzie, et al., 2008, p. 296).

Many other life-forms currently assumed to be separate 'species' can interbreed. A few of the many examples include grizzly and polar bears, camels and llamas, capercaillie and black grouse, red and black kites, dolphins and false killer whales.

The Biochemical Evidence

The DNA biochemical evidence, using hybridization and other biochemical studies, strongly disagrees with the current fossil-based phylogeny (evolutionary history) of many birds. For example, biochemical research for totipalmate birds (web-footed, like pelicans, boobies, gannets, cormorants, anhingas, frigatebirds, and tropicbirds) has produced a conclusion that is rejected by some ornithologists but greeted with surprise by most. DNA comparisons indicate that *Pelecanus* is the sister group of the shoebill (*Balaeniceps rex*, a large stork-like bird), and frigate birds are part of the *Procellarioidea*, which also includes penguins, albatrosses, petrels, and loons.

Evolutionists speculate that tropicbirds appear to be descendants of an ancient evolutionary divergence, which makes them a sister group of a large group of aquatic birds, including the other totipalmate taxa (Sibley and Ahlquist, 1990, p. 491-503). As more biochemical and genetic research on birds is completed, no doubt the conflicts with the fossil record will continue to create headaches for evolutionists.

The Genetic Evidence

The 2008 Chicago's Field Museum of Natural History Bird Tree-of-Life Research Project genetics study, the largest ever done, has, according to its authors, re-written the avian evolutionary tree. The research shows, according to the genes examined, that many birds that look very much alike are genetically very dissimilar. Examples include falcons which are not closely related to other birds of prey, but that are similar morphologically to hawks and eagles (Hackett, et al., 2008).

Conversely, some birds that look very different from each other, such as woodpeckers, hawks, owls and hornbills, are genetically all closely related to 'Passerines' (perching birds, including the many different songbirds). Contrary to conventional conclusions that hummingbirds are not closely related to pelicans or other water birds ,the genetic evidence indicates that hummingbirds evolved from drab nocturnal nightjars and tropicbirds (white, swift-flying ocean birds, like terns). Furthermore, the Hackett study concluded that flamingos, tropicbirds and grebes, all of which are closely related, did not evolve from water birds.

Furthermore, perching birds, parrots, and falcons, which are morphologically very dissimilar, are genetically very similar; thus the study concluded they descended from a recent common ancestor. Hackett, et al. (2008) also concluded that shorebirds are not a basal evolutionary group. This refutes the long established view, used in most bird guide books, that all modern birds evolved from shorebirds! The study also concluded that modern birds evolved relatively very rapidly within a few million years during an explosive radiation, sometime between 65 million and 100 million years ago. This genomic evidence of rapid avian evolution, somewhat like the 'Cambrian Explosion' of all major phyla, is a significant problem for Darwinian gradualism.

The Argument for the Origin of Birds by *Fiat* Creation

The last view presented here is that birds and theropods were created separately and therefore did not evolve. This explanation best fits the fossil record and all of the other known facts. One is the enormous gap between birds and dinosaurs, because

> ...over the decades researchers who doubted the dinosaur-bird link also made good anatomical arguments. They said dinosaurs lack a number of

features that are distinctly avian, including wishbones, or fused clavicles; bones riddled with air pockets; flexible wrist joints; and three-toed feet. Moreover, the posited link seemed contrary to what everyone thought they knew: that birds are small, intelligent, speedy, warm blooded sprites, whereas dinosaurs—from the Greek for "fearfully great lizard"—were coldblooded, dull, plodding, reptile-like creatures (Stone, 2010, p. 56).

Since detailed evidence of dinosaur anatomy is lacking, comparisons are very problematic. Attempts to compare skeletons of extant and extinct animals have provided only conflicting theories of bird evolution, as we have so often seen. Although fused clavicles have been found in some dinosaurs, crucial differences between birds and dinosaurs remain. Many evolutionists continue to hope that some day they will dig up fossils to provide conclusive evidence for one of the proposed theories for bird evolution, but after almost two centuries of looking and billions of fossils uncovered, this hope does not seem very likely to bear fruit (Witmer, 1995, p. 44). Professor Witmer concludes that many of the clues to bird evolution

> ...point to different and conflicting stories. Deinonychus does indeed resemble the Jurassic bird Archaeopteryx. But what about *Troodon*? What about Protoavis? And what about the "time problem"? Where are the Jurassic relatives of *Deinonychus* and *Troodon*, if they existed at all? These questions still need to be answered. There are points of agreement, however. The ancestor of birds was probably a small theropod dinosaur, probably resembling *Deinonychus* (Witmer, 1995, p. 46).

Conclusions

An enormous unbridgeable gap, both fossil and morphological, still exists between birds and all other animals. The earliest known bird, Archaeopteryx, has been dated back to the Late Jurassic, around 150 to 145 million years ago, by evolutionists. Yet it has the same cranial characteristics and flight feathers as modern birds. The fossil record and other evidence are very clear: "evolutionary change in avian morphology primarily occurs in terms of minor size adjustments, while changes in shape are very rare" (Björklund, 1994, p. 739). It is notable that some modern finches, sparrows, and weavers can all interbreed, as can many other 'families' of birds like ducks and falcons. Genesis correctly states that life forms can only breed 'after their kind'; however, much built-in genetic variety exists. This is not 'evolution' since it is neither accidental, nor slow, nor does it involve adding new genetic information. Instead it simply shows existing genes were rapidly reshuffled to suit habitat and food requirements, as in the different beaks of 'Darwin's finches' (Snow, 2006).

The evolution of birds has stymied Darwinists since 1859 and remains a critical problem for the theory of evolution. It is clear from the evidence that "morphological change in birds in general consists of changes in growth such that species become larger or smaller than their ancestors but reclaim their ancestral shape" (Björklund, 1994, p. 727). It is also clear that "many points [of evolution] are still under fierce contention, and a lack of fossil material leaves some enormous blank spots" (Cusack, 2008, preface).

As Feduccia et al. (2005) note, although there is much heated debate "that birds are derived from within the archosaurian assemblage: whether birds are derived from 'dinosaurs' depends largely on how one defines the Dinosauromorpha" (2005, p. 125). For this reason Ruben wrote that when attempting to interpret.

The claim by some evolutionists, such as Chiappe, that "the century-old debate on bird ancestry has largely been resolved" is clearly false—he argues for the maniraptoran theropod theory against all of the other theories noted and critiqued in this review (2009, p. 252). More accurate is the observation by evolutionist, Biology Professor Lawrence Witmer, that "we will probably never be lucky enough to find the fossils of the true ancestor of birds" (1995, p. 11). The fossil, DNA, and other evidence reveals that the first bird was a bird, and no convincing evidence exists to support the idea that birds evolved from reptiles or any other non-bird animal.

References

Alexander, David E., Enpu Gong, Larry D. Martina, David A. Burnhamc, and Amanda R. Falk. 2010. "Model tests of Gliding with Different Hindwing Configurations in the four-winged Dromaeosaurid *Microraptor gui.*" *Proceedings of the National Academy of Sciences.* 107(7): 2972-2976. February 16.

Aymar, Gordon. 1935. *Bird Flight; Evolution, Biology, Migration, Aerodynamics.* New York: Dodd, Mead.

Benton, Michael. 2014 How Birds Became Birds. *Science.* 345(6196):508-509.

Björklund, Mats. 1994. "Processes Generating Macroevolutionary Patterns of Morphological Variation in Birds: A Simulation Study" *Journal of Evolutionary Biology* 7:727-742.

Chatterjee, Sankar. 1997. *The Rise of Birds.* Baltimore, MD: The Johns Hopkins University Press.

Chiappe, Luis M. 1995. "The First 85 Million Years of Avian Evolution." *Nature,* 378:349-355.

_____. 2009. "Downsized Dinosaurs: The Evolutionary Transition to Modern Birds." *Evolution Education Outreach.* 2:248-256. April 16.

Colbert, Edwin, H., Michael Morales, and Eli C. Minkoff. 2001. *Colbert's Evolution of the Vertebrates: A History of the Backboned Animals Through Time. Fifth Edition.* New York, NY: John Wiley and Sons.

Coyne, Jerry A. 2009. *Why Evolution is True.* New York, NY: Viking/Penguin Group.

Cusack, Denys. 2008. *On the Origin of Birds: A Journey Through Time.* North Charleston, SC: BookSurge Publishing.

Dingus, Lowell and Timothy Rowe. 1998. *The Mistaken Extinction: Dinosaur Evolution and the Origin of Birds.* New York: W.H. Freeman and Company.

Feduccia, Alan. 1996. *The Origin and Evolution of Birds*. New Haven, CT: Yale University Press.

_____ 1999. *The Origin & Evolution of Birds*. 2nd Edition, New Haven, CT: Yale University Press.

_____, Theagarten Lingham-Soliar, and J. Richard Hinchliffe. 2005. "Do Feathered Dinosaurs Exist? Testing the Hypothesis on Neontological and Paleontological Evidence." *Journal of Morphology* 266:125-166.

Gurevitch, Jessica and Dianna K. Padilla 2004. "Are invasive species a major cause of extinctions?" *Trends in Ecology & Evolution* 19(9): 470-474. September.

Heilmann, Gerhard. 1926. *The Origin Of Birds*. London: Witherby.

Holmes, Thom and Laurie Holmes. 2002. *Feathered Dinosaurs: The Origin of Birds*. Berkeley Heights, NJ: Enslow Publishers.

James, Frances C. and John A. Pourtless IV. 2009. *Cladistics and the Origin of Birds: A Review and Two New Analyses*. Washington, D.C.: The American Ornithologists' Union.

Kavanau, J. Lee. 2010. "Secondary Flightless Birds or Cretaceous Non-Avian Theropods?" *Medical Hypotheses*, 74:275-276.

Lee, Michael, Andrea Cau, Darren Naish and Gareth Dyke. 2014. Sustained Miniaturation and Anatomical Innovation in the Origin of Birds. *Science*. 345(6196):562-566.

Long, John and Peter Schouten. 2008. *Feathered Dinosaurs: The Origin of Birds*. Oxford, NY: Oxford University Press.

MacKenzie, Leslie, David K. Arwine, Edward J. Shewan and Michael J. McHugh. 2008. *Biology: A Search for Order in Complexity*. Arlington Heights, Il. Christian Liberty Press.

O'Donoghue, James. 2010. Bird evolution: 150 years of flying feathers. *New Scientist*. 208(2790):36-40. December.

Oregon State University Press release. 2010. *Bird-from-dinosaur Theory of Evolution Challenged: Was it the Other Way Around?* February 10.

Ostrom, John. 1973. "The Ancestry of Birds." *Nature*, 242:136.

Padian K and Chiappe LM. 1997. "Bird Origins" in Currie PJ & Padian K. *Encyclopedia of Dinosaurs*. San Diego: Academic Press. pp. 41–96.

Peterson, Roger Tony. 1963. *The Birds*. New York: Time-Life.

Ruben, John. 2010. "Paleobiology and the Origins of Avian Flight." *Proceedings of the National Academy of Sciences*. 107(7): 2733-2734. February 16.

Senter, Phil. 2010. Using creation science to demonstrate evolution: application of a creationist method for visualizing gaps in the fossil record to a phylogenetic study of coelurosaurian dinosaurs. *Journal of Evolutionary Biology*. 23: 1732–1743.

Sereno, Paul C., Ricardo N. Martinez, Jeffrey A. Wilson, David J. Varricchio, Oscar A. Alcober, and Hans C. E. Larsson. "Evidence for avian Intrathoracic Air Sacs in a New Predatory Dinosaur from Argentina." *PLoS One* 3(9):e3303.

Sibley, Charles and Jon Ahlquist, 1990. *Phylogeny and Classification of Birds: A Study in Molecular Evolution*. New Haven, CT: Yale University Press.

Snow, Philip. 2006. *The Design and Origin of Birds*. Leominster: Day One Publications.

Steele, Philip. 1991. *Extinct Birds and Those in Danger of Extinction*. New York, NY: Franklin Watts.

Stevens, Richard W. 2009. "Can Evolution Make New Biological Software?" *Creation Research Society Quarterly*, 46(1):17-24.

Stone, Richard. 2010. "Dinosaur's Living Descendants." *Smithsonian*, 41(8):55-62, Dec.

University of Montana. 2009, "How a New Theory of Bird Evolution Came About." *ScienceDaily*. March 3.

Whetstone, K. N. and L. D. Martin. 1979. "New Look at the Origin of Birds and Crocodiles." *Nature*, 279:234-236.

Witmer, Lawrence. 1995. *The Search for the Origin of Birds*. New York: Franklin Watts.

Woodmorappe, J. 2003. Bird evolution: discontinuities and reversals. *TJ* 17(1):88-94.

Wood, Todd, Kurt Wise, Roger Sanders and N. Doran. 2003. A Refined Baramin Concept. *Occasional Papers of the Baraminology Study Group*. July 25.

_____2006. The Current Status of Baraminology. *Creation Research Society Quarterly*. 41:149-158. December.

_____2011. Using creation science to demonstrate evolution? Senter's strategy revisited. *Journal of Evolutionary Biology*. 24: 914-918.

Yoon, Carl Kaesuk. 2009. *Naming Nature: The Clash Between Instinct and Science*. New York: Norton.

Chapter 12

Bats — Flight, Echolocation, and Other Features

Introduction

On a warm summer evening in many regions of the country, what at first appear to be birds flying around often are actually bats. The main clue that they are bats is their rapid, erratic, darting flight. Bats are very unique fur covered animals that are highly beneficial for humans. They have a critical role in the ecosystem as dispersers of seeds, pollinators of flowers, and helping control harmful insects. Bats are so unique that it has been difficult to classify them. They fly like a bird, but can walk like a penguin. As late as 1748 they were classified as birds, and even as rodents and primates by Linnaeus. Bats now are classified, not as birds, but mammals placed in their own separate order, Chiroptera. Chiroptera is Greek for "hand-wing" because bat "wings" are flat sheets of tissue connected to their hands.

Bats are classified as mammals because the females nurse their pups with nipples located on the bat's sides under their wings. The bat's body, but not its "wings," is covered with hair as are almost all mammals (Graham, 1994). Bats are also the only mammals that can fly on their own power. Most bat kinds use a complex echolocation (sonar) system to locate their prey and navigate around in their dark world (Simmons, 2005, p. 527).

Fully one in five mammals living on earth today is a bat—the only mammal kind containing more species than rodents (Sears, et al., 2006, p. 6581). Bats exist in an extraordinary diversity of lifestyles and morphologies. They are found in abundance in warm latitudes, live on every continent except Antarctica, and thrive everywhere except where it is extremely hot or cold (Simmons, 2005). Depending on the species, they subsist on a diet of insects, nectar, pollen, fruit, small vertebrates, fish, blood, and nuts (Carroll, 1998, p. 278). Both their cranial morphology and dentition is very specialized to fit their diet. Some types, such as fruit bats, are very common; other kinds, such as insectivorous sac-winged bats, are very rare (Greenhall, 1965).

The approximately 1,000 known bat species currently are grouped into 18 living and six extinct families (Simmons, 2005, p. 527). Bats, like dogs, have an innate genetic ability to produce enormous variety, but also, like dogs, clear genetic limits exist. All bats are divided into two suborders, megabats (megachiroptera) and microbats (microchiroptera). Megabats are large, mostly non-echolocating, diurnal fruit-eating or nectar-drinking mammals that live in the tropics (Fleming, 1985). They are found only in the Old World, mostly in the tropics of Asia, Africa, and Australia.

The smallest microbat is about the size of a bumblebee and the weight of a dime. The about 1,000 species range from a little over an inch (2.5 centimeters) to about 5 inches (12 centimeters) long. Most are echolocating (the only microbat exception is the Rousettus) and most are insect-eating, night-flying animals (Williams and Mies, 1996, p. 4). The largest megabat, the flying fox, has a wingspan that is approximately two meters across. The microbats are very diverse and widely distributed small-sized bats

Evolution of Bat Theories

Darwin, in his chapter on the difficulties of evolution, cited bats as his first example, questioning if it is "possible that an animal having, for instance, the structure and habits of a bat, could have been formed by the modification of some animal with wholly different habits" (1859, p. 171). He added that it would require a "long list" of animals that possessed clear transitional traits to "lesson the difficulty [of evolution] in any particular case like that of the bat" (1859, p. 180). Naturalists still face the same problem today. Thewissen and Babcock conclude that the origin and early evolution of bats is one of the greatest controversies in modern biology because the "fossil evidence for bat origins is extremely sparse" (1992, p. 340). Actually it is nonexistent.

The problem is not the fossil record, but the fact that none of the existing fossils support bat evolution. Many excellent well-preserved fossils of bats exist, dated by evolutionists all the way back to the Eocene. As a result, unconstrained by the fossil record, many conflicting theories of bat evolution exist. Because of a lack of fossil evidence for their evolution, the whole evolutionary history of bats "has been obscured by controversial phylogenetic hypothesis" (Teeling, et al., 2005, p. 581).

One theory is that bats first evolved in Laurasia, possibly in North America, from a small placental mammal (Teeling, et al., 2005; Carroll, 1998, p. 277). The argument for this view is, because the bones in a bat's wing are very similar to mammal hand bones, bats must have evolved from some shrew-like animal that could glide from tree to tree like flying squirrels (Williams and Mies, 1996, p. 2). Sears, et al., wrote that the current general consensus is that the common ancestor of bats was a small quadrupedal mammal with limb morphology similar to that of mice (2006, p. 6581). The problem with this view is, as leading bat fossil expert Carroll concluded, "the fossil record does not provide evidence of the transition" from "small placental mammals" to bats (1998, p. 277).

Others argue from anatomical evidence that bats evolved from primates, flying lemurs, or even tree shrews (Lin and Penny, 2001). Another claim is that bats and Phenacolemers, flightless mouse-sized animals that are claimed to share a common ancestor with bats (Hamrick, et al., 1999). It even is proposed, based on neuroanatomy, that "megabats are more closely related to primates than to microbats" (Lin and Penny, 2001, p. 684).

Yet still others, using molecular evidence, conclude that bats are more closely related to cetferungulates instead of primates (Lin and Penny, 2001, p. 687). Teeling concluded, based on molecular evidence, that "living bats last shared a common ancestor at, or just after, the Cretaceous-Tertiary boundary" (Simmons, 2005, p. 527). University of Chicago Biologist Van Valen wrote over 30 years ago that we can only hypothesize about the origin of bats, and it is difficult to go beyond hypothesizing because bats "have no Archaeopteryx as of yet" (1979, p. 103). He then speculates on the possible evolutionary histories of bats, stressing the tentative nature and problems with existing speculations. His conclusions are still valid today.

Darwinists' major explanation for the total lack of valid evidence for bat evolution is that bats are not common in the fossil record, partly because they have small, light skeletons that do not preserve well. Actually the "earliest-known bats are represented by excellent fossil material, including virtually complete skeletons of *Icaronycteris index* from the early Eocene (50 Myr BP) of western Wyoming and *Palaeochiropteryx tupaiodon* from the middle Eocene (45 Myr BP) 'Grube Messel' of Western Germany" (Novacek, 1985, p. 140).

The *I. index* appears to be a fully modern bat. Enough excellent examples exist to determine that the present evidence does not support bat evolution from any non-bat animal. Unusually complete bat fossils dating by evolutionists all the way back to the Eocene have been found in locations that range from the Green River formation in Wyoming to the Messel Shale in Germany (Carroll, 1988). So far, all of the fossils exhumed from these sites are modern-looking microchiropterans.

The oldest fossil bats, which have been dated by evolutionists at around 54 million years, are not "dramatically different from living bats," but rather, in most ways are indistinguishable from modern bats (Perkins, 2005, p. 314). Burton describes the Eocene fossils "as fully evolved and structurally adapted for flight as any recent forms" (Burton, 1980, p. 494). Carroll adds that the skeletons of "early Eocene species are almost indistinguishable from modern forms" (1988, p. 278).

Older fossils that may reveal insight into bat evolution from non-bats have not yet been found, and the earliest bats existing in the fossil record all clearly are bats. For this reason, despite their large number today — they make up more than 20 percent of all extant mammals — "their evolutionary history is largely unknown" (Teeling, et al., 2005, p. 580). Lin and Penny add that not only is the evolutionary history of chiroptera uncertain, but "even the monophyly of this group has been questioned" (2001, p. 684).

The story of the evolution of each bat type is the same. For example, Fenton notes that although protein comparisons "suggest vampire bats evolved more than 10 million years ago" the "fossil record sheds no light on the evolutionary origin of vampire bats" (1998, pp. 94-95). Fenton then outlines his theory of vampire bat evolution, stressing that it "is just that — a theory. Now we wait to see who comes up with a better one" (1998, p. 97). The same problem is true of all other bat kinds.

Evolution of Flight in Bats

Many evolutionists assume that flight in higher animals evolved four times in all of history, once in insects, once in pterosaurs, once in birds, and once in bats (Carroll, 1998, p. 277). Because of its complexity, it commonly is assumed by many researchers that bat echolocation could have "evolved only once in bats" (Simmons, 2005, p. 527). This is a concern to evolutionists because "bats' evolutionary success is in large part" due to "their power of flight" (Wimsatt, 1957, p. 106). Because the evolution of flight is recognized as very improbable, a single origin of flight in mammals is postulated (Teeling, et al., 2005, p. 581). Although all bats are capable of true powered flight, some can glide like raptors (Williams and Mies, 1996, p. 2).

It is for this, and other reasons that "some workers believe that flying foxes, which are actually Old World fruit-eating bats, are more closely related to humans and other primates than to the small bats that Americans see flying overhead" (Thewissen and Babcock, 1992, p. 340). Specifically, they argue that lemurs are ancestral to fruit bats.

The design of bat "wings" is so radically different than bird wings that they are technically not even called wings by bat biologists, but rather "alar membranes." Darwin recognized this, thus wrote "the bat's wing is a most abnormal structure (1859, p. 150). The many ways that a bat "wing" is very different than a bird wing include that a bird wing is a highly specialized organ dedicated to the task of flying. In contrast, the bat "wing" is a thin skin membrane stretched over very elongated "fingers" (see Figure 12.1). As shown in Figure 12.1, the bones that support four of these "fingers" are similar to greatly elongated phalanges of mammals (Seeley, 1967, p. 24). To achieve strength and light weight, these bat wing long-bones have a unique design similar to a steel construction "I-beam."

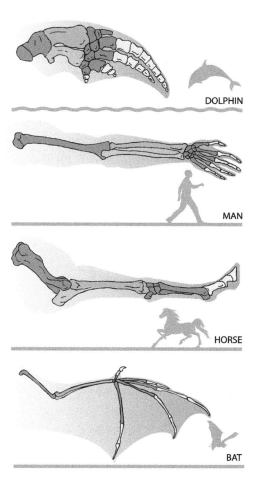

Figure 12.1 — Comparison of Bat Forelimb Structure with Other Mammals[1]

Otherwise, the "wing" bones of a bat resemble those in the hand and arm of a human. Consequently, bats have been placed in class Mammalia, order Chiroptera, which literally means "hand-wing." Bat legs are also part of the wing membranes and cannot

---

[1] Image Credit: NoPainNoGain / Shutterstock.com

effectively be used separately. In contrast to the bird wing design, the alar membrane stretches from the third finger, which in bats is disproportionately long, to the foot, and then to the tail. In birds, feathers are attached to the wing along a limb called a wing proper.

The bat flight system varies in different bat types, as it also does in birds. Bats do not have one alar membrane type, but rather, a family of alar membranes, just as birds have a family of wing types. The alar membrane is clothed with the same short hairs as the bat's body (Seeley, 1967, p. 24). Most bats can fold their elongated digits together like a folding hand fan so they can be carried at the bat's sides as they walk on land. The fifth, more normal sized digit, terminates in a claw that can be used for walking (Seely, 1967, p. 24). The wing claw also can function to catch prey and transfer it to the bat's mouth while in flight. Bats achieve this transfer so effectively that by this means they can locate, pursue, catch, and eat several insects within a few seconds (Griffin, et al., 1960).

Flight lift in bats is provided both by the "wing" down stroke and also by changing the wing curvature and the down stroke angle (Graham, 1994, p. 16). Bats have highly sensitive receptor cells on their "wings" which provide them with constant feedback to allow them to instantly adjust their wings according to changing flight conditions. These receptors use Merkel cells, a touch sensitive cell common in the skin of most mammals and even humans. Fine hairs extending out from their Merkel cells enable bats to accurately sense the air flow traveling across their wings. The Merkel cell feedback is used to adjust various wing traits, such as wing curvature. If the wing is curved too much or too little, lift will be lost, causing a stall and, if not adjusted soon enough, the bat will plummet to the ground. The wing position also must be adjusted. It is now known that effective flight is not possible without this entire irreducibly complex system, of which we have described here only a few of the basic components.

The fossil record shows no evidence for the evolution of bat flight—nor any evidence of the evolution of any other kind of animal flight (Bergman, 2003). Rather, the "earliest known members of these [bat] groups had ... advanced flight apparatus" (Carroll, 1998, p. 277). Furthermore, the "earliest fossil bats resemble their modern counterparts in possessing greatly elongated digits to support the wing membrane, which is an anatomical hallmark of powered flight" (Sears, et al., 2006, p. 6581).

The length of the primary supportive elements of the bat wing, Sears, et al., concluded "have remained constant relative to the body size over the last 50 million years" (p. 6581). They add that the "absence of transitional forms in the fossil record led us to look elsewhere to understand bat wing evolution" (2006, p. 6581). Hecht concluded that "the origins of bats have been a puzzle. Even the earliest bat fossils, from about 50 million years ago, have wings that closely resemble those of modern bats" (1998, p. 14).

Unconstrained by empirical evidence for bat flight evolution, researchers are free to develop various evolution-of-flight theories. One current theory of bat flight evolution is that, first, a shrew-like mammal evolved membranes that connected their limbs and tail, which allowed the animal to glide. The next step postulated in bat flight evolution was movable proto-wings, then the membranes became thinner, and four of the phalanges gradually became longer and better adapted to flight. The last step was the evolution from a fixed wing to the modern movable and highly controllable wing (for an illustration of this process, see Graham, 1994, pp. 10-11).

These just-so stories are not supported by either molecular or fossil evidence. Nor are they supported by a mechanical evaluation— the flight system must function to aid survival and, until it is functional, a bat would not be able to fly, or even glide, nor could it survive very well as a terrestrial animal because the wing membranes would severely interfere with effective ground locomotion.

Some have theorized that flight evolved independently in megachiroptera and microchiroptera. Others disagree with this view. Van Valen notes that, although major differences in megabat and microbat flight systems exist, all "major external adaptations for flight are the same in these two groups, and almost all differ from those of other flying animals" (1979, p. 103). Even more important, Van Valen adds, is the fact that the "earliest fossils of bats do not provide evidence for this view."

Sonar in Bats—Seeing with Ears

Another major unresolved problem is the evolution of sonar, a complex echolocation system used by a wide variety of animals from many kinds of bats to a handful of birds plus whales, dolphins, and porpoises (Perkins, 2005, p. 314; Au, 2004; Graham, 1994, p. 11). The complex sonar system is a critically important reason why bats have achieved their enormous numerical and ecological niche success today.

Sonar echolocation is an enormously "complex system involving specialization of the respiratory system, ear and brain" (Simmons, 2005, p. 527). This is illustrated by the fact that bats which fly in large swarms must effectively tune out both the echoes of their companions and the "multiplicity of odd reverberations of sound from the irregular facets of the walls and ceiling" in the caves in which many bats live (Novick, 1970, p. 32).

Much is known about echolocation, but scientists disagree on even the most broad outlines about how it could possibly have evolved (Denzinger, et al., 2004; Simmons and Stein, 1980; Springer, et al., 2001). Because the basic animal groups that use echolocation all are believed to have evolved independently, some argue that sonar also must have "evolved independently among widely disparate groups of creatures" that have the advantage of this system (Perkins, 2005, p. 314). The problem with this view is that it is very unlikely sonar evolved even once, and to postulate that it evolved numerous times strains the credibility of objective researchers. The problem with all sonar evolution theories is that the fossil record "shows a sophisticated sonar system was present in the earliest records of microchiropteran history" (Novacek, 1985, p. 140).

The sound used for echolocation is produced by a thin vocal membrane especially designed to produce echolocation sound. The sound is usually emitted through the mouth, but some bats have a complex structure called a "nose leaf" to create the sound for their sonar. Sonar systems produce sound waves that are between 20 and 80,000 Hz, which is just outside the range of normal human hearing (20 to 20,000 Hz). The sound that bounces off objects is reflected back to the bat and the echo is picked up by the bat's large funnel-shaped ears designed effectively to receive the sound reflection.

The bat's transducer system then calculates the location of the object by determining the delay between the sound emission and the echo's return. This system allows for accurate navigation in total darkness. Most bats have excellent vision and, at the least, all have functional eyes—echolocation helps them to live nocturnally and in caves or other dark places, such as house attics (Graham, 1994, p. 6). Some bats, such as flying foxes, use their excellent vision for most of their activities.

Guided Missile Prey Capture Strategy

Bats usually capture their prey while in flight (Wimsatt, 1957, p. 108). As noted, bats use sound rather than sight to track prey by emitting a series of ultrasonic pulses to evaluate their environment. When the pulses hit an insect, they bounce back to inform the bat of the insect's exact location. Insects move both very rapidly and very erratically, as anyone who has tried to swat a fly or mosquito knows, requiring a highly accurate echolocation system to be effective.

The main system that bats use, laryngeal echolocation, is "one of the most innovative features in the evolutionary history of mammals." This system often is accurate enough to detect a single fine hair (Springer, et al., 2001, p. 6241). The echolocating strategy that bats use to track and catch erratically moving insects is similar to the system used by guided missiles to intercept evasive targets. It also is very different from the system that humans and many animals use to track moving objects.

A research team used infrared video and sound recordings of bats intercepting both free flying and tethered insects to reconstruct the bats' flight and tracking maneuvers. By this means the researchers determined that bats do not use the constant bearing method that baseball players use. Instead, bats constantly change their flight and speed in *response* to the insect's rapid movements. The bat locks on to its target and keeps its compass direction to the target constant, changing its flight direction to achieve that end. This strategy is termed parallel navigation after the parallel trace for the bearing lines. In the 1940s, engineers working on the problem of programming guided missiles to destroy their targets developed a very similar technique (Ghose, et al., 2006, p. 865). The bat's strategy for catching erratically moving targets, such as insects, is called the time-optimal method.

The system humans and many animals use is to sight the target, then move at a fixed speed in a straight line with constant bearing toward the target. Constant bearing keeps the person focused on a moving target, such as a baseball that moves in a highly predictable fashion, and allows the batter to move in a straight line to close in on the target (Ghose, et al., 2006, p. 865). His eyesight then tracks the ball's movement to enable him to move in on a collision course with it.

As noted, insects don't move in a predictable straight trajectory like baseballs, but dart about erratically, and may be in the open air for only seconds at a time. For this reason, bats must work out in advance the path required to catch an insect, not where it is now, but where the insect is projected to be in the future. After the bat calculates where the insect will end up in a second or so, it must adjust its flight path accordingly.

Adaptive behaviors, such as agile flight and head-aim control, and adjustments in the timing patterns of sonar vocalizations, all are finely coordinated to allow the bat to effectively capture free-flying insects even in complete darkness. Bats require this system because both they and their prey move in all three dimensions—up-down, left-right, and forward-backward—plus time, whereas terrestrial life usually moves in only two dimensions—left-right and forward-backward—plus time, making their movement far more predictable.

Other bats, such as certain megabats, use a very different type of echolocation based on tongue-clicks instead of vocal cords. This fact has always caused problems for Darwinism—did the two echolocation types evolve separately, or did one type evolve first, and then diverge later into the two distinct echolocation types?

The two systems are so radically different that many evolutionists believe sonar evolved independently several times in bats alone. A competing view is that echolocation evolved in the bat's common ancestor, but was lost during megabat evolution, and some bats then evolved the new tongue-click system, a very different—and evidently inferior—form of echolocation (Springer, et al., 2001). No evidence exists for either of these just-so stories.

Another major problem for Darwinism is, if laryngeal echolocation is so critical to a bat's success, why would it be "lost" and then replaced with an inferior system? In addition, why is any type of echolocation rare in animals, and why has it not evolved in many more animal types such as birds? (Speakman and Racey, 1991).

Furthermore, why has it evolved so infrequently, in megachiroptera? The largest bats, including old world fruit bats, do not have the advantage of sonar (Griffin, 1958, p. 41). Was it lost or never evolved in these bats? When it exists in bats, why is it used primarily for gross navigation in sighted animals rather than for prey detection, a field in which it is obviously very useful (Speakman and Racey, 1991)?

Another problem is that megabats have a very different complex of nerves than microbats. The megabat system is in many ways more similar to primates, and, in contrast, microbats have the "simple siomorphous pattern of retinotectal connections so far found in all vertebrates except primates" (Pettigrew, 1986, p. 1304). For this reason, some evolutionists have concluded that the common belief that all bats evolved from a common ancestor is incorrect. Rather, megabat's nervous system either evolved from primates or evolved to be very similar to primates by parallel evolution.

Since the latter is unlikely, some biologists argue that megabats in fact did evolve from primates, and thus are living primates. Pettigrew (1986, p. 231) proposes that "an early branch of the primate tree must have developed the power of flight long before the hominid branch even dreamed of it." This does not solve the origin of bats problem because, if true, the very bat-like megabat wing and many other bat features must have evolved independently by parallel evolution.

The Molecular Evidence

Teeling, et al., reviewed the molecular evidence to determine if "multiple origins of laryngeal echolocation within bats or a single origin of echolocation with subsequent loss in megabats" better fits the evidence (2005, p. 581). The molecular data have not been able to support whether laryngeal echolocation evolved independently in different microbats lineages, or if it evolved in the common ancestor of bats and was subsequently lost in megabats (Springer, et al., 2001, p. 6241).

Biochemical analysis of DNA data also has challenged the existing theories of bat evolution, requiring "a complete rethinking of our understanding of the evolutionary history of bats, including new evolutionary explanations for the more than 20 different anatomical specializations shared by living echolocating bats" (Simmons, 2005, p. 527). Once thought to belong to the same group as primates, if classified by the molecular evidence, bats are in the super-order Pegasoferae along with cats, cows, horses, hedgehog, and even whales. One molecular study concluded that within this super-order, bats are more closely related to horses than cows are (Okada, 2006).

Figure 12.2 — Egyptian Fruit Bat[2]

Conclusions

The existing bat fossil record provides no evidence for bat evolution from a lower, non-flying life form. The bat fossil record, although not as large as that for some other life forms, is dated by

---

[2] Photo Credit: Rosa Jay / Shutterstock.com

evolutionists back to around 54 million years ago. Bats appear abruptly in the fossil record as fully formed bats, motivating Van Valen to conclude that "although the time bats became bats can't yet be specified, their early evolution was undoubtedly rapid" (1979, p. 110). The oldest known complete fossil bat is a lcaronycteris dated by Neo-Darwinists back to the Eocene, over 50 million years ago. Since then, their evolution has been "near stagnation" (Van Valen, 1979, p. 110).

A total lack of any evidence for the evolution of bat flight and the evolution of two distinct types of echolocation also are major impediments to accepting the Darwinian explanation of bat origins. New fossils have supported this conclusion, and it is unlikely that more discoveries will alter it. Nor does the molecular evidence provide support for existing theories of bat evolution.

References

Au, Whitlow W.L. 2004. Introduction: "A Comparison of the Sonar Capabilities of Bats and Dolphins." Edited by Annette Denzinger, Cynthia F. Moss, and Marianne Vater.

Bergman, Jerry. 2003. "The Evolution of Feathers: a Major Problem for Darwinism." *TJ* 17(1):33-41.

Burton, Maurice. 1980. *The New Larousse Encyclopedia of Animal Life*. New York: Bonanza Books.

Carroll, Robert L. 1988. *Vertebrate Paleontology and Evolution*. New York: Freeman.

_____. 1998. *Patterns and Processes of Vertebrate Evolution*. New York, NY: Cambridge University Press.

Darwin, Charles. 1859. *The Origin of Species*. London: John Murray.

Denzinger, Annette, Elisabeth K.V. Kalko, and Gareth Jones. 2004. Chapter 42: "Ecological and Evolutionary Aspects of Echolocation in Bats" in *Echolocation in Bats and Dolphins*. Chicago, IL: The University of Chicago Press. Edited by Annette Denzinger, Cynthia F. Moss, and Marianne Vater.

Fenton, M. Brock. 1998. *The Bat: Wings in the Night Sky*. Buffalo, NY: Firefly Books.

Fleming, Theodore H. 1985. "A Day in the Life of a *Piper*-eating Bat." *Natural History*, 94(6):52-59, June.

Ghose, Kaushik, Timothy K. Horiuchi, P.S. Krishnaprasad, and Cynthia F. Moss. 2006. "Echolocating Bats Use a Nearly Time-Optimal Strategy to Intercept Prey." *PLoS Biology*, 4(5):0865-0873, May.

Graham, Gary L. 1994. *Bats of the World*. New York: Golden Press.

Greenhall, Arthur M. 1965. "Trinad and Bat Research." *Natural History*, 74(6):14-21.

Griffin, Donald R. 1958. "More about Bat 'Radar.'" *Scientific American*, July, pp. 40-44.

_____, F. A. Webster, and C.R. Michael. 1960. "The Echolocation of Flying Insects by Bats." *Animal Behavior*, 8:141-154.

Hamrick, Mark W., Burt A. Rosenman, and Jason A. Brush. 1999. "Phalangeal Morphology of the Paromomyidae: The Evidence for Gliding Behavior Reconsidered." *American Journal of Physical Anthropology*, 109(3):397-413, July 1.

Hecht, Jeff. 1998. "Branching Out." *New Scientist*, 160(2155):14, October 10.

Lin, Yu-Hsin and David Penny. 2001. "Implications for Bat Evolution from Two New Complete Mitochondrial Genomes." *Molecular Biological Evolution*, 18(4):684-688.

Novacek, Michael J. 1985. "Evidence for Echolocation in the Oldest Known Bats." *Nature*, 315:140-141.

Novick, Alvin. 1970. "Echolocation in Bats." *Natural History*, 79(3):32-40.

Okada, Nirihiro. 2006. *Proceedings of the National Academy of Sciences* 10:1073.

Perkins, Sid. 2005. "Learning to Listen: How Some Vertebrates Evolved Biological Sonar." *Science News*, 167:314-316.

Pettigrew, John D. 1986. "Flying Primates? Megabats have the Advanced Pathway from Eye to Midbrain." *Science*, 231:1304-1306.

Sears, Karen E., Richard R. Behringer, John J. Rasweiler IV, and Lee A. Niswander. 2006. "Development of Bat Flight: Morphologic and Molecular Evolution of Bat Wing Digits." *Proceedings of the National Academy of Science*, 103(17):6581-6586.

Seeley, H.G. 1967. *Dragons of the Air*. New York: Dover Publications.

Simmons, James A. and Roger A. Stein. 1980. "Acoustic Imaging in Bat Sonar: Echolocation Signals and the Evolution of

Echolocation." *Journal of Comparative Physiology A: Sensory, Neural, and Behavioral Physiology*, 135(1):61-84.

Simmons, Nancy B. 2005. "An Eocene Big Bang for Bats." *Science*, 307:527-528.

Speakman, J.R. and P.A. Racey. 1991. "No Cost of Echolocation for Bats in Flight." *Nature*, 350(6317):421-423.

Springer, Mark S., Emma C. Teeling, Ole Madsen, Michael J. Stanhope, and Wilfried W. de Jong. 2001. "Integrated Fossil and Molecular Data Reconstruct Bat Echolocation." *Proceedings of the National Academy of Science*, 98:11-6241-6246.

Teeling, Emma C., Mark S. Springer, Ole Madsen, Paul Bates, Stephen J. O'Brien, and William J. Murphy. 2005. "A Molecular Phylogeny for Bats Illuminates Biogeography and the Fossil Record." *Science*, 307:580-583.

Thewissen, J.G. and S.K. Babcock. 1992. "The Origin of Flight in Bats." *Bioscience*, 42(5):340-345, May.

Van Valen, Leigh. 1979. "The Evolution of Bats." *Evolutionary Theory*, 4(3):103-121.

Williams, Kim and Rob Mies. 1996. *Understanding Bats: Discovering the Secret Lives of these Gentle Mammals*. Marietta, OH: Pardson Corporation/Bird Watcher's Digest Press.

Wimsatt, William A. 1957. "Bats." *Scientific American*, 197(5):105-114, November.

Chapter 13

Whales — Speculation and Evidence

Introduction

The term whale is a common noun that can refer to all marine mammals called cetaceans that are members of order cetacea, including dolphins and porpoises. Whales are divided into toothed whales and baleen whales, the latter employing enormous brush-like structures to effectively filter its diet of small organisms from ocean water (Ober and Garrison, 2005). Of the 76 known whale species, 66 are toothed whales and ten are baleen whales. Toothed whales (*odontoceti*) are divided into three main families: pilot whales, narwhal whales, and delphinidae such as dolphins and killer whales (orca). In this chapter, the term whales excludes both dolphins and porpoises.

Baleen whales (Suborder *Mysticeti*) are divided into six main families, fin whales, minke whales, blue whales, humpback whales, rorqual whales, right whales, and gray whales. Some whale species grow to be only about 20 feet long, but blue whales, the largest living animal currently in existence, can grow up to 100 feet long and weigh as much as 150 tons. Toothed whales are smaller on average than Baleen whales and range from three to 32 feet long.

The Origin of Whales

The origin of whales presents an extremely difficult evolutionary scenario. Numerous sequences leading to whales have been proposed, but no one theory of whale evolution is generally accepted. Historically, whales were classified as a type of fish and it was not until Linnaeus reclassified them as mammals that their origin became a major issue (Slijper, 1962). One current theory is that sea animals (fish) evolved into terrestrial animals, then whales evolved from some terrestrial ungulate ancestor, or from some extinct wolf-like animal, back into a sea animal. From which terrestrial animal whales evolved is a major controversy. Charles Darwin proposed that whales evolved from bears. He wrote that "I can see no difficulty in a race of bears being rendered, by natural selection, more and more aquatic in their structure and habits, with larger and larger mouths, till a creature was produced as monstrous as a whale (Darwin, 1859, p. 184)."

Other suggested precursors of whales include a cow-like animal, a hippopotamus-like animal, a hyena-like animal called a pachyaena, a wolf-like animal called pakicetid, or even a cat-like animal called a sinonyx (Domning, 2001). The hippo theory, long the leading candidate because of its DNA similarities with whales, recently has lost favor because the proposed hippo precursor lived in the wrong part of the world, and too recently, to be a whale ancestor.

Yet another theory is that whales descended from a primitive group of hoofed carnivorous mammals called mesonychids (Zhou, et al., 1995; Prothero, 1999). Since the 1960s, based on dental similarities and molecular data, it was widely believed that whales evolved from an extinct archaic ungulate mesonychid (Thewissen, et al., 1998, p. 452; Harder, 2001, p. 180). Other experts noted that mesonychians cannot be the ancestor of whales for many reasons, including all "phylogenetic studies indicate that pakicetids are more closely related to living cetaceans than to artiodactyls and mesonychians" (Thewissen, et al., 2001).

New findings placed mesonychians in the artiodactyla family (even-toed ungulates, including camels, hippos, pigs, and ruminants) based on *Artiocetus clavis* and *Rodhocetus balochistanems* fossils (Milinkovich and Thewissen, 1997). When this theory was announced, Muizon wrote that it was "based on solid anatomical data, and contradict[s] the previous hypotheses of both palaeontologists and molecular biologists." This theory was soon displaced by other theories.

The latest theory, as of 2007, is that whales evolved from an Indohyus, a putative 48 million-year-old terrestrial animal about the size of a small raccoon that looked like an antler-less African long-tailed mouse-deer (Thewissen, et al., 2007). Some even have described this animal as an overgrown long-legged rat-like animal looking nothing like a whale. The main evidence that it was a whale ancestor is Indohyus' thickened ear bone, a design that so far is found only in cetaceans (Thewissen, et al., 2007).

All of these proposed theories have major problems. For example, whale evolution from artiodactyls is supported mainly by DNA sequences. This theory is problematic because all artiodactyl teeth have three lobes, a trait lacking in both cetaceans and mesonychians, requiring a complicated tooth evolution that "includes reversals, convergences or both" (Milinkovich and Thewissen, 1997, p. 623). Ellis's conclusion that "all known fossil whales seem to be fully developed aquatic mammals; we do not know the steps that led to their return to the sea" (1987, p. 8) still holds true.

Figure 13.1—Artist's reconstruction of an extinct Indohyus[1]

Proposed Evolution from Terrestrial Mammals

Because whales are mammals, their evolution was assumed to have occurred through some type of terrestrial mammal. Evolving from a land tetrapod into a sea mammal requires hundreds of major land-adapted traits to be converted into sea-adapted designs. Nonetheless, their evolution from a fish appears even less probable due to the enormous anatomical differences between fish and whales. Obvious differences include: fish obtain oxygen by gills, but whales use lungs to breathe air; fish lay eggs; whales give birth to their young live and breastfeed—in other words whales are mammals.

Numerous other examples of problems with the current whale evolution theories include evolution from a terrestrial animal to an aquatic whale requires radical changes in the integument system, lactation, breathing, diving, feeding methods, nervous system, eyes (they must be protected in water), hearing, and evolution from a walking to a swimming mode of existence. Other obvious examples include loss of body hair, body streamlining, transformation of

---

[1] Image Credit: Nicolas Primola / Shutterstock.com

forelimbs into flippers, loss of hind limbs, evolution of flukes for swimming, and backward nostril design.

To convert a land tetrapod to a fish-like mammal (whales were first classified as mammals only in 1693 by naturalist John Ray) requires thousands of other changes. All of these systems are interrelated and function as a unit, requiring altering the interrelationships of the entire system. Both size and structural changes necessary for a large dog-sized tetrapod animal to evolve into a whale (a humpback whale is larger and heavier than a city bus) are summarized below:

1. **Body Size**: The body size changes required to evolve from a small terrestrial mammal to a whale are enormous—from a 50-pound dog-sized animal to up to a 150-ton sea animal, and from a few feet long to up to a 100-foot-long animal. The tongue of a blue whale alone weighs as much as an elephant. These changes require not only size modifications, but major design changes in every body organ and structure.

2. **The Heart**: The size changes require evolving a heart from the size of a human fist to one about the size of a Volkswagen Beetle. The heart valves would have to evolve from about the size of a dime to the size of an automobile tire rim. Each tooth would have to evolve from a few ounces to over a kilogram (2.2 pound) in weight. A human heart beats about 70 times a minute, a whale heart only nine times a minute, but the force of each beat is many times stronger than in humans.

3. **Weight-bearing**: Land-dwelling animals consume about 40 percent of their energy just to support their bodies and move around the land, but sea-dwelling creatures use water for support and only need energy to move around in water (Zahn, 1988, p. 28). For this reason, the transition from land to water requires major muscular and skeletal system design changes. Whales must not only lose their legs, but also evolve flippers, pectoral fins, a fluke,

an aerodynamic body design plus a brain and the appropriate nervous and muscle system to service these many new structures and their requirements.

4. **Heat Retention**: Land temperatures often change rapidly and can fluctuate over a wide range. For this reason land-dwelling life must possess a physical mechanism that can withstand, or adapt to, enormous temperature changes. Not only do the temperature changes in the sea occur very slowly and within a much narrower range, but ocean water is very cold, and water's high thermal conductivity is a major problem for warm-blooded mammals (Heyning and Mead, 1997, p. 1138). Organisms with a body system regulated according to land temperatures demands must evolve a whole new system to accommodate the frigid ocean water temperatures. As warm-blooded animals, whales have various heat conservation structures such as counter-current heat exchangers to minimize heat loss. In contrast to land mammals, whales also largely lack hair and sweat glands and have a thick layer of fibrous fat called blubber to help insulate them from the icy cold water, all of which involve major marine environmental adaptations (Heyning and Mead, 1997, p. 1138).

5. **Water**: Water is essential to metabolism and must be used economically due to its relative scarcity on land. Land animals require a system designed to permit ration and regulation of water loss while preventing excessive evaporation. Because the skin of land-dwelling animals is not suitable for an aquatic habitat, land-dwelling creatures sense thirst, a function not required by sea-dwelling creatures. In contrast although marine animals also must regulate body water, they must do so in very different ways than terrestrial animals.

6. **Kidneys**: Because water must be used economically by terrestrial animals, they require a very efficient kidney system. The body's protein metabolism system either excretes or breaks down wastes to other, less toxic, compounds. The metabolic breakdown of protein produces toxic amounts of ammonia, which is then

converted into urea and, in the end, reduces the amount of water excreted. In addition, a complex system of ducts and other structures are required for the kidney's proper functioning.

In contrast, sea-dwelling organisms discharge waste materials, including ammonia, directly into their aquatic environment. In short, in order to evolve from water to land, living things must develop whole new complex organ systems to deal with water regulation. Then, to evolve back into aquatic animals another whole new, very different system must evolve, especially to deal with salt removal, since whales live in a toxic saltwater world.

7. **Breathing Opening**: Terrestrial animals breathe through their nose and mouth. In contrast, to take in air, whales have a unique nostril called a blowhole complex (some whales, such as a humpback, have two) on the top of their head. Each whale breath must take in thousands of times as much air as humans, enough for the whale to remain submerged for as long as an hour. They would have to evolve a hole on top of their head that connects directly to the lungs and a strong muscular flap valve system which covers the blowhole to prevent sea water from flooding into their lungs when they descend below the saltwater surface.

8. **Respiratory system**: Fish "breathe" by means of gills that function by removing oxygen that is dissolved in the water. Consequently, they cannot live for more than a few minutes out of the water. In order to survive on land, they would have to acquire a complex lung system. To evolve back into a sea animal, they would need to re-evolve a new gill system or evolve a new means of taking in oxygen from the water, as a whale does, via a lung system that is very different than in land animals. The orthodox theory teaches that fish evolved a gill system, then a lung system when they evolved to live on land, then a whole new lung system design when the pre-whale land animal evolved back into a marine animal. One major adaptation is not only their enormous lung capacity, but also a very efficient oxygen exchange system to allow

it to stay under the water for a long time.

9. **Pressure**: Terrestrial animals must deal with only about 14 psi on land, but deep diving whales submerge as much as 1,640 feet below the water surface requiring it to deal with the enormous pressure existing at these depths. Its enormously thick muscular body and its strong frame skeleton both are designed to withstand pressure level this high (Zahn, 1988, p. 28). Some whales also can remain submerged for as long as two hours. This feat is achieved by its ability to reduce its lung volume as the pressure increases, significantly slowing down the heart rate to reduce oxygen use and the ability to store large amounts of oxygen in the muscle hemoglobin (Ellis, 1987, p. 8). It also shuts down blood circulation to unessential areas. When the whale is swimming on the water surface, it takes in enormous amounts of air that is compressed, countering the deep-sea pressure. The blowhole is closed with a special muscle plug that allows the animal to maintain the required internal pressure.

10. **Hearing**: To evolve from a land animal into an aquatic whale, the external ears must evolve into an internal hearing system that can function under water and eardrums that can withstand the very high pressure existing in water as deep as 1,640 feet. This environment requires a radically different hearing design system. The ear auricle would have to disappear, then later re-evolve so as to allow the animal to live in an aqueous environment.

11. **Vision**: The eyes and lenses not only must evolve to become far larger in a whale, but also must withstand the enormous pressures of the deep ocean and produce a far higher refractive index to achieve water vision. Whales are one of the very few mammals that shed tears, which is one of several mechanisms that they use to protect their eyes and body from the seawater's high salt concentration.

Among the many other major changes required for a terrestrial animal to morph into a whale include the evolution of a "tail," actually a powerful dorsal fin called a "fluke," and its accessory structures. A fluke is a very different structure than that used by either fish or mammals. Fish tails use bones that move from side-to-side by muscles and, in contrast, flukes are wide cartilaginous structures lacking bones. They are moved by powerful muscles connected to the whale's spine. From tip-to-tip, flukes can be longer than six feet. The fluke's up and down movement can propel the whale at speeds of over 30 mph.

The whale forelimbs, called flippers, also are essential for both steering and turning. They are designed with bumps called *tubercles* on the leading edge of its flippers to break up the vortices, reducing drag, which normally is a problem. Furthermore, the tubercles create lift, allowing the animal to tilt its flippers at a small angle without stalling. The same lift is how birds, and heavier than air airplanes, are able to fly. The likelihood that all these many dramatic physiological changes required to swim could have happened concurrently enough in the one organism to function when evolving from land to water is virtually impossible.

Reproduction

Whales give birth to one live young calf at a time. The mother has specially designed nipples to allow her calf to lock onto her with its specially designed mouth to enable the mother to pressure force her milk into it. The calf must drink two to three gallons of milk in only a few seconds to allow them to surface for air. A calf can drink up to 100 gallons of fat rich milk in a single day.

Blue Whales

The blue whale, in contrast to bottom feeders, swims along the sea surface with its mouth open wide. In one gulp it can suck in as much as 50 tons (45,359.2 Kg) of water, enough to ingest four tons or about 40 million krill, a shrimp-like animal about the size of your little finger. Humpbacks emit clouds of bubbles in a circle below schools of small fish. The bubbles trap the fish, the whale then lunges up with its mouth open and, lastly, its throat expands to make room for the food and water that was ingested. The design changes for this complex system to function are just a few of the thousands of major functional alterations required to evolve a whale from a small terrestrial dog-like mammal.

Baleen Whales

One of the most striking requirements for a land animal to become a baleen sea whale is the transformation of teeth into the hundreds of enormous comb-like shaped baleen structures. These structures are used to give this whale the unique ability to obtain nourishment by straining zooplankton from seawater. The combs, which are up to seven feet long, are spaced one-quarter of an inch apart and overlap. They are fringed on one side, a design feature that functions to effectively catch plankton such as krill.

Baleen whales have two blowholes that pull in seawater containing plankton. Next, their throat contracts, forcing the water out and retaining the plankton on the baleen filter (described above) which are then swallowed. These whales filter thousands of gallons of seawater daily to obtain the over two tons of krill they require to survive. Gray baleen whales swim at the sea bottom and devour large quantities of sediment. They then rise to the surface to rinse out the muck and sediment from their mouths and swallow their catch of small fish (Esperante, et al., 2008).

Whale Evolution

Up until 1993, the claimed evidence for whale evolution consisted of a few partial skulls with no non-cranial material (Miller, 2003, p. 173). Nevertheless, evolutionists consider the fossil evidence leading to whales among their best examples of one

> of the most remarkable series of transitional fossils [that] documents the amazing story of whale evolution. From about sixty-five to thirty-seven million years ago in the Paleocene and Eocene Periods, there lived a group of land-dwelling mammals, which, though they were ungulates (hoofed animals), were carnivorous and may have behaved like hyenas. Called "mesonychids," these creatures would not be anyone's first guess as a likely ancestor of the sperm whale. Yet in 1979 ... in Pakistan ... Phillip Gingerich made a remarkable find: an animal that, though only coyote-sized, had the distinctive anatomical traits of a whale, and so was named "*Pakicetus*" (Parsons, 2004, p. 160).

Discussions of whale origins must assume that various extinct creatures were whale ancestors. These initial assumptions usually are subsequently retracted as a result of more fossil finds. One example is mesonychids, which, after *Archeocetes* was discovered in Eocene strata, were determined not to be a viable whale transition (Rose, 2001). Another example is the whale putative ancestor, *Basilosaurus,* which was at first thought to be a serpent-like reptile, but was later reclassified as a "whale-like" mammal (Evans, 1987, p. 2). This animal, however, does not provide support for whale evolution because no clear fossil connections exist between *Basilosaurus* and the *Archeocetes* and modern whales, whether with teeth (Odontoceti) or baleen. Gaskin put this fact bluntly:

> Archaeoceti could not be considered as direct ancestors of either modern baleen whales or modern toothed whales..... it was unlikely that they gave rise to the ancestral forms of either group. The Archaeoceti may be regarded as a less successful independent line which died out perhaps 10 million years ago (Gaskin, 1972, p. 3).

Other evidence supports the conclusion that the archeocetes are members of another mammal category unrelated to modern whales.

Details Regarding the Whale Fossil Record

More than 26 fossil species now have been claimed by one or more paleontologists to be whale ancestors, thereby proving the evolution of whales from a fully terrestrial to a fully aquatic animal. They have been assigned by some researchers to four families: Pakicetidae, Ambulocetidae, Remingtonocetidae, and Protocetidae. Depending on the authority, the major skeletal finds used to prove whale evolution include the *mesonychids, Pakicetus, Ambulocetus, Rodhocetus, Prozeuglodon,* and *Protocetids.* All of these animals, judging from their teeth and other features, were active hunting carnivores in contrast to all whales except Delphinidae that consume krill and other small marine organisms, including small fish.

1. The family *Pakicetidae* (genera *Pakicetus, Nalacetus,* and *Ichthyolestes*) contains fully terrestrial even-toed ungulate artiodactyl tetrapods. *Pakicetus* was about the size of a wolf, *Ichthyolestes* the size of a fox, and *Nalacetus* in-between (Gingerich, et al., 1983; Gingerich, et al., 2001). Artist reconstructions picture

Pakicetus as appearing very similar to a medium-sized dog. A major reason for considering this dog-like animal a whale ancestor is its possession of certain inner ear traits, as judged from the animal's skull characteristics, as cetacean. The first Pakicetus fossil find consisted of a lone skull and a relatively complete skeleton found in 2001.

Although Pakicetus had a few minor whale characteristics, most of its traits were very different from whales. One study of Pakicetus's anklebones determined that it had many similarities to artiodactyls (Thewissen, et al., 2001). Furthermore, the teeth of this wolf-sized land animal "closely resemble those of land-dwelling mesonychids — so closely that paleontologists ... had always regarded such teeth as belonging to mesonychids until they found the jaws those teeth came from" (Parsons, 2004, p. 160).

Pakicetidae nostrils were not even close to where a modern whale blowhole is located, but were in the same place as a dog's nostrils. A major evidence for its whale ancestry is its ears, which are dissimilar to the ears of both terrestrial and aquatic animals, and thus are interpreted as intermediate (Gingerich, 2003). Based largely on these few conclusions, the whole animal is interpreted as an intermediate whale transition. Evidence, though, has established that, except for one small bone, it lacks the sensitive auditory components present in whales. Thewissen, *et al.*, from his study of the Pakicetidae bones and structures determined that its auditory system is well developed for airborne sound, not underwater hearing (2001, p. 278).

2. *Ambulocetus nations* is an otter-sized mammal that, in spite of being named a "walking whale," based on reconstructions from fossil bone fragments, looks nothing like a whale. Enough of the skeleton has been uncovered to conclude that it had tiny front limbs and longer hind limbs with hoofs, large feet, and a strong tail. It had a long non-whale-like tail and lacked evidence of a fluke, a critical structure present in all whales. Nor did it display evidence

of a whale's posterior, its flippers, its blowhole, nor most of the other unique whale traits. It was actually an amphibious carnivorous animal with legs and a body that looks very much like a nine-foot long crocodile. Its eyes also were in the wrong place— on top of its crocodile-like head and not on the side of its head as is true of whales. It also had crocodile-like webbed feet, and its fossil spine indicated that it could undulate like a modern otter to walk on land.

Further research has forced the original theorist, University of Michigan Professor Philip Gingerich, to conclude that he now has doubts that *Ambulocetus* is in the direct line of whale evolution (Werner, 2007, p. 144). In short, he now thinks it is not a whale ancestor at all, but on a different part of the evolutionary tree. It is not considered a crocodile ancestor either because modern crocodiles date around the time that *Ambulocetus* lived, but it could well have been a member of the crocodile family. Evidence does exist that *Ambulocetus nations* had ankle bones similar to those of artiodactyla, but this does "not unambiguously support either of the predominant hypotheses of cetacean relationships" (Thewissen, et al., 1998, p. 452). This finding only confuses whale evolution because it requires "extensive convergence or reversals" in evolution to account for the contradictory evidence (Thewissen, et al., 1998, p. 452).

3. The *Remingtonocetidae* were similar to the *Ambulocetids,* which may be an evolutionary dead end (Miller, 2003). The cranial anatomy is well-documented, but so far only one complete upper molar and a complete lower premolar and molar are known (Bajpal and Thewissen, 1995; Thewissen and Bajpai, 2001, p. 463). This evidence indicates that the animal had a long, slender crocodile morphology and may be a member of the ambulocetus or crocodile family.

4. *Protocetids* are a diverse group of cetacean, and one of the most well known examples is Genus *Rodhocetus* (Chadwick, 2001,

p. 67). Although very dolphin-appearing, judging by the fossils, the animal also looked very much like a crocodile-dolphin hybrid. It had very small hind legs and once was believed to have a fluke-like tail similar to the whale fluke, an assumption that has not been supported by fossil evidence—no evidence of any fluke structure exists on any of the known Rodhocetus fossils. It even lacks the ball vertebrae required for a fluke, a significant problem because all cetaceans have ball vertebrae and flukes.

Furthermore, no evidence exists for the bone structure required for the flippers that exist on all whales. It did have nostrils that were located slightly higher on the skull than that of a crocodile, but not anywhere near the modern whale blowhole, and no evidence exists that their nostrils functioned like a blowhole. Its skull is much closer to that of a crocodile and very dissimilar to a whale. The first *Rodhocetus* fossils were found in Pakistan in 2001 by Philip Gingerich.

5. *Archeocete*: This proposed link between an extinct Archeocete class and whales is not supported by fossil evidence. Unlike modern toothed whales, the Odontoceti archeocete fossils had teeth that were differentiated into incisors, canines, and molars called polyform teeth (thus were heterodonts), which indicates that they were terrestrial mammals. All whales have monoform teeth and only one tooth type exists in a single animal. No evidence of a fossil connection has been found between either the Archeocete teeth or pelvic structures and Odontoceti toothed whales.

6. *Basilosaurus* was an up to 70-feet-long serpent-like fully aquatic animal with sturdy front flippers and small well-developed hind legs, complete with jointed knees and toes that were used as copulatory organs. Originally discovered in the late 1800s in the United States, *Basilosaurus* was named "king lizard" because of its resemblance to a large lizard. Stahl concluded that *Basilosaurus* "could not possibly have been ancestral to any of the modern whales" for numerous reasons, including its very non-whale

serpentine body form and its teeth shape, often an important means of both identification and classification (Stahl, 1974, p. 489).

Lawrence Barnes of the National History Museum noted that it lived contemporaneously with modern baleen whales (mysticetes) and toothed whales (odontocetes, thus could not be in the evolutionary line to modern whales (quoted in Werner, 2007, p. 144). *Basilosaurus* was likely an extinct marine animal and not a transitional form.

7. *Dorudon atrox*, a 20-foot-long cetacean with a fluke and small back legs, is another putative whale evolutionary link. The animal is very similar to a small Basilosaurus and for this reason is thought by some mammalogists to be a juvenile Basilosaurus. The most complete skeleton shows small hind limbs, feet, and toes very similar to those of Basilosaurus, indicating that *Dorudon* is a juvenile Basilosaurus.

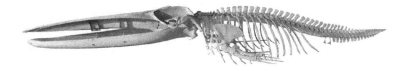

Figure 13.2—Whale Skeleton[2]

Whales with Teeth

Fossil teeth comprise the central evidence in the whale fossil record and present problems for whale evolution. One example is that Pakicetus teeth resemble those of Protocetus and Indocetus, not whales (Berta, 1995; Bajpai and Gingerich, 1998). Whales with teeth first appeared in the fossil record only in the Eocene, estimated by evolutionists to be 30 million years after the Archeocetes became extinct (Evans, 1987, p. 21; Alexander, 1975,

---

[2] Photo Credit: David Herraez Calzada / Shutterstock.com

pp. 434-435).

Evans concluded that the Eocene archeocete fossils were "replaced" by members of four different fossil whale orders in strata judged to be Oligocene. Two separate types of Odontoceti may have existed, those with polyform teeth, such as the *Squalodontidae,* and others with no dental differentiation (monoform teeth). Only the monoform dentition groups still exist today.

Darwinists claim that whale teeth evolved from the "differentiated" form existing in fossil whales to the "undifferentiated" teeth found in modern Odontoceti. This evolution scenario requires a series of fossils linking a long, serpent-like creature with tiny back legs (such as the *Basilosaurus)* to modern toothed whales. Furthermore, the comparison of these unrelated and unlinked life forms is not based on scientific data. Last, evidence exists that they lived at the same time as whales and therefore could not be a whale precursor.

The claim that true polyform teeth existed in certain fossil Odontoceti requires more study (Ridgway, 1972, p. 6). Toothed *Squalodontidae* fossils found in late Oligocene possessed teeth grouped into functional incisors, canines, premolars, and molars. For this reason, evolutionists are forced to claim that teeth became more numerous and *less* specialized as the pre-whales evolved into modern Odontoceti whales (Gaskin, 1972, p. 3).

Another problem is that when the fossil finds are compared, one type of putative whale fossil is found almost exclusively, or exclusively, in only one part of the world, such as Pakistan, and another claimed transitional form is found exclusively, or almost exclusively, in a *different* part of the world (Thewissen, 1998).

Summary of the Whale Fossil Record

Although some claim there exists "near unanimity among specialists that the ancestors of the Cetaceans also were the ancestors of the land mammals known as the Artiodactyla, of which modern representatives are the camels and rhinoceroses," much controversy exists (Gaskin, 1972, p. 5). Although many evolutionists believe the whale evolution fossil record to be one of the best documented for all animals, biologists have been unable to fill the enormous void between land mammals and whales with valid evidence, even though over two million putative fossil whale bone fragments have been discovered. None of these fossils document a clear viable transitional species, and all of those proposed are problematic. The best example of a transitional form is the modern-day dolphin; but, since dolphins are contemporaneous with modern whales, they cannot be whale precursors.

No clear fossil lineage exists between the Artiodactyla and modern whales, and evolutionists admit that "the fossil record which could confirm the origin of the cetaceans from terrestrial or freshwater mammals still has many gaps" (Gaskin, 1972, p. 5). Banister and Campbell accurately summarized the fossil record claims, noting that the "origins of present-day cetaceans are poorly known" (1985, p. 294). This still is true in 2016.

The origin of the first baleen whales is also obscure (Esperante, et al., 2008). Baleens appear fully formed in the fossil record for the first time in the Middle Oligocene (Gaskin, 1972, p. 4). No fossil evidence exists to support the supposed transition from ancestral land-dwelling mammals with teeth to baleen whales, in spite of the fact that the teeth which distinguish them preserve better in the fossil record than any other body part.

In view of the lack of transitional forms, Colbert concluded that "whales ... appear suddenly in early Tertiary times, fully adapted ... for a highly specialized mode of life" (Colbert, 2001, p. 392). Another evolutionary biologist added: "We do not possess a single fossil of the transitional forms between the aforementioned land animals [carnivores and ungulates] and the whales" (Slijper, 1962, p. 17). The lack of transitional forms is ignored by evolutionists who make such irresponsible claims such as that whales "enjoyed at the outset a series of extraordinarily rapid evolutionary changes that by middle Eocene times made them well adapted for life in the ocean" (Colbert, 2001, p. 392).

Molecular Studies

Molecular studies have supported some whale evolution theories and not others. So far, as a whole, there exists a "wide gulf between the morphological and molecular evolutionary studies" on the question of which mammals are the whales' closest cetacean relatives (Luo, 2000, p. 235). Luo adds that "there is a big disagreement between morphological and molecular studies ... on the broad picture of ungulate-cetacean evolution" (2000, p. 236).

Naylor and Adams noted, after evaluating the molecular studies, that "the phylogenic position of cetacea within the mammalian tree has long been a subject of debate" (2001, p. 444). Nikaido, *et. al.*, (1999) concluded, based on a study of insertions of short and long interspersed elements, that the Hippopotamuses are the closest extant relatives of whales.

Spaulding, *et al.* (2009, p. e7062), in an evaluation of extinct taxa using both morphological and molecular evidence, argued that the fossils closest to whales are Indohyus. They also determined that Mesonychids were more distantly related, and that the closest living relative was a hippo, and concluded that "mesonychia is only distantly related to Artiodactyla" (2009, p. e7062). When taxon sampling is altered or other criteria are used for comparisons, the taxonomic arrangement may be changed (2009, p. e7062).

Whale Pelvis Bones

The so-called "pelvic girdle" of whales and porpoises is located in the general region where hip bones exist in land mammals (Bejder and Hall, 2002). Many Darwinists argue that these bones prove that whales evolved from a terrestrial animal with functional hind legs. Scheffer described these whale hips as "a pair of slender bones floating in the muscles near the sex organs" (1976, p. 8). Actually, the whale pelvic bones are "freely floating in muscle tissue just in front of the anus" (Evans, 1987, p. 4).

The Evolutionists Arguments

The evolutionary explanation for the whale pelvic bones is that they are the useless vestigial remains of the pelvic girdle and the hind legs that existed when the whale ancestor was a terrestrial tetrapod (Young, 1962, p. 667; Ridgway, 1972, p. 7; Alexander, 1975, p. 431; Watson, 1981, p. 33; and Evans, 1987, pp. 4-5). Certain extinct whales did have pelvic bones, but this fact alone does not prove whale ancestors were terrestrial. The fact is, an enormous number of critical anatomical features separate whales from terrestrial animals, and no good evidence of transitional forms exists. Many extinct animals have existed with a wide variety of features that cannot be used to prove anything about evolution.

Bejder and Hall argued that simple evolutionary changes in *Hox* gene expression or *Hox* gene regulation are unlikely to have caused hind limb loss, but selection "acting on a wide range of developmental processes and adult traits other than the limbs are likely to have driven the loss of hind limbs in whales" (2002, p. 445). They argue that hind limbs likely "began to regress only after the ancestors of whales entered the aquatic environment" (2002, p. 445).

Before the limbs could regress, the pre-whale would have had to have an effective method of swimming—and once it did, why would the limbs regress? Chadwick wrote that, as the "rear limbs dwindled, so did the hip bones that supported them" (2001, p. 69). An example of this line of reasoning from an online discussion group is as follows

> whales' hip-bones prove (or suggest strongly) that an "intelligent designer" did not create whales. ...an "intelligent" design uses functioning parts for rational purposes. Hip bones have a function: to support legs. Whales have no legs. Whales have no use, function, nor need for hip bones. And yet they have hip bones... Ergo... The "ID" notion can't explain it. It can only beg the question. "Maybe there is a use we are unable to perceive." Maybe. But "Maybe" is not an explanation; the ID concept has no explanatory value. Evolution, on the other hand, is easily capable of embracing the concept of vestigial organs and structures, and "explains" the mystery... Whales are descended from animals that had legs (Silas, 2002).

Crapo concluded, "it is clear that the empirical data fit neatly within an evolutionary argument while posing an unresolved problem for creationists" (Crapo, 1984, p. 6). Russian zoologist Alexy Yablokov wrote that from the "time of Charles Darwin to the present, the two small bones in whales in the place of the well-developed posterior extremities of terrestrial mammals, have been considered to be a fine example of vestigial organs" (1974, p. 233).

Awbrey (1983, p. 6) asserted without citing his evidence that the fossil record of whales supports the pelvic bone degeneration theory because not two, as seen today, but rather three whale pelvic elements are discernible in the fossil record. If the fossils demonstrate a modification from three bones in whales' hips to two, this would not in itself demonstrate that the whale pelvis is now a useless structure.

Although Awbrey asserts that the pelvis has been reduced by evolution and "no longer connects the hind legs to the axial skeleton" he admits that the two small bones have a function — namely "to support the reproductive and rectal muscles" (Awbrey, 1983, p. 6). Their support role fits either the design, or the descent with modification view, but either way, they are not vestigial.

A major problem is that far less is known about cetaceans than about many other animals. Furthermore, "the exact identity [i.e., are they the ischium, ileum or pubis?] and development of the elements of the pelvic vestige in extant cetaceans have not been established. Such identification is critical to fully understand the events underlying the evolution of the cetacean pelvis" (Pabst, *et al.*, 1998, p. 393). The whale hip bones may not correspond to any of the bones Pabst *et al.* listed, and may serve an entirely different function.

The Function of the Hip Bones of Whales

Creationists also once explained the whale hip bones as evidence of degeneration, but this view is no longer valid because a clear function has now been determined for these bones. The whale hipbones have a role similar to the hyoid bone in humans — to serve as an anchor for various muscles and other structures. A good example is the North Sea Beaked Whale in which the putative "pelvis" is present only in males where it is used to anchor the muscle set attached to the penis (Watson, 1981, p. 33).

In other whales, the whale "pelvis" bones, together with the separate putative limb bones, serve as an attachment for the penis corpora cavernosa (Young, 1962, p. 667). Tajima, *et al.*, concluded from an anatomical study of the porpoise pelvic bone that its function in male finless porpoises is to support the penis (2004, p. 761).

Work by Yablokov also documents that the whale pelvic bones serve a critical copulation function, and the "pelvis" in toothed whales is differentially located in males compared to females in order to make "penis erection possible in the male" and aid in "effective contraction of the vagina in the female" (Yablokov, 1974, pp. 234-235). These bones also support certain internal organs and also serve as attachment points for several muscles, as does the coccyx in humans (Williams, 1970, p. 33).

The major contradiction for the evolutionists is that they once argued that the whale hip is a useless leftover from when its ancestors were terrestrial, just as predicted by evolution. But then when function for the hip was found, they still argue that this proves the whale hip was derived from the terrestrial ancestor's hip. Hence, this demonstrates the 'just so story' nature of evolution—it explained nothing, just merely adjusts its so-called predictions when the data change

Although Darwinists now acknowledge that these "formerly held vestiges" play "important functions" in the whale, they argue that the bones "still demonstrate descent with modification" (Conrad, 1983, p. 9). Of course, if Darwinism is true, all organs and structures would demonstrate descent with modification because evolution teaches that *all* organs evolved from other simpler organs. In conclusion, like the human hyoid bone, the two small pubic bones in the whale provide structural support for various organs and muscles (Awbrey, 1983, p. 6).

The Whale Limb Bones

In addition to the small but functional whale hip bones, some whales also have structures resembling limb bones. In some whale species, anterior to the tail exist "rudiments of a femur and even a tibia," both of which are attached to the girdle (Alexander, 1975, p. 431). Blue whales often have a "pelvis" with tiny bones attached to it. In addition, a tiny tibia-like bone is sometimes found in the bowhead whale (Watson, 1981, p. 33). Young described the whale hind legs as "bony nodules.... representing limb bones" (1962, p. 667). Andrews described a case of a 31-inch-long whale hind limb that he concluded showed a "remarkable reversion to the primitive quadripedal condition" (1921, p. 2).

Many aquatic animals, such as crocodiles, have fully functional limbs that serve as both paddles to swim and feet to walk. So why did whales lose these limbs and paddles? Awbrey, asserted that these whale leg bones are atavisms that can be explained only in terms of mega-evolution:

> In many cetacean species, an occasional individual also has one or more poorly formed leg bones that form no joint with the pelvis. When present, these bones are arranged in the typical tetrapod order of femur, tibia and tarsus, and metatarsal. The paired protrusions enclosing these leg bones range from tiny bumps to cylindrical structures up to four feet long (Awbrey, 1983, p. 6).

No clear fossil data supports Awbrey's claim that these small bones indicate the descent of whales from an ancestor that possessed fully formed legs. Byers characterized the lack of fossil data for loss of legs in whales as follows:

> The oldest Cetacean fossils are found in Upper Eocene deposits, and in none of these fossils are leg bones better developed than they are in modern specimens. There is nothing aberrant or unusual in these fossils. I have yet to find anything in the fossil record that is surprising or difficult for a creationist to explain (Byers, 1983, p. 2).

One other proposal for these whale "leg" bone abnormalities is that they are simply the result of mutations and/or teratogens. Evidence for this includes the fact that they are very rare in many whale species—the case he examined "is the only recorded case" that he knew of among cetaceans, even though "hundreds of thousands of whales have been killed, especially in the last fifty years" (Andrews, 1921, p. 6). If they are in fact mutational or developmental abnormalities, they tell us very little about whale phylogeny. Until more cases are studied, it is difficult to draw firm conclusions about their function or origin.

Conversely, in some species of whales, the "leg" bones are typical. The most plausible explanation, as noted above, is that the "limb" bones are part of a larger structure that serve as copulatory guides and as an anchor for the genitalia muscles (Chadwick, 2001, p. 73). An example is the *Basilosaurus*, the giant aquatic marine animal with a serpent-like body, flippers, and very small hind limbs discussed above. The "well-developed" hind limbs of *Basilosaurus* have been considered evidence that it was a late transitional stage to the legless modern whale (Chadwick, 2001, p. 73).

In 1990, Gingerich, *et al.*, discovered several new skeletons of *Basilosaurus* in Egypt. They contained comparatively well-preserved examples of the limb and foot bones. From their research on these skeletons, Gingerich, *et al.*, also concluded that they function as copulatory guides to assist the animal in sexual reproduction — obviously a critical role for *Basilosaurus* (1990, p. 154). One reason for this conclusion is the fact that, relative to body size, the putative hind limbs of *Basilosaurus* appear too small to be of much use in swimming, or body support on land, but their use for the

> maintenance of some function is likely for several reasons: most bones are present; some elements are fused, but remaining joints are well-formed with *little suggestion of degeneracy; the patella and calcaneal tuber are large for insertion of powerful muscles; and the knee has a complex locking mechanism.* ... The pelvis of modern whales serves to anchor reproductive organs, even though functional hind limbs are lacking. Thus hind

limbs of *Basilosaurus* are *most plausibly interpreted as accessories facilitating reproduction.* Abduction of the femur and plantar flexion of the foot, with the knee locked in extension, probably enabled hind limbs to be *used as guides during copulation, which may otherwise have been difficult in a serpentine aquatic mammal* (Gingerich, 1990, p. 156, emphasis mine).

Whale Fetus Teeth

Modern whales are divided into whales *with teeth* (*Odotoceti*) and baleen whales (*Mysticeti*) which, instead of teeth, use comb-like plates attached to their mouth roof to strain food from sea water. Adult baleen whales lack teeth, but when a fetus they possessed tooth-buds in the upper and lower jaws. Ever since Darwin wrote about the presence of teeth in fetal whales, which, when grown, "have not a tooth in their heads" (1859, p. 450), the whale fetus tooth-buds commonly have been labeled vestigial. It is assumed this proves that the baleen whales' ancestors had teeth, and that these embryonic "teeth" are unnecessary because they are not present in the adult.

The modern claim that fetal baleen whales' teeth are "derived from toothed ancestors, is suggested not only by paleontological evidence, but also by the fact that teeth are still found in ... [whale] embryos. The teeth are absorbed as the fetus develops the whalebone characteristics of this suborder" (Ridgway, 1972, p. 507). Darwinists argue that these tooth buds in fetal baleen whales falsify the design model and can be explained only by evolution: the whale teeth are "evolutionary leftovers" that "clearly refute design" (Awbrey, 1983, p. 6). In contrast to this claim, fetal baleen whale tooth buds now are known to have several documented functions, a topic we will now cover.

Functions of Whale Tooth buds

Vialleton concluded that, although "teeth in the whale do not pierce the gums and function as teeth, they ... actually play an important role in the formation of the bone of the jaws to which they furnish a *point d' apui* on which the bones mold themselves" (1930, p. 164). Kaufmann elaborated on Vialleton's findings about the whale teeth function, noting that the temporary development of whale teeth "guides the formation of their jaw. The teeth are multiplied and the length of the jaw is patterned after this multiplication. This could apply to the baleen whale; after the jaw is properly formed, the teeth are completely reabsorbed into the bone structure" (Kaufmann, 1983, p. 4).

Dewar also elaborated on Vialleton's research, concluding that "Darwin was wrong and Vialleton was right," because the position of these fetal teeth and their form and number are very "different from those of other Cetacea [and] show that in the whalebone whale, far from being merely the relics of an extinct ancestor, they have an individuality and a causality peculiar to them, since they are multiplied and adapted to the length of the jaw" (Dewar, 1957, pp. 171-172).

Dewar argues that "the toothless whales first acquired a number of additional teeth, then lost them and developed in their place the extraordinary baleen plates that occur in the mouth." He concludes that Vialleton's assertion was confirmed in a paper by Dr. John Cameron (1918), which showed that "one of the functions of the developing teeth is to enable the jaw to be properly molded." This was

> illustrated by a photograph of a microcephalic idiot of whom the jaws recede like those of an ape, because of the poor development of the teeth. 'In many of these individuals' he writes (p. 179) 'the teeth never develop at

all: The effect of this defective dentition is reflected in the corresponding feeble degree of development of the jaws..... The superior and inferior maxillae (jaws) in the early stages of their ossification, it may be recollected, are fragile bony shells enclosing the dental germs. For example, the lower jaw at birth is simply a thin trough of bone enclosing the developing teeth. The cause (of the poorly developed jaws) is a deficiency or actual total failure of development of the dental gums, the effect being that the investing jaws likewise fail to execute their normal growth and evolution (Dewar, 1957, pp. 171-172).

Several studies using different animals have found that a poorly developed jaw resulted in improper fetal teeth development. Instead of teeth that never erupt from the gums, it is more accurate to consider the tooth-like structures as being a part of a jaw developmental system. Similar scaffolding systems actually are rather common in embryology. Examples include the webbing between the fingers in humans and certain animals.

In a penetrating analysis of the argument that embryonic teeth in baleen whales are evolutionary vestiges, Dubois reviewed the logical fallacies inherent in the vestigial organ concept. He concluded that it is "highly unlikely from an evolutionary point of view that the baleen whales would have developed the extra teeth only to begin the process of losing them," and while Darwinists attempt to construct a

scenario to 'explain' such an occurrence, such scenarios are the evolutionary equivalent of the creationist's God could have done it that way; and in terms of actual explanatory value are equally worthless. Further, that the teeth seem to be 'adapted to the length of the jaw' militates against the assertion of vestigiality since one of the characteristics of vestigial structures is that they are no longer adaptive and therefore in the process of being discarded. I have actually seen one person maintain that even the degree to which a structure has not yet been lost is controlled by considerations of adaptive value. I find this incredible. If a structure is useless, how can it be of any adaptive value to maintain it? If it is not useless, then it is not vestigial (Dubois, 1985, p. 14).

Dubois argued that the vestigial question in this case would never exist except for two factors,

> First the evolutionary viewpoint generates certain artifacts—evolutionists must have evolutionary evidence, and 'vestiges' are a phenomenon which would seem to supply it—but given the number of structures which have been alleged to be vestigial and are so no longer, it may be said that this viewpoint has generated a 'problem' to be 'solved' which is entirely spurious. Second, there seems to be some under appreciation of the fact that not all structures are directly useful to adults (Dubois, 1985, p. 14).

In one study of the development and degradation of the temporary tooth buds in baleen whales, Ishakawa and Amasaki found that "the degradation pattern was a little different from that of deciduous tooth buds in terrestrial species" (1995, p. 665). The same claim made about whales losing their teeth is also made about chickens, animals believed by many Darwinists to have descended from toothed dinosaurs. If birds descended from toothed ancestors, Darwinism would predict that there should be evidence of vestigial, defective and nonfunctioning, but still present, enamel-protein genes in many birds, such as chickens.

A study of the chicken genome has found no evidence that this bird has enamel-protein genes. The reason is that no living bird, or any known Tertiary bird, has well-developed teeth except Archaeopteryx and some Cretaceous birds. If, as evolutionists suppose, modern birds are derived from toothed ancestors, then their young should exhibit fetal teeth as whalebone whales do, but no known bird embryo shows evidence of teeth. The supposed rudimentary teeth that have been described in parrots are not teeth but papillae. Birds lack embryonic teeth because they are not necessary for molding their very slender jaw (Dewar, 1957, pp. 171-172).

The Cetacean Vibrissal Apparatus

The "vibrissal apparatus" (hairs, such as the whiskers cats use to sense the physical environment) in cetaceans are assumed to be remnants of a former total hairy covering of an earlier evolutionary stage. The remaining "hairs" located on the heads of whales are "usually considered a very clear example" of a vestigial organ (Yablokov, 1974, p. 235). Subsequent research has shown that these structures are not vestiges but rather are very complex functional sensory organs with a well-developed nerve supply connected to each "hairlet" (Yablokov, 1974, p. 235).

The blue whale (*Balaenoptera musculus*) has about ten thousand nerve fibers combined in large bundles and connected to each vibrissa. New research on the behavior responses of blue whales that resulted from touching their vibrissae has shown the evolutionary claim that vibrissae are only "remnants of a previous hair cover" is incorrect. The vibrissae actually play a major role as tactile organs, especially for determining the presence of food (Yablokov, 1974, p. 235).

Recent investigations by Yablokov and others have confirmed this claim. The results of detailed histological investigations of vibrissae from five baleen whale species have documented that they are complex sensory organs (Yablokov ,1974, p. 235). The hair follicle extends deep into the dermal layer of the skin and is embedded in connective tissue fibers that differ considerably in size from similar structures used in the connective tissue of the cetacean dermis. The pelvic bones and vibrissae are two examples showing not only do these putative "vestigial organs have a function ... but they are highly specialized structures, perfected for carrying out complex and delicate functions as in the case of the pelvic bones in the present toothed whales, or vibrissae in baleen whales" (Yablokov, 1974, p. 240).

Conclusions

The review presented here agrees with Stahl who wrote that "ascertaining the terrestrial stock from which the whales came is exceedingly difficult" (Stahl, 1974, p. 486). Colbert et al., added that like bats, "whales (using this term in a general and inclusive sense) appear suddenly in early Tertiary times, fully adapted by profound modifications" (2001, p. 392). The fossil and other evidence of whale evolution contradicts the following uninformed claim:

> We also have great series of transitional fossils for many of the most dramatic transformations of evolutionary history. For example, we have an amazingly clear record of the evolution of whales, from a bear-like land mammal, to river predators that were shaped like giant otters, to primitive whales, to modern whales (Loxton, 2007, p. 85).

Instead, Colbert's half-century old statement that "no intermediate forms are apparent in the fossil record between the whales and the ancestral Cretaceous placentals" is closer to the current state of knowledge (1955, p. 303). In fact, determining a terrestrial animal that could have evolved into a whale has been, and still is, a "source of spirited debate" (Harder, 2001, p. 180).

One reason for this conclusion is that the various claims postulated for all claimed whale transitional animals are very problematic (Camp, 1998). Another reason is that no evidence exists for useless vestigial organs as once claimed for whales, and the enormous gap between whales and their putative ancestors has only widened with further research (Woodmorappe, 2002). The research work on genetic comparisons finds that there exist major conflicts between the existing whale genetic evolutionary tree and the fossil record (Spaulding, 2009; Xiong, *et. al.*, 2009).

Furthermore, even the extremely long time periods that evolutionists postulate cannot explain the evolution of ocean-going whales: "There is, in short, neither the time nor the mechanism that could begin to account for so rapid and dynamic an evolutionary transformation from that small [postulated evolutionary whale ancestor] mammal to the extraordinary whale in so (relatively) short a period as twelve million years" (Le Fanu, 2009, p. 120).

References

Alexander, R. McNeill. 1975. *The Chordates*. Cambridge University Press, Cambridge, England.

American Museum of Natural History. 2009. Getting A Leg Up On Whale and Dolphin Evolution: New Comprehensive Analysis Sheds Light On The Origin Of Crustaceans. *ScienceDaily*. September 25.

Andrews, Roy Chapman. 1921. A Remarkable Case of External Hind Limbs in a Humpback Whale. *American Museum Novitates*, 9:2-6, June 3.

Anonymous. 2001. Whale Evolution. WGBH Educational Foundation and Clear Blue Sky Productions. http://www.pbs.org/wgbh/evolution/library/03/4/1_034_05.html.

Awbrey, Frank T. 1983. Giving Evolutionists Some Space: Vestigial Organs Demand Evolution. *Origins Research* 6(1):6.

Bajpai, S. and P. Gingerich. 1998. A New Eocene Archaeocete (Mammalia, Cetacea) from India and the Time of Origin of Whales. *Proceedings of the National Academy of Science*, 95(26):15464-15468.

Banister, Keith. and Andrew Campbell, eds., 1985. *The Encyclopedia of Aquatic Life*. Facts on File, New York.

Bejder, Lars. and Brian K. Hall. 2002. "Limbs in Whales and Limblessness in Other Vertebrates: Mechanisms of Evolutionary and Developmental Transformation and Loss." *Evolution and Development*, 4(6):445-458, Nov-Dec.

Berta, A. 1995. What is a Whale? *Science*, 263:180-181.

Byers, R. C. 1983. In: Do vestigial organs demand evolution? Edited by G. Howe. *Origins Research* 6(2):2.

Camp, Ashby. 1998. The Overselling of Whale Evolution. *Creation Matters*. 3(3):1-5. May/June.

Cameron, J. 1918. The Histogenesis of Vertebrate Striated Muscle, including a Contribution to our Knowledge Regarding the

Structure and Functions of the Cell-Nucleus. *Transactions of the Royal Society of Canada*, 12: 81-98

Chadwick, Douglas. 2001. Evolution of Whales. *National Geographic*, 200(5):64-77, Nov.

Colbert, E. H., M. Morales, and E.C. Minkoff. 1955. *Evolution of the vertebrates*. Wiley, New York.

_____. 2001. *Evolution of the Vertebrates: A History of the Backboned Animals Through Time*, 5th edition. Wiley-Liss, New York.

Conrad, Ernest. 1983. True Vestigial Structures in Whales and Dolphins. *Creation/Evolution*, 10:9-11.

Crapo, Richley. 1984. Vestigial Organs Revisited. Edited by G. Howe. *Origins Research* 7(2):1 ff.

Darwin, Charles. 1859. *The Origin of Species*. John Murray, London.

Dewar, Douglas. 1957. *The Transformist Illusion*. Dehoff, Murfreesboro, TN.

Domning, D. 2001. New 'Intermediate Form' Ties Seacows Firmly to Land. *Reports of the National Center for Science Education*, 21(5-6):38-42.

Dubois, Paul. 1985. Further Comments on Baleen Fetal Teeth and Functions for Yolk Sacs. *Origins Research* 8(2):13-14.

Ellis, Richard. 1987. *The Book of Whales*. New York: Alfred Knoph.

Esperante, Raúl, Leonard Brand, Kevin E. Nick, Orlando Poma and Mario Urbina. 2008. "Exceptional Occurrence of Fossil Baleen in Shallow Marine Sediments of the Neogene Pisco Formation, Southern Peru." *Palaeogeography, Palaeoclimatology, Palaeocology*, 257:344-360.

Evans, Peter. 1987. *The Natural History of Whales and Dolphins*. Facts on File, New York.

Gaskin, D. E. 1972. *Whales, Dolphins and Seals*. St. Martin's Press, New York.

Gingerich, P.D., N.A. Wells, D.E. Russell and S.M.I. Shah. 1983. Origin of Whales in Epicontinental Remnant Seas: New Evidence from the Early Eocene of Pakistan. *Science*, 220:403-406.

Gingerich, P.D., B. H. Smith, and E. L. Simons. 1990. Hindlimbs of Eocene Basilosaurus. *Science* 249:154-157.

Gingerich, P.D., M. Haq, I.S. Zalmout, I.H. Khan and M.S. Malkani. 2001. Origin of Whales from Early Artiodactyls: Hands and Feet of Eocene Protocetidae from Pakistan. *Science*, 293:2239-2242.

Gingerich, P.D. 2003. Land-To-Sea Transition in Early Whales: Evolution of Eocene Archaeoceti (Cetacea) in Relation to Skeletal Proportions and Locomotion of Living Semiaquatic Mammals. *Paleobiology*, 29(3):429-454, Summer.

Harder, B. 2001. New Fossils Resolve Whale's Origin. *Science News*, 160(12):180.

Heyning, J.E. and J.G. Mead. 1997. Thermoregulation in the Mouths of Feeding Gray Whales. *Science*, 278:1138-1139.

Ishakawa, Hajime and Hajime Amasaki. 1995. Development and Physiological Degradation of Tooth Buds and Development of Rudiment of Baleen Plat in Southern Minke Whale, *Balaenoptera acutorostrata. The Journal of Veterinary Medical Science*, 57(4):665-670.

Kaufmann, David. 1983. When is a Vestige not a Vestige? *Origins Research*, 6(2):4.

Le Fanu, James. 2009. *Why us? How Science Discovers the Mystery of Ourselves*. Pantheon Books, New York.

Loxton, Daniel. 2007. Evolution. *Skeptic*, 13(2):80-89.

Luo, Z. 2000. Evolution, in Search of the Whale's Sisters. *Nature*, 404:235-239.

Milinkovitch, M.C. and J.G.M. Thewissen. 1997. Evolutionary Biology: Even-Toed Fingerprints on Whale Ancestry. *Nature*, 388:622-623.

Miller, Keith. 2003. *Perspectives on an Evolving Creation.* Eerdmans, Grand Rapids, MI.

Naylor, G.J.P. and D.C. Adams. 2001. Are the Fossil Data Really at Odds with the Molecular Data? Morphological Evidence for Cetartiodactyla Phylogeny Reexamined." *Systematic Biology*, 50(3):444-453, June.

Muizon, Christian. 2001. Walking with Whales. *Nature*. 413: 259-260.

Nikaido, M.A., A. Rooney and N. Okada. 1999. Phylogenetic Relationships among Cetartiodactyls based on Insertions of Short and Long Interspersed Elements: Hippopotamuses are the Closest Extant Relatives of Whales. *Proceedings of the National Academy of Science*, 96:10261-10266.

Ober, William C. M.D. and Claire W. Garrison, R.N. 2005. *Biology*. McGraw Hill, New York.

Pabst, D., S. A. Rommel, and W. A. McLellan. 1998. Evolution of Thermoregulary Function in Cetacean Reproductive Systems. In *The Emergence of Whales: Evolutionary Patterns in the Origin of Cetacea*, G.M. Thewissen (editor). Plenum Press, New York, NY.

Parsons, Keith. 2004. *The Great Dinosaur Controversy: A Guide to the Debates*. ABC-CLIO, Santa Barbara, CA.

Prothero, Donald. 1999. "Mesonychids" in *Encyclopedia of Paleontology. Volume 2: M-Z*, pp. 716-717. Fitzroy Dearborn, Chicago, IL. edited by Ronald Singer.

Ridgway, Sam. 1972. *Mammals of the Sea*. Charles C. Thomas, Springfield, IL.

Rose, Kenneth. 2001. The Ancestry of Whales. *Science*, 293:2216-2217.

Scheffer, Victor. 1976. *A Natural History of Marine Mammals*. Scribner, New York.

Silas. 2002. Posted June 13, 2002 on an internet online discussion. *Proof of Design? Astronomical Enigma*

[Archive] - *Bad Astronomy*. www.bautforum.com/archive/index.php/t-1292.html-345k.

Singer, Ronald. (editor). 1999. *Encyclopedia of Paleontology. Volume 2: M-Z.* Fitzroy Dearborn, Chicago, IL.

Slijper, Everhard Johannes. 1962. *Dolphins and Whales.* University of Michigan Press, Ann Arbor, MI.

Spaulding, Michelle, Maureen A. O'Leary, and John Gatesy. 2009. Relationships of Cetacea (Artiodactyla) Among Mammals: Increased Taxon Sampling Alters Interpretations of Key Fossils and Character Evolution. *PLosONE.* 4(9):e7062.

Stahl, Barbara. 1974. *Vertebrate History: Problems in Evolution.* Dover, New York.

Tajima, Yuko, Yoshihiro Hayashi and Tadasu K. Yamada. 2004. Comparative Anatomical Study on the Relationships between the Vestigial Pelvic Bones and the Surrounding Structures of Finless Porpoises (Neophocaena Phocaenoides). *Journal of Veterinary Medical Science*, 66(7):761-766, July.

Thewissen, J. G. M. 1998. *The Emergence of Whales; Evolutionary Patterns in the Origin of Cetacea.* New York: Plenum.

Thewissen, J.G.M., S.I. Madar and S.T. Hussain. 1998. Whale Ankles and Evolutionary Relationships. *Nature*, 395:452.

Thewissen, J.G.M. and S. Bajpai. 2001. "Dental Morphology of Remingtonocetidae (Cetacia, Mammalia)." *Journal of Paleontology,* 75(2):463-465.

Thewissen, J.G.M., E.M. Williams, L.J. Roe and S.T. Hussain. 2001. "Skeletons of Terrestrial Cetaceans and the Relationship of Whales to Artiodactyls." *Nature*, 413:277-281.

Thewissen, J.G.M., M.J. Cohn, L.S. Stevens, S. Pajpai, J. Heyning, and W.E. Horton, Jr. 2006. "Developmental Basis for Hind-Limb Loss in Dolphins and Origin of the Cetacean Bodyplan." *Proceedings of the National Academy of Science,* 103(22):8414-8418.

Thewissen, J.G.M., L. Cooper, M. Clementz, S. Bajpai, and B.N. Tiwari. 2007. Whales Originated from Aquatic Artiodactyls in the Eocene Epoch of India. *Nature*, 450: 1190-1194.

Vialleton, L. 1930. *L'Origine des Etres Vivants*. Librarie Plon, Paris.

Watson, Lyall. 1981. *Sea Guide to Whales of the World*. Dutton, New York.

Werner, Carl. 2007. *Evolution: The Grand Experiment*. New Leaf Press, Green Forest, AR.

Williams, John Gary. 1970. *The Other Side of Evolution*. Williams, La Vemge, TN:.

Woodmorappe, John. 2002. "Walking Whales, Nested Hierarchies, and Chimeras: Do They Exist?" *TJ*, 16(1):111-119.

Xiong, Ye, Matthew C. Brandley, Shixia Xu, Kaiya Zhou, and Guang Yang. 2009. Seven New Dolphin Mitochondrial Genomes and a Time-Calibrated Phylogeny of Whales. *BMC Evolutionary Biology*.

Yablokov, Alexy. 1974. *Variability of Mammals*. The National Science Foundation, Washington D.C.

Young, Patrick H. 2003. Whales Still Have No Ancestor. *Creation Research Society Quarterly*, 39:213-218.

Young, J. Z. 1962. *The Life of Vertebrates*. Oxford University Press, New York.

Zahn, K. *Whales*. 1988. New York: Gallery Books.

Zhou, X., R. Zhai, P.D. Gingerich, and L. Chen. 1995. "Skull of a New Mesonychid (Mammalia, Mesonychia) from the Late Paleocene of China." *Journal of Vertebrate Paleontology*, 15(2).387:396-398.